Social Interaction in Language Teacher Education

Studies in Social Interaction
Series Editors: Steve Walsh, Paul Seedhouse and Christopher Jenks

Presenting data from a range of social contexts including education, the media, the workplace, and professional development, the *Studies in Social Interaction* series uncovers, among other things, the ways in which tasks are accomplished, identities formed and communities established. Each volume in the series places social interaction at the centre of discussion and presents a clear overview of the work which has been done in a particular context. Books in the series provide examples of how data can be approached and used to uncover social-interaction themes and issues, and explore how research in social interaction can feed into a better understanding of professional practices and develop new research agendas. Through stimulating tasks and accompanying commentaries, readers are engaged and challenged to reflect on particular themes and relate the discussion to their own context.

Series Editors
Steve Walsh is Professor of Applied Linguistics at Newcastle University

Paul Seedhouse is Professor of Educational and Applied Linguistics at Newcastle University

Christopher Jenks is Assistant Professor of English and Intensive English/TESOL Coordinator at the University of South Dakota

Titles available in the series:

Social Interaction in Second Language Chat Rooms	Christopher Jenks
Social Interaction and L2 Classroom Discourse	Olcay Sert
Social Interaction and Teacher Cognition	Li Li
Social Interaction and English Language Teacher Identity	John Gray and Tom Morton
Social Interaction in Language Teacher Education	Fiona Farr, Angela Farrell and Elaine Riordan

Visit the Studies in Social Interaction website at
edinburghuniversitypress.com/series/ssint

Social Interaction in Language Teacher Education

Fiona Farr, Angela Farrell and Elaine Riordan

EDINBURGH
University Press

Edinburgh University Press is one of the leading university presses in the UK. We publish academic books and journals in our selected subject areas across the humanities and social sciences, combining cutting-edge scholarship with high editorial and production values to produce academic works of lasting importance. For more information visit our website: edinburghuniversitypress.com

Edinburgh University Press Ltd
The Tun – Holyrood Road,
12(2f) Jackson's Entry,
Edinburgh EH8 8PJ

Typeset in 10/12 Minion Pro by Servis Filmsetting Ltd, Stockport, Cheshire, and printed and bound in Great Britain.

A CIP record for this book is available from the British Library

ISBN 978 1 4744 1262 9 (hardback)
ISBN 978 1 4744 1263 6 (webready PDF)
ISBN 978 1 4744 1264 3 (paperback)
ISBN 978 1 4744 1265 0 (epub)

CONTENTS

FIGURES, TABLES AND CHARTS

FIGURES

TABLES

CHARTS

ABBREVIATIONS

A	Assessed
BSR	Bachelors of Sport and Recreation
C/a	Community of Activity
C/e	Community of Explanation
CA	Conversation analysis
CADS	Corpus-assisted discourse studies
CEFR	Common European Framework of Reference
CIC	Classroom interactional competence
CL	Corpus linguistics
CMC	Computer-mediated communication
CoP	Community of practice
CPD	Continuous professional development
DA	Discourse analysis
EAP	English for Academic Purposes
EFL	English as a Foreign Language
ELT	English Language Teaching
ELTE	English Language Teacher Education
ESL	English as a Second Language
ESP	English for Specific Purposes
EST	Experienced student teacher
IELTS	International English Language Testing System
IRF	Initiation response feedback
KaL	Knowledge about language
L	Lecturer
L1	First language
L2	Second language
LCIE	Limerick Corpus of Irish English
LIBELCASE	Limerick-Belfast Corpus of Academic English
LIWC	Linguistic Inquiry and Word Count
LSWE	Longman Spoken and Written English
LTE	Language teacher education
LTI	Language teacher identity
MLE	Mediated learning experience
MOOC	Massive open online course

NST	Novice student teacher
O	Obligatory
PACK	Pedagogic and content knowledge
PDR	Professional development review
PPP	Presentation, practice, production
PT	Peer tutor
RP	Reflective practice
S	Structured
SLA	Second language acquisition
ST	Semi-structured
TEC	Teacher Education Corpus
TP	Teaching practice
TPACK	Technological, pedagogic and content knowledge
TPS	Teaching practice supervisor
TT/ST	Teacher talk/student talk
TTT	Teacher Talking Time
UA	Unassessed
V	Voluntary
WPM	Words per million
ZPD	Zone of proximal development

INTRODUCING THE CONTEXTS

1.1 INTRODUCTION

Our overriding aim in this book is to demonstrate by empirical means how novice and early career teachers can be understood as a community and as apprentices to the English Language Teacher Education (ELTE) community of practice (CoP), drawing on a combined corpus-linguistic/discourse analytic (CADS) approach. The research reported on is grounded in the sociocultural theory of teaching and learning (Vygotsky 1978), which places interaction and talk at the centre of student teacher learning although written modes and their roles are also considered of value. Previous studies in the field of genre analysis have revealed that discourse communities are characterised by specialised patterns of discourse and terminology (Swales 1987, 1990), and similar work has been conducted on CoP language features (Healy 2012; Healy and Onderdonk-Horan 2012; Riordan 2018; Vaughan and Clancy 2013). Community members can also be expected to share topics of professional interest and concern, as the work of Cutting (2000) and Vaughan (2010) has highlighted. However, due to a dearth of empirical research in this area, we still have only a partial understanding of the fabric of this community and the processes through which student teachers become socialised into its norms and practices.

To address this gap, we report on research which set out to probe and describe the types of interactions that typically take place in ELTE contexts, drawing on spoken and written data sourced from a wide and diverse range of contexts, as represented by the Teacher Education Corpus (TEC), which was compiled by the authors for this purpose. As will be demonstrated, the corpus data will be differentiated in the following four ways: (1) experientially, positioning teachers along the cline from novice to experienced; (2) educationally, examining pre- and in-service education programmes; and (3) by mode of interaction, with comparisons made between data from face-to-face (lectures, tutorials, feedback) and on-line modes of computer-mediated communication (blogs, discussion forums, chat and portfolios); and (4) by interactional relationship paradigms, for instance student teachers with peers, peer tutors, teaching practice supervisors, and lecturers. This book relies, therefore, on an empirical corpus-based approach to investigate the data from these contexts, providing examples of how data can be approached and used to uncover social-interactional themes and issues, in relation to ELTE specifically, but with further links made to ELTE as a micro-context of social interaction in general. Our ultimate aim in exploring these data sets is to understand how research in ELTE social interaction can feed into a better understanding of professional practices and, from this, to develop new practice-oriented and research agendas. With these goals in mind, we begin by reviewing the defining features of institutional, classroom, on-line and language teacher education discourse as representative of the contexts featured in TEC (see Chapter 4 for a full description of TEC).

1.2 INSTITUTIONAL DISCOURSE

The data for this book was sourced from a variety of modes of communication in which student teachers engaged in a third-level institutional setting, therefore it broadly represents institutional discourse. Institutional discourse has been the focus of a great deal of linguistic research with most studies undertaken in the third-level education context. University discourse analysis is most associated with the work of Biber and colleagues (Biber 2006; Biber et al. 2002), which provides a detailed linguistic analysis of different spoken and written academic registers. This includes thematic areas at the level of lexis and grammar, such as word classes, metalanguage, discourse connectors, stance and clause and phrase structure. These authors have also documented patterns of variation in spoken and written university discourse. For instance, the use of metalanguage, which is subject specific lexis, was shown to occur with greater frequency and variety in written rather than spoken academic registers while the latter display a variety of narrative forms such as discussions and explanations (Biber et al. 2002). In general, spoken academic discourse relies on a smaller set of words due to factors pertaining to real time production, although these items do occur with high frequency. There is also a marked difference in lexical density across academic disciplines, for instance the humanities and social sciences are characterised by large sets of word types while business and engineering have relatively fewer technical terms, but they are highly technical in nature. Moreover, in the latter, everyday words are often assigned technical meanings (Biber 2006: 36–46). Spoken academic registers also contain linguistic features that derive their meaning from the wider textual and situational content, especially pronouns and direct situational references. There is also a high tendency towards procedure-focused language by contrast with textbooks, which tend to convey content (Biber 2006). Within the broad context of institutional discourse, various sub-genres have emerged that can be linked to particular micro-contexts, some more traditional and established than others. In the following section, we explore the distinguishing features of classroom discourse which represents the former type.

1.3 CLASSROOM DISCOURSE

In general, classroom teaching in the third level context displays greater similarity with other spoken discourses rather than with written academic genres, although it can feature both procedural and content-based language as well as teacher-centred stance, which is a predominant feature of teacher-led academic spoken registers (Biber 2006: 186–210). More recently, there has been a growing interest in the interactional features of spoken discourse in higher education, with lectures and small group teaching in classrooms being the main focus to date, for instance Walsh and O'Keeffe (2007) and Walsh et al. (2011) used a combined corpus linguistics and conversation analysis approach to explore the features of interaction in small group teaching. The latter study (Walsh et al. 2011: 336) identified four types of third level classroom talk as determined by broad functional categories, that is: procedural talk, didactic talk, emphatic talk and argumentational talk. Procedural talk orients to the interactional function of informing, and being informed about procedural matters. This often involves long turns by the tutor, with minimal verbal contributions from students. In this context, the tutor typically performs the role of both questioner and answerer as he talks through a procedure. Didactic talk, on the other hand, is associated with the function of eliciting information from individuals or groups, or giving evaluative feedback. In this context, turn-taking is tightly controlled by the tutor, and reminiscent of classic initiation response feedback (IRF) descriptions (Sinclair and Coulthard 1975) of classroom discourse with display questions, student nomination and short utterances by students featuring prominently. The third type, empathic talk, has the function of indicating shared space between participants. In this context, students typically recount experiences they are having as part of the course of study, with these accounts often accompanied by evaluations of situations and behaviour. The tutor accepts and builds on these accounts, converting them into pedagogical material in the form of reflective statements about appropriate behaviour, roles and identities in the professional practice of the discipline. This type of talk is characterised by the frequent use of interpersonal discourse markers to provide supportive responses to the speaker and to mark shared knowledge, and with hedges indicating that pragmatic work is going on (Carter and McCarthy 2006). In terms of turn-taking, empathic talk is more symmetrical than either procedural or didactic talk, with a greater balance struck between tutor talk and student talk. By contrast, argumentational talk is one where shared space is disputed rather than used to build empathy, with turn initial negation, assertions and counter-assertions commonly used for this purpose.

Aside from corpus-based conversation analysis (CA) research of this kind in the university context, most studies of interactional classroom discourse have been undertaken in the second language (L2) education field from a pedagogical-oriented perspective. Walsh's work in the L2 classroom context has been instrumental in exploring classroom interactional competence (CIC), defined as the ability to use interaction to mediate and assist learning (Walsh 2002: 23). This research has also highlighted more widely the importance of learners being afforded interactional spaces in order to enhance participation and increase learning opportunities (Walsh 2013: 54). This is seen to be dependent on the ability of teachers to manage learner contributions in a positive and focused way, with scaffolding being a key strategic skill that can be developed to achieve this. These practices are consistent with Vygotskyan theory in education and teacher education which emphasises the key mediating role played by a more expert other to help learners and student teachers to co-construct understanding (Daniels 2007; Vygotsky 1978; for a fuller account, see Chapter 2). From this discussion of the features of traditional academic registers and classroom discourse, we turn next to the characteristics of newer forms of academic discourse as have developed in line with the integration of technologies in education.

1.4 ON-LINE ACADEMIC DISCOURSE

Computer-mediated communication (CMC) is a further avenue that linguists have turned their attention to in recent years. Meskill (2009: 51) notes that CMC offers 'vast instructional possibilities both for learners and those preparing to teach them'. In this sense, it can cater for two needs at once; that is, as a means through which teaching occurs, and as an end in itself. As far as the former is concerned, Lamy and Hampel (2007: 7) have observed that CMC allows learners to engage with the communicative aspect of their study by exchanging language on-line rather than in conversation classes, as was the case previously. On-line learning tools and environments have also created opportunities for informal and autonomous learning as well as facilitating the social side of learning by making interaction more common (Meskill 2009). Moreover, the enhanced interaction and collaboration afforded by CMC has encouraged and supported reflective dialogue between teachers and mentors (Lamy and Hampel 2007: 73), as well as aiding the development of content or subject knowledge (Burgess and Mayes 2008). Amongst the various types of CMC that have emerged, there are those that are now commonly found in work environments. While some aspects of CMC are similar to face-to-face discourse, there are also differences (Levy and Stockwell 2006: 84). CMC can involve aspects that make it similar to written language (Lapadat 2002; Sotillo 2000). In these ways, it cuts across the boundaries of speech and writing (Vásquez 2011a).

A key distinction is made between communication in synchronous (for example, chat discussions) and asynchronous on-line modes (for example, discussion fora, blogs and portfolios). For instance, features of synchronous on-line communication among students and teachers include lags in turn-taking (as users do not have visual cues to help with conversational structuring) (Kern 1995; Meskill 2009), short turn lengths (Kern 1995; Riordan 2018), and the use of strategies to compensate for lack of visual cues, such as emoticons (Negretti 1999). Also observed is the open sharing of information between users (Riordan 2018), and a more balanced distribution of talk (Beauvois 1998; Burnett 2003; Chen et al. 2009). Researchers have identified features that make this type of discourse similar to spoken language in terms of style and register, such as the high degree of informality reflected, the display of social presence and its use for entertainment purposes. Conversely, it has also been found to feature a higher level of lexical density and more complex syntactic structures than written language (Castro 2006; Kern 1995; Riordan 2018; Riordan and Murray 2010).

As far as the distinct educational benefits of these two types of on-line communication are concerned, synchronous discussions have been seen to help students to get to know one another, to share information and to ask teachers/lecturers questions. By comparison, asynchronous modes offer more in terms of the development of critical thinking and reflection, as time is allowed for more deliberated thought. Interestingly, students have been found to be more active in on-line discussion fora than instructors/facilitators (Wang et al. 2010; Wegerif 1998; Wickstrom 2003). Discussions in this type of on-line mode can also foster collaboration (Romano 2008), critical thinking (McLoughlin and Mynard 2009; Szabo and Schwartz 2011), and learner autonomy as students can read and re-read posts as required (Kaur and Sidhu 2010). Accordingly, they can play a key role in social learning (Wegerif 1998), individual learning (Krentler and Willis-Flurry 2005; Szabo and Schwartz 2011) and professional development (Montero et al. 2007). As such, they have become widely used in educational contexts to facilitate student discussions around course content and tasks and have the wider aim of fostering collaborative dialogue and social learning.

Another commonly used asynchronous tool is the blog, which has been described as 'a major player of the Web 2.0 wave' (Deng and Yuen 2011: 441). Blogs can be used either individually or collaboratively and have been found to be useful for peer collaboration (Dippold 2009; Sert and Asik 2019), reflection, community building, self-expression, and the enhancement of reading and writing skills (Coutinho 2010; Dippold 2009; Ducate and Lomicka 2008; Murray and Hourigan 2006; Murugaiah et al. 2010). As such, they have been proven to aid in the construction of knowledge and reflective practice (Elliott 2009). While there has been criticism that blogs tend to promote descriptive rather than critical reflection among certain groups (Lucas and Fleming 2011; Murray and Hourigan 2008; Yang 2009), others have argued that levels of reflection can improve over time (Stiler and Philleo 2003). While the use of language in asynchronous forums would, in general, seem to mirror that of writing (Lapadat 2002), blogs have been found to reflect a more informal and emotionally expressive style (Riordan 2012). Having reviewed the defining features of traditional, and newly emergent, discourse modes as are now commonly used in third level education, we turn next to discursive practices that are specific to the language teacher education context.

1.5 LANGUAGE TEACHER EDUCATION DISCOURSE

In this section, we summarise some of the key findings that have emerged from data-led approaches to the study of language teacher education discourse. These can be categorised in relation to the following areas, which are of relevance to the research reported on in this book: language, participation levels, identity work and reflective practice. The language of ELTE has been explored extensively by Farr (2011) in the context of post-observation teaching practice (TP) feedback interactions. For this, corpus-based techniques were used to analyse both spoken and written feedback by TP supervisors following practice teaching by student teachers. From this, four recurrent linguistic categories were identified in the data, relating to direction, reflection, evaluation and relational aspects. Comparisons made between spoken and written feedback data revealed fewer indicators of reflection in the written tutor reports. This was attributed to the absence of students' voices, whereas the spoken data was found to be more conducive to explicit elicitation and reflection (Farr 2011: 78). A further main finding of the study was that direction was softer in spoken feedback than in the written reports for face-saving reasons, with issues of power seen to be at play. Similarly, in the case of evaluation, the written reports reflected higher levels of direct criticism than the spoken feedback. More evidence was also found of praise and cathartic discourse in terms of small talk, apologising, irony and language in the latter, which was seen to be aimed at addressing the emotional state of the student teachers involved (Farr 2011).

Investigating more informal discourse, Riordan (2018) analysed data from peer tutor-guided face-to-face discussions, on-line chat and discussion fora, and blogs and e-portfolios from student teachers on MA and PhD TESOL education programmes. Through the use of a similar corpus approach, the discourse features of each type of talk or writing were explored and identified. This signalled the saliency of discourse functions such as narration, cognition, affect and evaluation. Further qualitative analyses revealed evidence of reflective thought and cognition in the student teachers' narratives, which were found to be higher in the spoken and on-line asynchronous modes of communication. Meanwhile, the novice teachers were seen to collaborate, offer emotional support and attend to each other's face needs through their use of affective and evaluative expression. From this, the discursive practices found in these sub-corpora were identified as 'that of sharing, collaborating, narrating, reflecting and engaging affectively'. They were also seen to be 'shaped by speaker roles and positions, tasks, discourse functions, and mode of communication' (Riordan 2018: 203).

These studies (Farr 2011; Riordan 2018) also investigated engagement and participation by student teachers in the various modes under investigation. In post-observation feedback settings, Farr (2011, based on her 2005 thesis) recorded participation levels of 65 per cent / 35 per cent, with the TP supervisor contributing twice the amount of talk as the student teacher. This is consistent with the later findings of Vásquez and Reppen (2007: 161), although in both studies it was noted that there was a rise in student teacher talk over time, which researchers attributed to their increased confidence over the course of their programme of study. Individual speaker style was also seen to play a part by Vásquez and Reppen, who observed differences in the amount of talk generated by individual teachers. Meanwhile, in similar research undertaken by Copland (2010), it was noted that student teachers often experienced difficulties when asked to give feedback to peers because 'they did not wish to, or did not know how to, or because they were unable to' (Copland 2010: 471). Conversely, when Riordan (2018) compared participation by student teachers and a peer tutor, significantly higher levels (80 per cent / 20 per cent) were recorded for the former. From this, the conclusion was reached that informal settings can encourage student teachers to participate more openly and actively. It was further acknowledged that other factors might be at play such as the level of formality, the topic of conversation and the rights, or indeed assumed rights, of speakers, as well as power differentials. These factors were identified by Copland (2012) to explain varying levels of student teacher participation level in ELTE settings.

Two further themes addressed in the research literature in ELTE that are of immediate relevance to the research reported on in this book, are identity work and reflective practice. A number of studies have been undertaken to explore teacher identity formation, some in the formal context of student teacher post-observation meetings (Le and Vásquez 2011; Urzúa and Vásquez 2008; Vásquez 2009, 2011b; Vásquez and Urzúa 2009) and others in the more informal setting of peer tutor-guided discussions (Riordan 2018; Riordan and Farr 2015). A recurrent theme in the findings has been the tension between novice and experienced teacher identity. By way of explanation, Vásquez and Urzúa (2009: 16) have observed that novices are 'performing a skilful, confident, optimistic professional self, while at the same time acknowledging, expressing, and possibly working through limitations'. Issues and processes surrounding the formation of teacher identity are explored as a main theme to shed light on the complex processes involved and what this may reveal about the teachers' socialisation into the CoP. Reflective practice is a further well-documented theme in the ELTE literature, although to date only a limited number of studies have been undertaken to empirically explore how best it can be fostered and the types of qualitative outcomes that can be achieved (Farrell 2016a; Mann and Walsh 2017; Riordan 2018). Amongst these, we find research carried out in the context of post-observation feedback meetings by Vásquez (2007) and Urzúa and Vásquez (2008), and Riordan's more recent study (2018) which investigated the role and effectiveness of peer tutor-guided discussions in fostering reflection amongst novices and more experienced student teachers on MA and PhD in TESOL education programmes, drawing on a CoP theoretical framework. In this book, these studies will be revisited as we explore the TEC data with a view to enhancing our understanding of the role that scaffolded reflection and collaborative dialogue can play in facilitating student teacher socialisation into the ELTE CoP, and their professional identity formation and growth.

1.6 OUTLINE OF THE BOOK

In this book, it is our intention to demonstrate how corpus linguistics and discourse analysis can be used in a combined and complementary way to illuminate the discursive practices of student teachers across a range of face-to-face and on-line modes of communication afforded to them on pre-service (MA) and continuous professional development (CPD) type (PhD) TESOL teacher education programmes. We will also explore the processes involved in teacher socialisation, teacher identity formation and teacher reflection as well as the mechanisms through which these processes can best be fostered and facilitated as part of a holistic approach to teacher education. To arrive at a more complete picture of the nature and role of social discourses in the ELTE context, we begin in Chapter 2 with the theoretical and pedagogical arguments for a data-led holistic approach to teacher education. This is followed in Chapter 3 by a review of the theoretical frameworks used by the authors to map the complex processes by which student teachers become active members and reflective practitioners in the ELTE CoP. The rationale for the CADS approach drawn on in the analysis is provided in Chapter 4 together with a detailed description of the data that was sourced from the various spoken and written modes that constituted TEC. Chapters 5 to 7 of the book present the research findings in the areas of student teacher socialisation (Chapter 5), teacher identity formation (Chapter 6) and the development of reflective teachers (Chapter 7). Finally, in Chapter 8 we summarise the main findings to emerge, and offer some suggestions as to their implications for future directions in ELTE and for further related research.

2

LANGUAGE TEACHER EDUCATION AND ANALYSING SOCIAL INTERACTION

2.1 INTRODUCTION

One of the primary motivations for writing this book relates to the need to start developing more robust evidence-based accounts of teacher education interaction to assist those working in the profession (as teachers, researchers and educators). Although we have moved some way forward, it is still true to say that although language teacher education (LTE) is much done, it is little studied (Freeman and Johnson 1998; Hammadou 1993), and 'for many reasons, there has tended to be very little substantial research in teacher education, both in education generally and in the field of language teaching' (Freeman 2001: 74). There are some notable recent exceptions and these will be discussed in this chapter. Even more compelling is the fact that the discourses and interactions of ELTE are being studied by few, in a context where language is not only the product but also the processing tool through which teachers become educated. No systematic formal qualification exists which teachers can undertake to move into the realm of teacher education. One of the consequences of this has been that the institutionalised imperative for publications in this field has not been present, hence the serious dearth of published materials to support its implementation, especially language teacher education. To compound this problem, the publications that are to be found are often based on theoretical and anecdotal experience. Few to date are based on robust and extensive corpora.

The time is ripe for exploiting larger amounts of relevant data through computational corpus-based techniques. Corpus-based research methodologies can be a powerful accompaniment to more traditional approaches to the study of interaction. Corpus-based research has developed in two independent but related ways since corpora have become more mainstream. Firstly, the quantitative approach focuses on large amounts of data, with specific attention being given to high frequency items and recurring patterns. This type of approach has been most appropriately applied to detailed linguistic analysis and the production of large reference works (dictionaries and grammar books). Secondly, there is a growing number of linguists coming from a background in discourse and conversation analysis who are using smaller corpora in qualitative ways to give their research a more statistical and empirical basis. The cited weakness of this latter methodology is that corpus data is, by its very nature, decontextualised, making emic interpretations notoriously difficult to defend. While this book uses corpora in a combined quantitative and qualitative way, it aims to address such methodological issues by drawing on a number of theories (discourse and conversation analysis, pragmatics and educational theories) and methodologies (corpus-based, survey and narrative account) in order to present a more robust methodological framework, which will progress research of this type.

This chapter situates the present research within language teacher education methodologies, philosophies and frameworks, which have changed over time and continue to do so. It provides coverage of the existing body of research evidence on social interaction in LTE contexts and provides readers with a survey of the literature. The aim is to review and discuss seminal publications and cutting-edge research in this type of social interaction. For example, the notion of social constructivism will be explored in some detail as well as the place of language as a mediational tool within this framework, and the role of interactional communities as facilitators of development.

2.2 LTE AND ITS DEVELOPMENT OVER TIME

In some ways, we have come full circle and beyond in terms of the approaches and underlying beliefs and practices in relation to LTE. In times past, the apprenticeship model of education was prevalent where a master was observed for the purposes of learning, assimilating and imitating. There was a process of socialisation into the 'craft', with time served on the peripheries in the first instance, in order to earn a more central place as part of the expert practitioner group, but only over time. And although this 'apprenticeship of observation' (Lortie 1975) continues to be central in LTE, it has acquired the added dimensions of formal content and pedagogic knowledge, critical reflective practices, and supervised, evaluated and reviewed practice teaching. When considering this carefully conceived melange, it is prudent to remember that what constitutes good teaching is not a matter of fact or certainty, but of judgement and evaluation by individuals, individuals who may not always agree. And while many parts of the world now implement a set of teaching standards, the interpretation and evaluation of those standards will inevitably differ, even if marginally, from one person to the next. The issue of teacher evaluation is a contentious one and is outside the scope of this book, so, for now, we return to the various dimensions of the broad context and abstract them into a number of the most relevant theoretical frameworks which have influenced and informed LTE in more recent times.

2.2.1 THEORETICAL INFLUENCES: THE WHY AND HOW OF LTE

Roberts (2016: 4) provides a useful summary of learning in terms of four views of the person and their implications for LTE. The four are as follows:

1. learning as determined by external influences, as in behaviourist learning theory: person as input-output system;
2. learning as the realisation of one's unique self, as in humanistic theory: person with self-agency;

3. learning as a cognitive process, where each of us constructs inner representations of the world which then determine our perceptions and subsequent learning: person as constructivist;
4. a social perspective on learning, where the individual adapts to and enacts socially constructed roles, and learns by means of social exchange: person as social being.

These four theories explain how and why we do things the way that we do in LTE contexts, in other words the underlying beliefs that inform our practical approaches. And while individual teacher educators or institutions may be more strongly persuaded by one, or some, over others, in general, the profession espouses all of these to be important and relevant. Roberts (2016: 4) argues that 'each dimension needs to be integrated for LTE to be effective, and that a broadly social-constructivist view offers the best overall framework with which to think about teacher learning'. This seems to be the most widely articulated stance at the present time. A closer look at each of them will help to explain why this is the case.

Behaviourist psychology, originally construed by Skinner (1953), is concerned with observable behaviour through a model of stimulus and response. Originally experimented on animals, this approach sought to predict and control behaviour through positive and negative reinforcement, for example, rewarding a dolphin with food for performing the correct trick in reaction to a stimulus in the environment, such as a whistle-blowing sequence. Within this approach all social behaviour is seen as being externally controlled and maintained. Skinner's views have met with sharp criticism from an ethical perspective because of the potential and tendency they have in radical realisations to attempt to control behaviour and deny individual rights. Although original intentions, such as eliminating deviant and criminal behaviour, may have been noble, the potential for deleterious mind control is obviously one to be shunned. Taking a much less radical approach, its potential in the LTE context can be seen through model-based activities, such as traditional micro-teaching or an apprenticeship/imitation approach. And its most notable iteration in the language learning context is through the Audio-Lingual Approach, which is often language laboratory-based. Although favoured in some geo-political contexts, using model-based methodologies exclusively has led to a number of criticisms, such as: no one model has been empirically proven to be the best model; they fail to take account of the various beliefs and values of different individuals; and they are retrospective and therefore may impede the development of creative or novel ideas.

Humanistic approaches (Rogers 1969) take the individual as the core holistic entity with both cognitive and emotional dimensions, combining to make personal choices about their own growth and development. Self-agency and freedom are key concepts which shape this approach, also mirrored in many western sociopolitical contexts of the 1960s and 1970s. Non-directive activities, such as counselling models of practice supervision (Freeman 1982; Randall and Thornton 2001) and co-operative development (Edge 1992) are some of its realisations in the LTE arena. Critics have condemned such a strong individualistic orientation because: it can fail to take account of the social or cultural context; it can lead to selfishness and lack of appreciation for others' wants and needs; not all individuals have high levels of self-awareness and they may need feedback from others to help identify the gaps which need to be addressed for their own effective development; and the use of counselling models in non-counselling settings by individuals who will probably not have the appropriate education and experience is questionable. So, as with behaviourism, a modified approach is deemed most appropriate, and partial self-agency is advocated in LTE contexts as an optimal approach.

Constructivism refers to the ways in which learners build knowledge based on their own experiences and subsequent reflections, and has been aligned closely with the philosophy of active learning, learning by doing, task-based learning, problem-based learning and so on. In terms of child development, Piaget's work was the original contributor to this theory (and later Dewey 1933), while the cognitive approach in learning contexts came about as a direct reaction to what was perceived as ill-conceived behaviourism. This gave impetus to a wave of research on teacher cognition in the 1980s, which has continued up to the present (for example, Borg 2006; Li 2017). There are two main criticisms, the first relating to the proliferation of associated theories and an accompanying set of vague terms, often overlapping with others, for example, teacher beliefs/cognitions/personal theories. Secondly, it has been suggested that it focuses on cognition to the detriment of affective dimensions of learning, and of the influence of culture and power in formal educational settings. A useful and simple guide to constructivism for teachers can be found at: https://www.thirteen.org/edonline/concept2class/constructivism/.

Social constructivism is the approach which is now most advocated for optimal LTE. It combines constructivism with a social dimension to learning, thereby alleviating the criticism that constructivism is overly focused on internal and individual cognitions to the detriment of external considerations. From a theoretical perspective, it emanates from the original work of Vygotsky on sociocultural theory. As this is the primary philosophical stance informing current practices, and also the theoretical framework for the analyses that follow later in this book, we will spend some time exploring it from a theoretical perspective in this chapter.

2.2.2 SOCIOCULTURAL THEORY AND EDUCATION

The relationships between thought, language, culture and society have been much discussed over the last century. Most notable deliberations and theories can be found in essays by the Russian lawyer, philologist and psychologist, Lev S. Vygotsky, which have been translated and edited by Michael Cole, Vera John-Steiner, Sylvia Scribner and Ellen Souberman (Vygotsky 1978). Vygotsky's works and those of his contemporaries and followers have long been used as the basis for research in the fields of education and applied linguistics in the former Soviet Union. Western researchers have only become deeply interested in the unified perspective of Vygotskian psycholinguistic theory and the centrality it places on societal context and interpersonal relationships over recent decades (Ahmed 1994: 157). There are two explanations for our relative late coming in this respect. Lantolf and Appel (1994: 27), in the context of second language acquisition (SLA) research, attribute it to the fact that we had minimum access to the works of Vygotsky until the 1980s, and also to the fact that SLA research has generally located itself in the natural science tradition, which is strongly predictive and quantitative. Although this tradition has led to valuable insights, it is now widely accepted that sociocultural approaches may lead to a fuller understanding of some of the many phenomena under investigation in second language studies. This has also been argued to be the case for language teacher education, despite some associated difficulties. In general, sociocultural theories of education and of cognitive development postulate that learning takes place in social interaction, and through the use of mediational tools such as language, both of which are historically, culturally and institutionally determined. Freeman (2016: 93) simplifies the key concept as follows:

> A starting point is the term socio-cultural itself, which combines people ('social') and how they participate in meaning making ('cultural') as the key elements in how people learn. Instead of making the individual the analytical focus, as we are accustomed to doing, a socio-cultural perspective reverses the focus, arguing that by taking part in activities in social contexts, individuals make meaning.

Three of Vygotsky's principles are particularly relevant to the present book: the social nature of learning, mediated activity, and the notion of a zone of proximal development including developmental theory. Each of these will now be explicated in some detail. They are addressed separately here for purposes of exemplification, but are, in fact, very much integrated and interrelated, as will become apparent as the discussion unfolds.

The Social Nature of Learning

Sociocultural theories of learning prioritise the social nature of learning as learners interact with those more capable. Although individuals are considered to possess a degree of knowledge, most of this is said to come from collective endeavours which raises the quality of each individual contribution (Mercer 1995: 2). Vygotsky's approach stipulates that cognitive development and resulting higher mental functioning in individuals have their origins in social interactions. Wertsch (1990: 113), quoting Vygotsky's 'general genetic law of cultural development' (Vygotsky 1983: 163), explains that any developmental function appear on two planes,

> First it appears on the social plane, and then on the psychological plane. First it appears between people as an interpsychological category, and then within the child as an intrapsychological category … It goes without saying that the internalisation transforms the process itself and changes its structure and function.

Interindividual activity occurs between those who have already mastered the required skills and those who are trying to do so, and subsequently leads to intraindividual mastery, and it has been postulated that movement from one plane to the other occurs universally regardless of context, culture, age or object of learning, through the process of scaffolding, which will be discussed in more detail below

(Marks-Greenfield 1984). It has been suggested that any activity is a socially constructed event, even if done alone (Walsh 2001). Language is a means by which people can think and learn together (Mercer 1995: 4). Subsequently, in the psychological world, language is used to mediate intrapersonal cognitive activity, to clarify and make sense of the interpersonally acquired knowledge and commit it to individual mental repertoires (Ahmed 1994; Walsh 2001). Language is the way in which we represent our own thoughts to ourselves. Cognitive development takes place through social activity; we learn from our peers and more importantly from those who may be more expert than ourselves. Knowledge is constructed jointly and socially before it is internalised and individualised, all through language. Vygotsky's 'theory of mental development' states that, 'development does not proceed solely, or even primarily, as the unfolding of inborn facilities, but as the transformation of these innately specified processes once they intertwine with socially determined factors' (Lantolf and Appel 1994: 5; see also Atkinson 2002; Kozulin 1998).

Particular emphasis is placed on the system used to facilitate social learning, that is, speech. The most obvious way of sharing and passing on knowledge is by talking. Vygotsky saw language as shaping and defining social activity and not simply as a facilitator of it. In this respect he was concerned with its contexts of use and not with speech as an abstract system. According to Wertsch (1990: 115),

> In today's terminology, his writings might be termed *discourse analysis* or *pragmatics* rather than linguistics. However, unlike many contemporary discourse and pragmatic analyses, which separate semiotic from other aspects of activity, his concern was always with how speech is interrelated with other aspects of social and individual activity.

Mediated Activity

Stemming from the centrality of social interaction in the process of learning, the notion of mediated action becomes important. If human mental development is primarily socioculturally determined then all humans construct their knowledge based on artefacts such as tools, symbols and signs (Lantolf and Appel 1994: 7). There are essentially two types of auxiliary devices which facilitate human achievement and accomplishment. Vygotsky (1978: 53–5) categorically distinguishes between 'tools' and 'signs' in mediated action. Firstly, tools are mechanical, concrete and physical in nature and include items such as pole vaults for sporting achievement (Wertsch 1998: 27). In the case of LTE, mechanical tools might include teaching aids such as whiteboards, overhead projectors, video recorders and computers (see, for example, Hawkins 2004 for a description of a listserv as a mediational tool on an LTE programme). The sign, on the other hand, 'acts as an instrument of psychological activity in a manner analogous to the role of tool in labor' (Vygotsky 1978: 52). The primary mediational sign at the disposal of sociocultural groupings, and the object of the research in this book, is language. Vygotsky stipulates that tools have an external orientation and seek to exert changes in objects, whereas signs are internally oriented, aimed at mastering oneself (1978: 55). Others following in sociocultural traditions have chosen to make similar distinctions but use terms such as 'mechanical tool' versus 'psychological tool' (Lantolf and Appel 1994: 8). Whatever the terminology, the notion that physical and mental functioning is socioculturally and historically mediated is primary. Wertsch (1998: 24–72) outlines the ten properties of mediated action, as follows:

1. Mediated action is characterised by an irreducible tension between agent and mediational means (tools). The whole is greater than the sum of the individual parts.
2. Mediational means are material. All tools are material, even language, and as such the agent has to develop skills to react to and manipulate them.
3. Mediated action typically has multiple goals simultaneously, which may, at times, be in conflict.
4. Mediated action is situated on one or more developmental paths. It is only possible as a result of developments which have been made in the past.
5. Mediational means constrain as well as enable action.
6. New mediational means transform mediated action, for example Wertsch argues that the introduction of the modern PC has changed social and psychological processes.
7. Relationships of agents towards mediational means can be characterised in terms of mastery. In other words, agents need to develop skills/aptitudes in order to be able to use tools.
8. The relationship of agents towards mediational means can be characterised in terms of appropriation. Here, appropriation is meant in the Bakhtinian sense of taking something and making it one's own (Bakhtin 1981: 294).
9. Mediational tools are often spin-offs. Many cultural tools were not designed specifically for the uses to which they are subsequently put.
10. Mediational means are associated with power and authority. Wertsch refers to work by Bakhtin (1981: 342–8), which distinguishes between 'authoritative' and 'internally persuasive' discourse. The basic idea is that the word of those in authority is binding on those with less or without authority.

The Zone of Proximal Development

So far, stemming from sociocultural approaches, we have seen the centrality afforded to the interactional nature of learning and the notion of mediated learning, and heard mention of the role of language in both. It is therefore entirely logical that Vygotsky, as part of his thoughts on human mental development, should have formulated a theory on how learning is supported and assisted by those capable of providing cognitive support. The basic idea behind his thinking in this respect is that the normal intellectual capacities of individuals can be extended through the appropriate supports from those more skilled at the task at hand. The role of the human as mediator is paramount and has given birth to conceptualisations such as the mediated learning experience (MLE) perspective of Feuerstein (Kozulin 1998: 59–79). There are two important characteristics of such situations. Firstly, there are at least two people present, only one of whom is considered to have expert knowledge, and secondly, speech mediates the interaction between both parties. From this, it is apparent that the learner has an actual and potential performance level and this is known as the zone of proximal development (ZPD). Vygotsky (1978: 86) defines the ZPD as, 'the difference between the actual development level as determined by independent problem solving, and the level of potential development as determined through problem-solving under adult guidance, or in collaboration with more capable peers'.

Within the ZPD children/learners move through various developmental stages. They move from one stage to the next with adult guidance in the form of 'scaffolding' (Bruner 1985: 25). Scaffolding is the cognitive support provided by an adult/tutor to aid a child/learner (Diaz et al. 1990; Donato 1994; Mercer 1995; Randall and Thornton 2001; Walsh 2001). This support comes in the form of dialogue so that a child can more easily make sense of difficult tasks. Scaffolded guidance, widely recognised as being an exclusively human activity, is the 'sensitive, supportive intervention of a teacher in the progress of a learner who is actively involved in some specific task, but who is not quite able to manage the task alone' (Mercer 1995: 77). In a traditional teaching or teacher education context this support is usually realised through linguistic means where there is generally an absence of physical aids and tools. It is then withdrawn appropriately as the competence of the learner reaches the required levels. The expert may upgrade or dismantle the scaffolding in light of the emerging capabilities of the novice (Rogoff 1990: 94), thereby allowing for a 'moving zone of proximal development' (Marks-Greenfield 1984: 131). The discursive mechanism of scaffolding is described by Donato (1994: 41) in terms of the characteristics outlined originally by Wood et al. (1976: 98). These features include the following:

1. recruiting interest in the task;
2. reducing degrees of freedom in order to simplify the task;
3. direction maintenance;
4. marking critical and relevant features of the task;
5. frustration control;
6. demonstrating and modelling an ideal version of the task to be performed.

This process recognises that comprehension must precede production, and also allows for the role of serendipity as trainees engage in what Wood et al. (1976: 90) call 'blind action', often resulting in accidental learning.

Traditionally, scaffolding has been examined from the perspective of a clearly identifiable expert and a clearly identifiable novice. However, Donato (1994) takes an interesting approach and examines whether it can occur between peers of different abilities. He investigates novice–novice scaffolding in the construction of dialogues in French among third level students in an American university and finds that it is very much evident. The results of this study show that speakers disinhibit each other and trigger mutual linguistic processing by means of scaffolding. They are, 'at the same time individually novices and collectively experts, sources of new orientation for each other, and guides through this complex linguistic problem solving' (Donato 1994: 46). In a later study, also discussing the notion of a group ZPD, Nyikos and

Hashimoto (1997) investigate the extent to which constructivist practices are a reality among students working together on final projects in a teacher education programme where such theories are explicitly advocated. Content analysis of written journals and reports is used to establish the factors influencing the extent to which a ZPD is formed: division of labour, writing and work styles, power relationships and role taking. These factors, necessary for the creation of an effective ZPD, operated differently, producing different results in the three individual groups under scrutiny, leading to the conclusion that a strongly supportive social component is a prerequisite to the potential for learning (or ZPD) (further examples of empirical studies employing these approaches include Antón 1999; De-Guerrero and Villamil 2000).

The notion of regulation and self-regulation through appropriate language use is central to the idea of supported learning. Vygotsky's developmental theory stipulates that through scaffolding, within the ZPD, higher psychological functioning is attained through a process where individuals move from being 'other-regulated' to being 'self-regulated' (Diaz et al. 1990: 127). It is necessarily normal for adult–child interactions to initially assume asymmetrical patterns of communication control as children are predominantly other regulated (Rommetveit 1985: 191). The transition from one to the other takes place within the ZPD through strategic use of dialogic interaction. However, self-regulated activity does not indicate the end of the developmental process in Vygotskian theory. Instead, he sees development as continuous and fluid and processes of other or self-regulation can re-emerge in the form of private speech for strategic reasons when an individual encounters a difficult task (for example, talking oneself through the assembly of a complex piece of equipment).

As can be seen from discussions so far, Vygotsky, during his short life, achieved much by way of formulating an approach and theory to explain how human functioning relates to and reflects its sociocultural and historical context. However, it has been suggested that there may be anomalies present, in particular with the construct of a ZPD. Kinginger (2002: 242–3), in her critique of conservative versus progressive philosophical approaches to education, highlights the problems ensuing from the ZPD as a 'rather metaphoric concept' and provides convincing evidence that the interpretation of this construct has been 'fraught with ambiguity from the start'. She continues by arguing that 'commentaries based on close reading of the original – of Vygotsky's own use of the ZPD – converge on a view of the ZPD concept as unfinished and inadequately linked to Vygotsky's overall developmental theory'. Additionally, and on a related note, it has been observed that his premature death prevented him from perhaps formulating a specific methodology which would allow his approach to be applied to real settings. Wertsch (1990: 115), identifies this issue thus,

The task of Vygotsky's socio cultural approach to mind was to specify how human mental functioning reflects and constitutes its historical, institutional, and cultural setting. In my opinion he clearly succeeded in producing an approach that is consistent with this goal, but he did relatively little in way of specifying how his approach would apply to concrete settings.

Furthermore, Wertsch goes on to show that the frameworks and organising principles proposed in the works of Bakhtin are most appropriate to extend Vygotsky's formulation of a sociocultural approach to mind. Nevertheless, many Vygotskian constructs have gained 'increasing prominence among scholars seeking to understand human development at the intersection of the personal and the social worlds' (Kinginger 2002: 243, see also Warford and Reeves 2003), and in particular the ZPD is seen as,

> the framework, par excellence, which brings all the pieces of the learning setting together – the teacher, the learner, their social and cultural history, their goals and motives, as well as the resources available to them, including those that are dialogically constructed together. (Aljaafreh and Lantolf 1994: 468, cited in Kinginger 2002: 243)

Clearly then, in this tradition, 'we see knowledge as constructed among members of learning communities ... and we question the nature of knowledge' (Hawkins 2004: 89). Essentially, notions of sociocultural context, collaborative learning, guided and self-direction and reflection should all feature prominently in the type of discourse examined later in this book.

Sociocultural Theory and Language Teacher Education

Farr (2011) explores in some detail the relevance and applications of sociocultural theory in language teacher education contexts, acknowledging that culture, individuals and institutions have a strong impact on local educational practices (Gill 1997). However, in a general sense, following the typical time lapse between theory and application, many contexts now take a social constructivist approach (Carlson 1999; Malderez and Bodóczky 1999; Randall and Thornton 2001; Smith 2001), with an emphasis on the joint construction of knowledge between teacher educator and student/novice teacher. In the extreme, one might find examples of teachers purposely adopting a non-expert role so that students are encouraged to take responsibility for the construction of their own knowledge (Mercer 1995: 52). This is in direct juxtaposition to the traditional cognitive paradigm involving teacher-transmitted knowledge, although it has been suggested that such a paradigm is still widely in practice on LTE programmes around the world (Bax 1997: 232). Smith (2001) suggests reasons why we should be moving towards social constructivism in our modes of instruction in ELTE, one of which is that modelling, or imitation, is appropriate if it takes place within the ZPD (see further discussion below). Imitation here is assumed in a relational versus behaviourist way, and can be achieved through supported collaboration. Smith justifies this approach on the basis that when many teachers encounter the real classroom for the first time they will end up 'teaching as they were taught, not as they were taught to teach' (Smith 2001: 222). Secondly, she links this with John Dewey's closely associated notion of 'direct experience' being the key to learning. By actively subscribing to these philosophies in their education practices, educators can provide direct experience with social constructivist activities, which will in turn provide a basis on which they can build their own teaching paradigms.

Despite the lip service paid to such philosophies, it would appear that many teacher education programmes, particularly at university level, are still very much knowledge transmission based. Schocker-von-Ditfurth and Legutke (2002: 163), commenting particularly on the German training context, suggest that, 'the dominant teaching formats at universities are transmission-oriented, and therefore contradict current ideologies of student-centredness and communicative methodology'. They base their observations on research and also on anecdotal evidence. Smith (2001: 227) suggests that collaborative work can be challenging and sometimes threatening for those more familiar with other approaches, both educators and student/novice teachers. Bax (1997: 237) identifies 'trainee frustration' at any perceived lack of input for fear of not acquiring important information. There are also financial considerations at play here. Education is expensive, and, in the neo-liberal institution, students are now clients in a consumer economy, where time and value for money are important. They may perceive that joint knowledge construction does not give them enough and that it takes too long. Thirdly, we often incorrectly equate maximum talk with maximum participation, and therefore, inadvertently, over-encourage it. Fourthly, there are some course components which do not easily lend themselves to collaborative explanation. For all of these reasons, strict and exclusive adherence to such practices is probably rare in LTE programmes.

However, the practice and reflection components of teacher education identify themselves as being a prime location for the implementation of co-construction of meaning and also for modelling. Farr (2011: 9) offers several reasons why this is considered to be the case.

Firstly, Edge (1992: 62), makes mention of three elements contained in the learning process: traditional intellectual learning, experiential learning, and thirdly, the notion of learning through 'the expression of our experience and understanding, the articulation of what we think and feel, (Edge 1992: 62, citing Dilthey 1976), as a way of bringing together intellectual and experiential learning. Obviously, this fits very closely with Vygotskian theories on social, collaborative and guided learning, and is what is purportedly practised in TP feedback. Secondly, individual expression is important for two reasons. It allows student teachers to take rightful ownership of their own experiences and feelings vis-à-vis a more authoritative figure, thereby counterbalancing some of the institutional power of tutor talk, and it nudges the tutor into assuming a more facilitative role while continuing to engender trust and confidence. It may also help to reduce the problem of different interpretations of reality and of the difficulties associated with discerning motives behind actions (Wertsch 1998: 15), particularly when they are the actions of others. A related justification can be found in the need to respect individual styles and approaches in language teaching (Edge 2002: 6).

Despite the criticisms outlined above in relation to the four influencing theoretical underpinnings, in practical terms, these beliefs and theories have led to what some have referred to as new learning, or new forms of learning. Anderson (1989) (cited in Lunenberg et al. 2007: 587) was one of the first to distinguish how new learning differs from more traditional approaches and suggests five main divergences:

1. development of flexible and de-contextualised expertise rather than recall of facts and context specific application of skills;
2. the teacher's role in mediating learning rather than conveying information to students (Brown et al. 1989);
3. students as active constructors of cognitive networks rather than receptors of information;
4. a focus on defining and representing problems and different solutions, rather than on the application of algorithmic procedures and single 'correct' answers;
5. a focus on the importance of social environments in which failure is accepted as a part of learning, self-regulated learning is valued (Zimmerman 2002) and other students are considered as resources for learning, as opposed to social environments which represent negative connotations concerning failure, a focus on teacher-directed learning, and a view of other students as hindrances to individual learning.

These are principles and approaches that are by now very familiar to the thinking and repertoire of activities of most teachers and teacher educators in many, though not all, parts of the world. We will return to the question of impact on change below when discussing the modelling role of the teacher educator.

2.2.3 FREEMAN'S DESIGN THEORY FOR SECOND LANGUAGE TEACHERS

In 2016, Donald Freeman published a book entitled *Educating Second Language Teachers*. In it, he situates his many, varied and rich experiences as a language teacher and language teacher educator, in conceptual discussions around the prevailing theoretical frameworks which have played an influencing role over the course of his professional life. In the final two chapters he presents a Design Theory for second language teacher education, as an alternative to 'second language teacher education … largely defined by prescriptive ideas about what the content should be and how it should be taught' (2016: 227). His Design Theory is heavily based on social practice theory, and aims to support the organisation and study of teacher education activities and programmes by explaining how things are done and helping to develop new ways of doing things. It is highly descriptive rather than prescriptive in orientation. Among its key premises is the idea that second language teacher education, although it shares many traits with general teacher education, is also different because 'unlike other content areas, in second language teacher education the content to be taught (language) is also the means of teaching it' (Freeman 2016: 227). While this framework was not designed for the analysis of spoken language data, in later analytical chapters we draw on some of Freeman's concepts to help interpret the TEC data.

Chapter 12 of Freeman's book presents an account of four of the six major components of the Design Theory. Chapter 13 elaborates on the fourth of these, 'communities', in much more detail, and presents the final two components. The following is a summary of the first four components (Freeman 2016: 231–6):

1. Providing tools and opportunities to use them, is the central purpose of teacher education. The example given is the presentation, practice, production (PPP) model, which, as a pedagogic tool can be used in planning a lesson (the opportunity to use it).
2. Social facts. This second component relates to recognising and using the tools appropriately in practice in ways which are normative and accepted in the teaching community. So, continuing with the PPP example, it is being able to use this tool to divide a part of the lesson into temporal elements with specific pedagogic purposes in practice.
3. Local and professional languages. This relates to appropriate social knowledge and use of language in the specific context of 1. The profession (for example, a language placement test) and 2. The local context (for example, the Junior Cert, as a state examination taken in Ireland at the age of fifteen or sixteen). Some language may cross between the two and be understood in both local and professional capacities, for example, the concept of Irish English. The language functions only if it can be understood within the relevant communities.
4. Communities. Professional in this case, communities with their theoretical origin in situated learning theory are described as a 'set of relations among persons, activities, and world, over time and in relation to other tangential and overlapping communities …' (Lave and Wenger 1991: 98). They are defined by what they say and what they do and essentially involve working together towards a common purpose.

Chapter 13 goes on to differentiate between two parallel types of community. The first he calls a Community of Activity (C/a), which is actual and visual and is defined by its participants and what it does. It is 'a group of people who are doing a recognized or recognizable activity – for example, queuing in line, having a classroom discussion … The particular form of activity has a past or heritage, which is what makes it recognizable' (Freeman 2016: 241). There are three aspects to a C/a: 1. actions are visible and 2. recognisable as meaningful, 3. and/or sensible to others within that community. Secondly, he identifies a Community of Explanation (C/e) 'where a group of people share common ways of reasoning about the world, or particular aspects of it' (2016: 241). A principal exponent of a C/e is the language which is used to make social facts. The alignment between both types of community is partial and changing (not everyone makes sense of everything in the same way all of the time).

The final two components of Freeman's Design Theory are:

5. Articulation, defined as 'the process of negotiating entry to a community of activity and explanation' (2016: 243). This takes place in the period when a newcomer

is working to be recognised as part of the community and acting as if they were. Learning happens through this 'acting', but in using/articulating social facts inappropriately it becomes clear that the individual is not yet a full member.

6. When articulation becomes full explanation in socially appropriate ways, it marks individuals as full members of the community. The articulations are no longer marked. So articulation is 'participating with', as a peripheral or partial member, whereas explanation is 'participating in', as a full member.

Freeman (2016: 252) concludes by rationalising why he has called this theory a design theory,

> The theory is meant to work in two ways. One is to serve in understanding what goes on, for better or worse, more or less effectively, in what is done in teacher education. In this sense, it should function descriptively to offer a set of terms to label what is done to a new set of social facts. This is its use as a 'theory'. The other use, which is closely connected to the first, is the 'design' dimension. Here the framework can function proactively to prescribe to ways of doing teacher education. However, these prescriptions will not be based on disciplinary history, professional whim, or institutional fancy. Instead, the design theory ought to provide a reasoned basis on which to evaluate, to reform, and to innovate in educating second language (as well as other) teachers.

These are laudable reasons, and the profession owes Freeman a debt of gratitude for taking all of his knowledge, beliefs and experiences and articulating them into a coherent theory. In later analysis chapters we will draw on parts of the theory and the terminology to explain the interactions under scrutiny.

2.3 CURRICULUM AND CONTENT: THE WHAT OF LTE

Having spent some time in the previous section on the pedagogic approaches now typically adopted in LTE and why they are deemed to be most appropriate, we now turn our attention to what typically constitutes the curriculum, or *what* is acquired by the novice teacher. Shulman (1986) originally distinguished between pedagogic (knowledge about methodologies, approaches, classroom management and so on) and content (in this case, knowing about the English language system, various theories of language and how it is constructed, the importance of culture and so on) knowledge (PACK), later expanded to include pedagogic content knowledge (knowing the most appropriate ways to teaching specific pieces of content to a particular group or individual). Mishra and Koehler (2006) argue that due to the ubiquitous nature of technology and its impact in pedagogy, a teacher's knowledge should now explicitly include technological knowledge, bringing us to the TPACK acronym. A model of TPACK has been presented incorporating the fundamental role of research and the impact of Wisdom of Practice (Chappell 2017) elsewhere (Farr and O'Keeffe 2019) and this model is reproduced in Figure 2.1 as it is relevant to the current discussion.

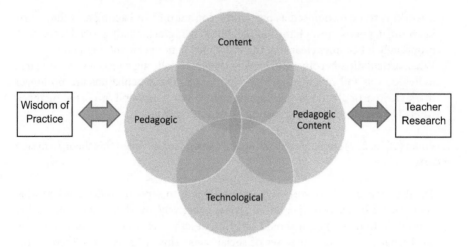

Figure 2.1   Teacher knowledge
Source: Farr and O'Keeffe, 2019.

These various, overlapping types of knowledge are acquired through a range of interactional contexts in LTE programmes, as well as through individual private study and critical reflection. Many of these contexts are explored empirically through the lens of language in later analyses chapters but for now it is worth summaris-ing in broad terms how the type of content articulated in Figure 2.1 is acquired by novice teachers undertaking a pre- or in-service programme. Typically, the content (language, pedagogy and technology) and research components are explored from a theoretical and methodological perspective in seminar or workshop modes, while hands-on practice takes place in the classroom as part of the TP cycle, which has a strong reflective and formative developmental focus (as discussed earlier). The practical application of the research methodology component is usually realised through teachers completing an empirical research project with a focus on either language use or classroom practice (such as an action research project), and writing this up as a report, a publication, or a thesis if conducted as part of a higher education qualification.

2.4 PARTICIPANTS: THE WHO OF LTE

The participants and the roles that they play are at the very heart of the analyses later in this book. While there are a number of important players in the process of LTE, the focus in this book is on those directly involved in the immediate formal institutional setting of the teacher education programme: the teacher educators, the TP mentors/supervisors, the student/novice teachers and the English language learners. It is the discourse that takes place between these groups in a range of interactional educa-tional settings which is analysed in the chapters that follow. We will take a moment now to think in more detail about these participants and the roles that they play.

2.4.1 TEACHER EDUCATORS/MENTORS

In our institutional context, the teacher educators and the TP supervisors are one and the same group of people tasked with performing different duties at different times. This overlap makes for an easy merge of roles and responsibilities, for example, the educator during the course of a grammar content workshop making reference to the practical methods of teaching a specific discoursal function to a target group of English language learners; or a mentor live observing a practice lesson who needs to assist the student teacher presenting the future perfect, or quietly right an incorrect semantic explanation. And while, in itself, these two overlapping roles do not generally cause consternation for a teacher educator, the range of roles they are required to fill can sometimes be a challenge, as can the responsibility of and pressure to be an effective role model. So what are these multi-dimensional roles?

Turney et al. (1982: 5) presented a tabular representation of seven provider roles, which we believe has expanded quite a bit over the past twenty-five years, depending on the professional context. Table 2.1 includes their original seven first and four at the end which we have added and discuss further at this point.

The impact of teacher education programmes on the classroom practices of teachers when they enter fully into the profession has been questionable. Research suggests strongly that under the pressure of a full teaching load in a busy and demanding educational institution teachers can often reach levels of anxiety that cause them to

Table 2.1   Teacher educator roles

Role	Duties
Instructor	Presenting, questioning, problem solving, guiding discussion
Manager	Planning, liaising, organising
Counsellor	Relating, responding, helping, handling difficulties
Observer	Establishing frames of reference, focusing, observing and recording interaction, analysis of observations
Feedback	Stimulating recall of the lesson/incidents, analysing performance, sharing interpretations, forward planning
Assessor	Communicating with learner-teachers, obtaining and assessing evidence, reaching summative assessments
Process leader	Guiding the process by which a group learns
Role model	Modelling new forms of learning, focusing on the process of learning as an agent of change
Developing professional	Committing and implementing a personal professional development plan to continually enhance teaching, judiciously integrating new methods and technologies
Researcher	Engaging in a programme of (action) research, disseminating outcomes, results, resources and so on, appropriately
Political professional	Influencing the political landscape at institutional and national level to safeguard and develop the profession and its communities

revert to teaching how they themselves were taught rather than implementing new forms of learning (as discussed earlier) they learn about on their education pro- grammes. This suggests that the many years spent doing an 'apprenticeship of obser- vation' (Lortie 1975), subconsciously absorbing the practices of our past teachers, has a strong impact. To break this cycle, Oxford (1997a: 46) outlines two techniques for integrating appropriate approaches into LTE. The first is the application of these learning-teaching practices within the programme, and the second is including the theories within the subject content of the programme. She concludes that using one to the exclusion of the other will reduce effectiveness. In other words, teacher educa- tors need to actively demonstrate these theories in their own practices so that future teachers can learn them and subsequently incorporate them into their own language learning classrooms. If student/novice teachers experience social constructivism in all aspects of their education programmes, they will have a better chance of inter- nalising and later practising it. LTE's role, then, if approached from a sociocultural perspective,

> is not so much to apprentice fledgling (or practicing) teachers to particular cultural models of teaching and schooling, it is to facilitate critical understandings of the implications and consequences of the decisions they make as to what they do, and how they do it. (Hawkins 2004: 90)

Lunenberg et al. (2007) also emphasise the importance of teacher educators focusing on the process of teacher education as much as on the content or output/product. Being a model of good practice/a role model is likely to have a longer-lasting impact as these practices become part of the assimilated repertoire a student teacher can draw on when confronted with the reality of the classroom. The Lunenberg et al. paper presents a number of case studies from the Netherlands, where a focus on the teacher educator as a model has been deemed fruitful as an agent of reform. They discuss both implicit modelling, which is basically a philosophy of 'walking the walk' as well as 'talking the talk', and explicit modelling, which is where the teacher educator articulates the pedagogic choices they are making, and why, in the form of a 'meta-commentary' (2007: 590). Unfortunately they conclude that, despite its potential 'at present one must have serious doubts about the competence of teacher educators to serve as role models in promoting new visions of learning' (2007: 586).

Closely related to the discussion of teacher educator as role model is a commitment to a structured, relevant and explicit ongoing professional development plan. This is now typically a requirement for continued membership of the profession through teacher recognition and registration schemes and, if it is something that teachers are required to do, then it must form part of the teacher educator's active agenda also. In contexts where this is a formal requirement, local protocol will dictate how this is managed. In our higher education context, there is no formal or obligatory insti- tutional CPD framework (yet), but expectations are explicit in processes like annual professional development reviews (PDRs) and of course in promotions' criteria. National guidelines from the National Forum for the Enhancement of Teaching and Learning in Higher Education are used by many to plan professional development activities and demonstrate their impact as part of such institutional processes. And, as an extension, being involved in research is a vital part of this same discussion on critical engagement. Formal research and publication is a requirement of working in a university setting, but even if this is not the case, some level of involvement in new insights, findings and evidence-based accounts is highly desirable as part of good role-modelling. And while conducting formal primary research may not be a priority for some teacher educators, or teachers (Borg 2009), staying abreast of what research is uncovering is easily done through scanning the journals or attending professional conferences. And initiating small-scale action research projects to inform one's own practice is not a big ask (Farr 2015). Farr and O'Keeffe (2019) suggest some accessible ways in which this can take place, using corpus-based methodologies. Personal involvement in research at any level gives a teacher educator a much more credible and authoritative voice in the eyes of their student teachers and their fellow professionals.

In addition to these local responsibilities there are a number of political agendas in which teacher educators are expected to take a leading role. To quote a good example, in the US context, Zeichner (2006) articulates his views about the challenges for the future of college- and university-based teacher education. In this context he contends that teacher educators should do four things:

1. work to redefine the debate about the relative merits of alternative and traditional certification programs;
2. work to broaden the goals of teacher education beyond raising scores on standardized achievement tests;
3. change the center of gravity in teacher education to provide a stronger role for schools and communities in the education of teachers;
4. take teacher education seriously as an institutional responsibility or do not do it.

This is a good example of what institutions or relevant government departments may expect, either implicitly or explicitly. If a teacher educator is to take on political agendas such as these, and many feel a duty to do so, it creates an added and very public layer of responsibility and pressure, to a set of already extremely complex professional demands.

It is clear from the range of expectations detailed in the previous paragraphs that the role of the teacher educator is a challenging one. Like teachers, they face full teaching schedules and administrative responsibilities, as well as the organisational load of running busy and demanding teacher education programmes. The challenges of becoming a teacher educator in the English higher education sector are clearly identified by Murray and Male (2005) in one of the few available studies which investigates teacher educators. They find that the transition from teacher to teacher educator and scholar, in the absence of a formal qualification with this as a specific focus, is difficult for a number of reasons, and it typically takes them between two and three years to establish their new identity. The two primary challenges identified by the twenty-eight participating teacher educators were establishing an appropriate pedagogy for the initial teacher education programmes with which they were charged, and becoming research active in a way that met with institutional and national metrics. In a more general sense, a challenge for teacher educators when trying to perform their many roles is the way in which they are typically judged as being effective. Common measures in the neo-liberal education system are student satisfaction ratings, research outputs and successful recruitment onto programmes, rather than explicitly on their effectiveness as a teacher educator as an agent of change and development for their students. The latter is of course much more intangible and a difficult metric to capture in any consistent way that can be benchmarked, and so is often excluded or at best gets some lip service unless there is an issue or a complaint. Given the various constraints, it is probably fair to say that language teacher educators must be very committed professionals to maintain the current standards, and they are still very much on a journey in terms of where they would like to be.

2.4.2 THE STUDENT/NOVICE TEACHER AND TEACHER COGNITION

Another central and all important party to the LTE context is the student teacher. The entire enterprise is focused on moulding and shaping and supporting their evolution into fully qualified teachers, who will continue to develop throughout their professional lives. The ways in which teachers, and, by extension, student teachers, have been viewed by the professional and research community has profoundly changed over the past thirty to forty years. And it is no coincidence that these perspectives have changed in line with evolving theoretical and methodological approaches to teaching, as discussed earlier in relation to LTE. Behaviourist methods such as audio-lingualism required little thought on the part of the teacher as it was based primarily on patterns and drills. Such methods were based on learned actions and behaviours. In such contexts teachers' observable actions and behaviours were the focus, as indeed were those of their learners. 'In fact, the less thought and the more patterned behaviour, the better' (Burns et al. 2015: 586). A change came in the late 1970s and 1980s when a range of more innovative, alternative, humanistic methods gained popularity on the international language teaching stage. Methods such as Gattegno's Silent Way, or Suggestopedia required teachers to align with a very specific way of thinking, and a specific set of beliefs and principles about teaching and learning. Teachers making decisions necessarily meant that some sort of cognitive activity was supporting their choices, and the notion of teachers as cognitive beings was born. Teacher cognition became even more discussed and researched in the eclectic post-method era of the 1990s, where informed decision-making was a crucial capacity given the array of options available, and this continues to be the case.

In fact, during the mid to late 1990s, when Fiona was just completing her MA in Teaching English as a Foreign Language (TEFL), as it was known at the time, she has a very clear memory of reading what seemed (even to her novice mind) to be seminal articles. These included Golombek's (1998) 'A study of language teachers' personal practical knowledge', which clearly signalled a change in how we thought about teachers and the cognitive processes underlying their observable actions in the classroom. Since that time, both conceptual and empirical publications on teacher

Table 2.2   Ontological generations in studying the language-teaching mind

Ontological Generations	Conceptual Unit of Study	Prevailing Research Methodologies	Exemplar Study
Individualist [1990 ff]	Decisions, thoughts, beliefs	Often quantitative, surveys (belief inventories), observation and stimulated recall interviews, frequency tallies	Johnson 1992
Social [1995 ff]	Meaning and explanations, situated in social contexts	Qualitative, introspective methods such as diary studies and in-depth interviews	Numrich 1996
Sociohistorical [2000 ff]	Thinking as a function of place and time, through interaction and negotiation with social and historical contexts	Qualitative, interviews and narrative inquiry Researcher positioning is important, and often the research process consists of co-constructed researcher-participant dialogue	Breen et al. 2001
Complex, chaotic systems [2010 ff]	Dynamic, emergent systems that involve the interaction of multiple interconnected elements	Qualitative, interviews, diary studies, analysis of interactions Research includes analysis of social, cultural, historical and political factors	Kiss 2012

Source: Burns et al. 2015: 589.

cognition have proliferated and have evolved the way in which we view teachers, as both individuals and socially and culturally bound beings operating in a specific set of circumstances. Burns et al. (2015) provide a relatively comprehensive account in their *Modern Language Journal* article 'Theorizing and studying the language-teaching mind: Mapping research on language teacher cognition'. Table 2.2 from this publication provides a neat summary overview of how research on teacher cognition has evolved since the early 1990s.

Table 2.2 clearly shows the shift from seeing the teaching mind as individualist to socially situated (aligned with the evolution of sociocultural thinking as discussed earlier). Closely following this, synchronic and diachronic notions of time in context were included, such as the lesson in the context of the present classroom/school and that considered in the historical context, as well as the strong view of learning as dynamic social activity (Johnson 2009: 1). However, this view of a dynamic system in context, coupled with the dynamic nature of the features of that activity (for example, changing views of language or language acquisition) has created a tension. From this tension has grown the view of complex systems, which are by their very nature chaotic. The focus then becomes the dynamic features of interactions in context. It is essentially here that the research reported in this book lies. We endeavour to complete the difficult task of analysing complex interactions in their sociocultural and his-torically mediated contexts, with the added dimension of technologically mediated modes in some cases. For this reason, there are no simple 'results' or 'findings' to be had or found. Rather it is a deconstruction for the purpose of enhanced understanding of the complexity of interaction, teaching and teacher education.

2.5 TASKS

1. Discuss any potential cons to taking a sociocultural approach in LTE contexts. Which of these are most likely to happen in a context with which you are familiar?
2. Read any of the literature quoted in this chapter, orally present a critical review to a peer and discuss.

REFLECTIVE PRACTICE IN LANGUAGE TEACHER EDUCATION

3.1 INTRODUCTION

Reflective practice (RP) has become an integral component on teacher education programmes today despite some historic shortcomings, which have remained only partially resolved. These shortcomings include the fact that RP has often over-relied on written modes to the detriment of face-to-face forms, that it has failed to foreground collaboration, and that its advocates have offered little empirical evidence to show how it can be scaffolded and facilitated within a community of practice (Farr and Farrell 2017; Mann and Walsh 2013, 2017). In this book we seek to address these deficiencies and to build on research that supports the need for a holistic and data-led approach to RP, undertaken from within the context of a teacher education CoP. The main aim is to demonstrate how (student) teacher interactions with peers, lecturers and tutors across a range of face-to-face and written RP modes, that are guided and structured to varying degrees, can enhance social and collaborative learning (discussed in detail in Chapter 2). This will also provide insight into the complex processes involved in student teacher socialisation into the ELTE teaching community and the development of reflective practitioners. From this, we can also evaluate the role played by the various modes, and their effectiveness in facilitating language teacher professional growth. The research reported on for this purpose draws on TEC, featuring members of a third level ELTE community (as discussed in more detail in Chapter 4).

As collaborative RP is argued for by the present authors as an effective means by which teachers are socialised into the CoP, it seems logical to begin this chapter with an overview of RP as a concept and approach in English language teacher education, as in education more widely. There follows a critical review of the wide-ranging benefits that can be expected for novice and experienced teachers from engaging in RP, and the various RP modes through which this can be achieved. At this stage, we also foreground some of the historic limitations of RP and we review empirically-based studies undertaken more recently which have begun to address these deficiencies from within a CoP research paradigm.

3.2 RP IN LTE

Reflective practice is one of three distinct models of teacher education that have emerged over the course of the last fifty years or so (Wallace 1991). In the first, the 'craft model', the experienced professional practitioner possesses all the knowledge and wisdom of the craft and novices study with the practitioner, and strive for professional competence via practice, in an 'apprentice' type relationship. This contrasts with 'the applied science model' which has been the most commonly used approach in teacher education, where experts (not necessarily practising, or practised in the field) convey knowledge to novices, which they, in turn, put into practice (see also Chapter 2). Finally, there is the reflective model, as developed from the 1990s onwards by Schön (1991) and influenced by the historic work of American educator John Dewey from the early part of the twentieth century (Dewey 1933). Here, teachers reflect on their teaching in order to systematically explore and address professional considerations relating to their classroom practices. This is ultimately with a view to improving outcomes and sustaining ongoing professional growth. The RP model of teacher education has been developed against the backdrop of the paradigm shift from behaviourist-oriented to constructivist-oriented traditions (see Chapter 2) in education and the move away from the concept of method becoming an integral component of general teacher education and in the ELTE domain (Browne 2000; Kumaradivelu 2001, 2003; Pennycook 2000; Prabhu 1990; Spiro 2013).

3.2.1 RP: CONCEPT AND PRINCIPLES

Notwithstanding the growth in the appeal of RP and its use in teacher education, the concept has remained subject to multiple interpretations, which can at times seem confusing and contradictory (for example, see Akbari 2007; Cornford 2002; Korthagen 2001; LaBoskey 1997; McGarr and McCormak 2014; Walsh and Mann 2015). As Freeman (2016: 208) recently observed '[RP] is probably the most widespread but least well understood' idea in second language teacher education. For instance, in its original conceptualisation by Dewey (1933: 7) it was perceived as being 'equal to professionalism and knowledge is based on scientific approaches'. Schön (1987: 5), by contrast, later envisaged it as an 'intuitive, personal, non-rational activity' thereby suggesting that it is experiential and practice-based.

Similarly, there are diverse perspectives concerning the exact praxis-oriented nature of RP as an approach and what should constitute the content or focus of reflection. However, despite this lack of consensus, we believe it is possible to arrive at a broad definition that manages to reconcile these distinct perspectives and to encompass both the reflective processes and the content component of RP. Hence, we define RP as the process by which teachers learn more about teaching and learning through deep and critical consideration of their own professional practice and that of others. This is consistent with Wajnryb's (1992: 9) earlier view that RP is an 'active, evidence-based process during which practitioners learn through the construction of personal meaning, and by constantly reassessing their thinking in different situations'. In a more recent study of RP in the TESOL teacher education context, Farr and Riordan (2012) also stressed that RP compels teachers to confront prior assumptions about teaching and learning, and to enquire into not just what works in the classroom but also why it works. In this regard, there is now a shared consensus that any RP process must involve a critical dimension, that is, it is a process by which 'one reaches newfound clarity, on which one bases changes in action or disposition' (Jay and Johnson 2002: 74). Work has also focused on the linguistic representation of reflective practice where Farr and Riordan (2012), and Riordan (2018) have presented exploratory frameworks that have raised awareness of the language through which RP is expressed (see also Chapter 7).

Despite the multitude of interpretations that the term RP has inspired, it is possible to extrapolate four core underlying principles which are now widely accepted in the teacher education field (Calderhead and Gates 1993; Dewey 1933; Farrell 2004; Firdyiwek and Scida 2014; Korthagen 2001; LaBoskey 1997; Schön 1987). The first is that practitioners typically engage in reflection as a means of understanding the nature of teaching, personal beliefs and values. The second is that the process/product of reflective practice needs to include some systematic analysis of a problem, event or interpretation under consideration, which can involve both individual and collaborative dialogue to arrive at a solution to the identified challenge. The third is that the RP process is recursive in nature, with each stage strongly dependent on all stages before it, and it involves a cyclical dimension (Cirocki and Farrell 2017: 8). Finally, the fourth principle is that RP is a voluntary process which, to be effective, must be approached with the correct frame of mind in the sense that teachers must show a willingness to question existing practices and make a full and wholehearted commitment to the overall process. Hence, Cirocki and Farrell (2017: 8) have observed that RP involves 'open-mindedness and engagement on the part of teachers to endorse promoting high-quality language instruction and deep reflection on this instruction'. RP can be engaged in by teachers at all stages of their careers, both on an individual basis and collectively with peers and/or mentors, within which a wide variety of RP approaches and models can be used, which we review in the following section.

3.2.2 RP: APPROACHES AND MODELS

Amongst the approaches to RP that have emerged in teacher education since the 1990s, we find two main types, that is, approaches which have focused on the process (the stages or levels) of reflection and those which are concerned with the content. In the 'process' category, theorists have been concerned with how RP can be achieved in terms of phases and stages. Building on the earlier work of Schön (1987), Farrell (2004: 31) has identified five phases in the RP process. The first is concerned with the efficient exploitation of technical knowledge and cognitive aspects; the second and third types centre on the key notions of reflection in action and reflection on action (see Schön 1991). In the former case, understanding and awareness are captured in the moment of teaching, whereas in the latter, consideration is given retrospectively to what has happened in the classroom. To these, Farrell (2004: 31) has added a fourth and a fifth type, that is, reflection for action, which is proactive in nature, and action research whereby teachers become researchers of their own practices.

Another well-known model is the three dimensional typography set out by Jay and Johnson (2002). The first stage, which they call descriptive reflections, 'involves the intellectual process of "setting the problem;" that is, determining what it is that will become the matter for reflection' (2002: 77). Here the teacher describes the issue, which could be a problem in class, a feeling, an experience or a theory. In the second stage, comparative reflections, the issue is explored from various perspectives to gain a better understanding. The third dimension, critical reflections, leads to the teacher making 'a judgement or a choice among actions, or simply integrates what one has discovered into a new and better understanding of the problem' (2002: 79). There are many more models describing various levels or stages of RP, including, for example, Korthagen (2004), Lee (2005) and Zwozdiak-Myers (2012).

Meanwhile, approaches that have focused on the content of RP, that is, what the reflection is on, have encompassed five main areas, with some overlap observed between them. The first is concerned with learners in terms of their beliefs, learning styles and strategies, interests, cultural backgrounds and their developmental readiness (Hillier 2005; Pacheco 2005; Richards and Farrell 2005; Richards and Lockhart 1996). The second focuses on teachers and explores teaching styles, belief systems and perspectives on teaching, and the affective dimensions surrounding their teaching (Akbari 2007; Hillier 2005; Richards and Lockhart 1996; Rodgers and Raider-Roth 2006; Stanley 1998; Zeichner and Liston 1996). The third type is concerned with teachers' cognitive development, and academic and research actions taken by teachers to develop professionally (Farrell 2004; Richards and Farrell 2005). The fourth type focuses on critical and contextual aspects whereby teachers examine the social and political consequences of their teaching (Zeichner and Liston 1996); and the fifth and final type centres on moral and ethical issues whereby teachers reflect critically on the moral consequences of their teaching (Hansen 1998). Within all of this, the practical aspects such as the tools and procedures by which reflection is guided and fulfilled, such as journal writing, surveys and classroom discussions, are explored (Richards and Farrell 2005; Richards and Lockhart 1996; Walsh and Mann 2015).

Farrell (2018) has designed a five-level model of reflection which covers the aforementioned topics where student teachers are encouraged to reflect on: (1) teaching philosophy, (2) teaching principles, (3) pedagogical theory, (4) classroom practice, and (5) beyond practice. In addition, the PENSER model (Problem Identification; Embracing; Noticing; Solving; Exploring; and Researching) introduced by Farr and Farrell (2017) offers a holistic framework through which teachers can systematically move from an awareness-raising focus on issues arising from their own behaviour and skills in the classroom towards more interpretive and critical understandings of their classroom experiences within a particular social and institutional context, to linking them to the wider societal context. This is with the overall aim of transforming practice, with action research serving as a key catalyst for change. This model has been successfully used on our MA TESOL programme, enabling the authors to systematically trace and evaluate the complex processes involved in RP, and the qualitative outcomes by empirical means. One of the key criteria for the design of the PENSER model was that it would create opportunities for teachers to engage in reflective practice across a range of complementary written and face-to-face modes. This was intended to help address a further main criticism levelled at historic models of RP which is that they tended to over-emphasise written RP to the neglect of face-to-face reflection (Mann and Walsh 2013, 2017). Hence, the PENSER model featured multiple RP modes including on-line portfolios and group discussions mediated by a lecturer/teacher educator (further details on multimodal approaches to RP can be seen in Section 3.3.3). There is now a growing recognition in teacher education that, while many individual methods have proven effective as tools to facilitate reflective thinking, no single pedagogical strategy is best or sufficient to teach reflective practice or to record its development in terms of the depth and outcomes achieved, as observed originally by Spalding et al. (2002: 1393). In the following section, we explore the benefits that can be gained for teachers at different stages of their professional careers when they engage in RP across various modes, drawing on studies that have provided empirical evidence to support this position.

3.2.3 RP: THE BENEFITS

As the potential benefits of RP for novice and experienced teachers alike have become more widely accepted, there has been an increased research interest in evaluating the outcomes of RP and how best these can be achieved (Black and Plowright 2010; Brandt 2006; Calderhead and Gates 1993; Crookes 2003; Farr 2010; Farr and Farrell 2017; Farrell 2004, 2016b; Gimenez 1999; Korthagen 2001; Schön 1983). Pacheco (2005: 2), for instance, has argued that reflection-driven exploration enables practitioners to make valuable links between theory and practice and to react, examine and evaluate their teaching. This in turn helps them to make more considered decisions or necessary changes to develop attitudes, beliefs and teaching practices. Ray and Coulter (2008) have observed that RP is most beneficial when it results in positive alterations in an individual's teaching practice as it reveals that learning has taken place, a view that is now widely shared (for example, see Tsui 2003). Tsui's (2003) work in the Hong Kong context has also been instrumental in bringing to light some of the benefits that RP can bring for novices, and early career teachers. The value of RP in the early days of teaching has also been supported by recent research undertaken by Farrell in the Canadian context (2016b) and by the work of Farr and Riordan (2012).

In educational circles, the early years are generally considered to be the most difficult in a teacher's career (Fantilli and McDougall 2009; Farrell 2016b; Gatbonton 1999; Mitchell 1997; Rodgers and Raider-Roth 2006). For instance, Pennington and Richards (2016) highlight the challenges that arise for novices in developing their teacher role and identity (see also Chapter 6 of this book) as they typically struggle to achieve the correct balance between maintaining discipline and focus, and developing a good relationship with learners. In this regard, Richards (2006: 60) has argued that most novice teachers take on a traditional or formal pedagogical role as their classroom 'default identity' as this provides the type of safe structure or hierarchy they feel they need in the early career. By contrast, a minority, adopt a more informal, personal and authentic identity. Zimmerman (1998: 91) has argued that this more informal type of orientation may be less effective for an inexperienced teacher who has not yet mastered instructional content and pedagogical skills, but that this will depend on the age of the students (see Chapter 6 for the linguistic exploration of teacher identity). We therefore argue, among others, that RP on such issues can stimulate thought and raise novice teachers' awareness and understanding of issues related to their identity.

The difficulties faced by novice English language teachers in their initial teaching practice have also attracted increased research interest more recently (Farr 2011; Farr and Farrell 2017; A. Farrell 2015; Farrell 2016b; Murphy 2015; Tsui 2003; Walsh 2006). Medgyes earlier observed that 'anxiety may be felt by any beginning teacher, whether native or non-native' (1994: 318). This has been supported empirically by RP oriented research by Farrell (2016b: 48), Farr and Farrell (2017) and Riordan (2018), which has demonstrated that novices from all backgrounds tend to be preoccupied in their reflections with issues relating to classroom management, how they are viewed by learners, and by their perceived lack of knowledge and skills, particularly as regards the teaching of grammar. They also typically report feeling uncomfortable with their position of authority, especially in situations where they find themselves teaching learners who are similar in age, or older (Farrell 2016b: 48). These findings also corroborate earlier classroom-based research undertaken by A. Farrell (2015), which signalled the importance of novices developing a teacher presence and that failure to do so might lead to a loss of learner confidence and place a strain on teacher–student relationships. The study undertaken by Farr and Farrell (2017) in the Irish TESOL teacher education context has highlighted further challenges posed for teachers by the changing nature of this profession and global developments surrounding the varieties of English taught. This is particularly acute for novices who already face many struggles in the teaching practicum, and at the early career stage. RP work has therefore tended to focus on challenges inherent in teachers' journeys and created an awareness thereof.

Moreover, while teacher professional development is intended to bring about change in teachers, it is commonly accepted that there is often little immediate evidence of change in teachers' practice and that such change takes place in the longer term (for example, see Pennington 1995: Waters and Vilches 2005). This is supported by RP research which has explored the processes by which language teacher roles evolve over time with novices moving from a focus on materials and classroom procedures to a growing concern with learners and interaction (Farr 2011; Farrell 2009). Key factors influencing teachers making changes to their practice include perceptions of the amount of risk involved, the communicability of the change, compatibility with existing practices, the number of gatekeepers involved, the perceived benefits of the change, the organisational, political, social and cultural context in which the change is being attempted, and whether opportunities are provided for those involved to critically explore the implications of such change for their professional practices (Richards 2001: 41–2). This carries implications for teacher education programmes in terms of how best we prepare those entering the profession as well as those seeking to progress their careers through continued professional development (CPD) initiatives. With the shift towards more learner-centred and communicative teaching approaches and the requirement for high levels of classroom interaction and target English use, good teaching today means that in addition to acquiring knowledge of linguistic and pedagogical theory, which is the hallmark of the L2 teacher's professionalism, those entering the profession need to develop insight and strategic competence in a wider range of areas than previously expected if they are to create the kind of supportive classroom environment and relationships in which learning can flourish and complex learner needs are met (A. Farrell 2015). This is where focused RP can play a role in encouraging teachers to deliberate on such issues.

In addition, developments in corpus linguistics have started to change the nature of the language we teach with the introduction of a more diverse range of varieties, genres and text types into the curriculum and the greater visibility of authentic and everyday English in course books and materials (Carter and McCarthy 2006). Corpus linguists have argued that this has created a more complex mediating role for teachers and the need for greater discernment and skill on their part in terms of how best to scaffold learners and the learning process, given the additional linguistic challenges that these developments pose (Carter and McCarthy 2006; Farr and O'Keeffe 2011; McCarthy 2008; O'Keeffe and Farr 2012; O'Keeffe et al. 2007; Prodromou 2003; Timmis 2002). This suggests a need for novice and experienced English language teachers alike to develop greater levels of critical language awareness and enhanced target English skills than previously needed if they are to discern and respond successfully to the ever more diverse and complex language needs of today's learners, as the work of Walsh has highlighted (Walsh 2003, 2006, 2011, 2013). RP can therefore be the means through which critical awareness can begin to develop.

Given the more globalised and culturally diverse nature of English Language Teaching (ELT) (see Byram 1997; Kramsch 1998; Spiro 2013), it has also become more common for today's TESOL professionals to teach learners from backgrounds and cultures whose experiences, expectations and beliefs may differ fundamentally from their own (Byram 1997; Kramsch 1998). Byram (1997: 12) has suggested that how well they cope with these additional cultural challenges depends on their ability to develop the type of intercultural sensitivity and strategic competence that enables them 'to move sensitively and intelligently from one culture to another'. Walsh (2006: 132) has advised that this can be achieved by developing greater critical awareness and skill in relation to the socio-pragmatic dimensions of language use. This means acquiring critical insight into the underlying conventions of politeness in different cultures, including their own, in areas such as directness/indirectness, and developing a high level of interpersonal skills. This can bring important affective gains in what has become an increasingly challenging psychological environment for teachers and learners alike (ibid.: 133). Changing sociopolitical trends surrounding the use of English worldwide also make it of paramount importance that novices develop insights into the critical dimensions surrounding the teaching of English today, as the existing standard English ideologies underpinning TESOL pedagogy come under increased scrutiny and challenge (Jenkins 2007; Kumaradivelu 1999; Matsuda 2012; Pennycook 2000). Accordingly, modern day practitioners are now expected to develop a more sophisticated level of linguistic, psychological, socio-pragmatic and critical insight and skill than previously anticipated.

These new requirements and demands have led to a re-examination of the knowledge base of TESOL teachers and a greater focus on integrating theory, research and opinion with empirical and reflective study of classroom practices (Farr 2011). As a result, reflective practice, classroom and action research are areas that have been added to the teacher education curriculum in order to expand the traditional knowledge base of teaching (Murphy 2015; see also Chapter 2 of this book). Similarly, there has been a move away from concern over content and pedagogical methodology to the more challenging and largely unexplored questions of how language teaching is learned with the aim of finding the best ways to teach it (Richards 2001: 72–4). This has led to a growing focus by RP researchers on the processes of teaching and teacher learning, the beliefs, theories and knowledge which inform language teaching, and the factors influencing teacher identity formation (Farr and Farrell 2017; A. Farrell 2015; Farrell 2016b; Morton and Llinares 2017).

The work of Farrell, in particular (Farrell 2016b, 2017), has been instrumental in bringing to light the harsh realities (many of which have been mentioned thus far) faced by novices entering the real classroom context and often being left to cope alone in a sink or swim type situation. To this end, Farrell has also demonstrated the benefits of creating RP opportunities for early career teachers for whom the English language teaching classroom can be a daunting and unsettling professional environment experience. Similarly, as mentioned earlier in this chapter, research by Farr and Farrell (2017) featuring the PENSER model of RP for use in the practicum context has highlighted the ways in which reflection-driven exploration of teaching on teacher education programmes can be facilitated through the use of a systematic framework by novice and experienced teachers alike to enable them to gain insights into the many professional challenges faced. Such an approach (Farr and Farrell 2017) has also been shown to provide a platform for self-appraisal and experimentation, which are considered crucial for ongoing professional development after student teachers complete teacher education programmes. Moreover, there is a growing body of research that has provided evidence that RP can help to build alert novices (Calderhead and Gates 1993; LaBoskey 1997; Tsui 2003), that is, student teachers who are better able to absorb course content, and to link this to their own personal experience as well as to their classroom practice. This is considered vital to inform appropriate action and change in professional practice for student and early career teachers.

There is also increasing empirical evidence to support the view that engaging in RP with more experienced peers can help with socialisation into the profession (Farr and Farrell 2017), which may in turn help to alleviate some of the recurring challenges we have discussed in this section. This is notwithstanding a growing recognition in teacher education circles that being an experienced teacher does not always equate with being an expert one (Tsui 2003). Indeed, experienced teachers, whose professional practices have been shaped by the prevailing English language dogmas, often need to be encouraged to explore changing norms and practices surrounding how and what they teach, which may seem to threaten existing beliefs held as fundamental truths (Farr and Farrell 2017). Nevertheless, there is a growing consensus that RP in collaboration with peers can provide a valuable forum for teachers to make sense of new demands and challenges in their teaching roles and practices, in what is a typically complex and daunting teaching environment (A. Farrell 2015: 89; Oxford 1997b: 443). This suggests that, where possible, opportunities should be created on teacher education programmes for student teachers to be exposed to individual and collaborative reflective practice with experienced practitioners, as well as with lecturers and peers for scaffolding purposes, as advocated by a growing number of RP researchers (for example, see Farr and Farrell 2017; Mann and Walsh 2017; Riordan 2012). This is discussed further later.

3.2.4 RP: COLLABORATIVE APPROACHES AND MODES

There is much to be gained for teachers at all stages of their careers from engaging in RP, both individually and collaboratively, for which there is now a growing consensus (Akbari 2007; Cunningham 2001; Farr and Farrell 2017; Farrell 2004, 2015). In this regard, Cunningham (2001) includes flexibility, practicality, professionalism and sustainability to the list of advantages RP can bring for professional development. In a similar vein, Farrell (2004: 5–6) has proposed that RP can promote self-authentication, existential self-realisation, empowerment and transformation as,

> through teachers engaging in systematic reflections of their work, by observing the acts of their own, and others, and by gauging the impact of their teaching on their students' learning, they can locate themselves within their profession and take responsibility for shaping their practice. (2004: 5–6)

In these ways, reflection-driven exploration of teaching can provide a systematic basis for novice and experienced teachers alike to explore and gain insight into the multiple issues and challenges they are likely to face in their professional practice in different contexts and settings from theoretical, practical and critically oriented perspectives. It can also provide a platform for self-appraisal and experimentation, which are considered crucial for ongoing professional development. Accordingly, RP has become an integral component on both pre-service and in-service teacher education programmes and in CPD initiatives where it is used by teachers at all stages of their professional development to promote independent and critical thinking so that they can better assess their own performances and mediate appropriate change (Farr 2011: 73).

As well as individual endeavours, peer group discussions have proven a worthwhile pursuit on TESOL education programmes for collaborative RP as they typically cater to both novice and experienced teachers (Farr and Farrell 2017; Ferraro 2000; Riordan 2018). Students on teacher education programmes can therefore engage in peer activities such as reflective practice groups, while also gaining the more experienced mentor scaffolding (see Chapter 2 for more on scaffolding) from lecturers on the course. Head and Taylor (1997: 9) have defined a teacher reflection group as 'any form of cooperative and on-going arrangements between two or more teachers to work together on their own personal and professional development'. This typically involves teachers 'undertaking an inquiry into their practice through verbally sharing, discussing, questioning and reasoning about their teaching experiences, either with their peers and/or with a reflective coach' (Ashraf and Rarieya 2008: 270). Zeichner (1995: 12) has argued that 'the lack of a social forum for the discussion of teachers' ideas inhibits the development of the teacher's personal beliefs because these only become real and clear to us when we can speak about them to others', echoing Vygotsky (1978) on meaning making via interaction. Moreover, novice teacher exposure to reflective practice usually occurs after teaching practice during supervisory conferences and typically involves feedback and assessment on the lesson taught. Being assessed by supervisors can create defensiveness and distress on the part of student teachers which may inhibit their ability to engage in frank and open discussion for reflective purposes (Farr 2011; Vacilotto and Cummings 2007). Notwithstanding the importance of post-observation feedback meetings, peer interactions offer another means for student teachers to share reflections without being judged by supervisors. Therefore, it is considered an advantageous supplement to supervisory conferencing on MA TESOL programmes, and therefore (as seen in Chapter 4) employed on our programmes.

The socialisation offered by collaborative RP may also lead to a greater appreciation of social presence and group learning as well as providing a suitable outlet for stress relief and emotional support (Farr and Farrell 2017; Farrell 2016b; Riordan 2018). Bullough et al. (2008: 1848) have alluded to the stressful nature of teaching as a profession, because 'to teach is to enter a world fraught with ill-structured, insistent, and emotionally-loaded problems'. Reflection has been regarded as one method of effective stress relief for teachers (Murray-Harvey et al. 1999; Riordan 2018). Zembylas (2003), for instance, has shown that group reflective practice can provide a valuable outlet for the expression of stress, uncertainty and fear, as well as offering a forum for teachers to provide emotional support to each other. Accordingly, it offers multiple emotional benefits for teachers by creating opportunities for them to articulate their views in a supportive environment with peers.

In addition, Kagan (1990) has raised the question of whether all forms of reflective practice should be considered worthwhile. Student teachers may perceive reflective practice as an obligatory exercise to fulfil course requirements and engage in only superficial reflection (Holmes et al. 2008). Group reflection involving peer discussions in a moderated environment such as TP preparation classes can provide the necessary structure to ensure that student teachers engage fully in the reflective process. It also provides a suitable and safe environment to encourage them to explore their own personal beliefs, experiences and uncertainties through autobiographical and philosophical disclosures to develop teacher cognition (Borg 2003). As Crookes has observed 'Teachers learn from each other and may possibly learn better when they have more opportunities to interact in a mutually supportive fashion' (2003: 7).

Farrell (2016b) has also stressed the importance of teachers engaging in reflection with peers through dialogue to articulate their underlying assumptions and beliefs because they are the driving force behind many of their classroom actions. This viewpoint reflects a widespread recognition in educational circles that teachers' beliefs impact on their professional practices, whether consciously or otherwise (Borg 2003; Woods 1996). As Borg (2003: 81) has observed, 'teachers are active, thinking decision-makers who make instructional choices by drawing on complex, practically-oriented, personalised and context specific networks of knowledge, thoughts and beliefs'. As a result of this realisation, teacher cognition (see also Chapter 2) has also become an important research paradigm in the field of second language teacher education, and in education more widely (Breen 2006). To this end,

Farrell (2016b: 132) has shown that collaborative reflective practice can be effective for teacher development because it provides a forum for teachers to express and explore their ideas, to receive feedback from peers, and to listen to shared and diverse perspectives. Mediated group discussion (see Chapter 2 for more on mediation) with a more expert other can also help teachers to develop critical thinking skills. This is important for novice and experienced teachers alike as it enables them to explore and challenge commonly held misconceptions and stereotypical viewpoints about teaching and learning. They can also be encouraged to engage with the research literature, or in action research projects to explore their ideas further and to report back to the group with the findings. This is likely to raise awareness of the ways in which empirical-based research in education can more accurately inform their professional practices, and introduces them to the research community.

To facilitate the RP process, a wide variety of collaborative RP modes have been employed. For instance, in addition to face-to-face modes such as group discussions with peers, or with reflective coaches/mentors (Ferraro 2000), teachers are often also encouraged to reflect on their teaching through written modes such as reflective journals or professional development portfolios and blogs (Dyment and Connell 2011; Farr 2015; Richards and Farrell 2005). More recently there has been a move towards research that has sought to explore different aspects of RP through the use of models featuring distinct and complementary face-to-face and written modes, such as the PENSER model mentioned earlier in this chapter (Farr and Farrell 2017). This has made it possible to identify and map the processes involved more holistically and to determine the precise benefits and limitations associated with different face-to-face and written modes. Studies in this area (Farr 2011; Farr and Farrell 2017; Riordan 2012) are important because, as many have pointed out (Akbari 2007; Cornford 2002; Walsh and Mann 2015), until fairly recently, there has been little empirical evidence to link RP with improved practice.

With this in mind, the research reported on in the chapters that follow demonstrates how data can work hand in hand with ongoing reflection and action in the highly complex relationships that teachers have with themselves, with their peers, and with teacher educators and mentors within a community of practice. It also provides evidence to suggest that by encouraging collaborative reflective practice whereby knowledge and experiences are shared, we can prevent teachers from focusing inwardly on themselves and their own teaching, which is one of the dangers of reflective practice in isolation (Farr 2011). Sharing reflective practice rather than solely practising it individually can also help student teachers to cultivate it as a habit. This may encourage them to create their own reflective practice group in their future careers to help them combat the isolation of the teachers' world (Shanker 1990), to mitigate the praxis shock in the early career years (Farrell 2016b) and to provide them with a sense of a community (Wenger 1998). This suggests that RP can be enhanced by encouraging practitioners to interact socially with peers, more experienced teachers and teacher educators acting as mentors. With these benefits in mind, we turn next to the notion of a CoP and explore how it can work with reflective practice to expand the knowledge base and to support the ongoing professional development of all teachers.

3.3 COMMUNITIES OF PRACTICE

3.3.1 CONCEPT AND PRINCIPLES

Communities of practice are groups of people with shared goals working collaboratively to promote learning through communication and interactions with other group members. This is with the inherent belief that the community knowledge as a whole is greater than an individual member's knowledge (Johnson 2001; Lave and Wenger 1991; Wenger 1998). Before exploring some of the key features of a community of practice, it is useful to distinguish the notion of CoP from those of speech community and discourse community, although at times they can overlap. The term speech community derives from sociolinguistics and relates to membership of primarily a sociolinguistic grouping. Hence, Gumperz (1982) originally perceived it as a linguistic community characterised by shared and distinct linguistic variables. This view is mirrored by variationist researchers who have sought to identify the distinctive linguistic norms associated with different geographic and social dialects (Labov 1972: 120–1). The concept of discourse community, on the other hand, as coined by Bizzell (1982), incorporates the notion of members sharing common interests, goals and specific genres or lexis (Swales 1987). For instance, Cutting (1999) uses discourse community as a framework in her analysis of the casual conversations of a group of university students working towards an MSc in Applied Linguistics. However, unlike the notion of speech community, homogeneity is not assumed for the group; rather it is unity of purpose that is the key overriding feature. Moreover, the notion of discourse community has mostly been associated with research into written texts and their production in terms of how and why communities develop genres.

The term CoP has been adopted as an alternative to speech community and discourse community and it is seen as more flexible as it has been applied to many groupings, social or institutional (Vaughan 2010). It was also intended in its conceptualisation by Lave and Wenger (1991) to relate to the process whereby novices, through observation of practices, and through gradual participation, progress towards full membership within the practice. Social and collaborative learning is therefore at the heart of the theoretical basis of communities of practice and crucial to enculturation, with newcomers supported and scaffolded in their engagement and participation within the community. Furthermore, it is not only the newcomers' proficiency with the activities that strengthens their membership of the community, but their understanding of the culture that surrounds these practices.

> From a broadly peripheral perspective, apprentices gradually assemble a general idea of what constitutes the practice. This uneven sketch of the enterprise (available if there is legitimate access) might include who is involved; what they do; what everyday life is like; how masters talk, walk, work and generally conduct their lives; how people who are not part of the community interact with it; what other learners are doing; and what learners need to do to become full practitioners. (Lave and Wenger 1991: 95)

The framework identifies three CoP practices (Wenger 1998). Firstly, mutual engagement is members engaging together to negotiate meaning; this engagement may be either harmonious or conflictual in nature. Secondly, a joint enterprise results from mutual engagement and negotiation; this joint enterprise is defined through members' pursuit of it. Thirdly, the CoP is characterised by members' shared repertoire. This may be linguistic or otherwise, such as shared practices, tools and norms which result from ongoing internal negotiation. A CoP therefore involves interaction, scaffolding, participation and engagement as key underlying practices. In this way, it creates a venue in which novice and experienced members alike can develop a deeper understanding of the norms and practices that underpin their professional lives, and achieve a greater a sense of belonging and professional identity (Wenger 1998). Riordan (2018) used four key components of the CoP framework and showed how they can be applied to exemplify how student TESOL teachers learn. These are, meaning, community, practice and identity. Hence, student teachers learn about teaching through observations, teaching practice and CPD activities (meaning); they learn by being included in the teaching community (community); they practise and continue to develop their skills and master the art of teaching (practice); and their identity as a teacher evolves through their engagement and interactions with others (identity).

A further key notion within the CoP construct is that of 'legitimate peripheral participation', whereby new members participate in the community peripherally initially but gradually increase their participation over time (Riordan 2018). As the research reported on in subsequent chapters will demonstrate, this is typically achieved in the TESOL teacher community of practice by trainees undertaking guided observations of classes taught by more experienced teachers, often followed by peer teaching and/or teaching practice. The assumptions that learning is shared and social, that it is experiential in nature and co-constructed through the negotiation of meaning are also inherent in the community of practice framework (see also Chapter 2 for a discussion on Freeman's Design Theory and his related ideas on community). Moreover, it is understood that while participation levels may vary in a CoP, interacting and engaging with one another socially provides a vital forum for community members to share emotions and feelings, which is vital for their emotional well-being. Acquiring knowledge of the resources and artefacts routinely used within the profession are also considered key requirements for the maintenance of the community, and the empowerment of its members (Cutting 2000; Vaughan 2010).

With this in mind, student teachers, experienced teachers and teacher educators on a TESOL teacher education programme can rightly be considered a CoP, one which can serve as a suitable venue for collaborative RP in order to facilitate the socialisation and professional identity formation of new members, to aid their developing understanding of norms and practices, and to enable them to make crucial connections between local and global practices (Wenger 1998; see also Fraga-Cañadas 2011). Therefore, we believe that engaging in RP within a CoP can bring enhanced benefits for teachers at all stages of their careers, particularly with regard to teacher identity formation. This is discussed further below and in Chapter 6.

3.3.2 THE BENEFITS OF RP IN COPS

Key links have been made in the research literature between RP in CoPs and teacher identity formation and professional growth (Farr and Farrell 2017; Farrell 2016b; Morton and Llinares 2017). As will be seen in Chapter 6 and mentioned earlier in this chapter, teaching involves many identity roles which practitioners must become familiar with due to the complex and multifaceted nature of teaching, as well as underlying global influences. Teacher identity is likely to be shaped by many factors including personal attributes and biography, gender, culture, age, working conditions and the institutional and classroom culture. It also involves the acquisition of new modes and discourse as well as the struggles in a particular situated community in relation to its norms and practices. The role of institutional expectations, policies and constraints are also powerful determinants of teacher identity (Pennington and Richards 2016). From this, a shared consensus has emerged in the academic literature whereby teacher identity is viewed as fluid and evolving rather than fixed or imposed (Riordan 2018). Moreover, it is negotiated through experience and the sense that is made of that experience (Sachs 2005: 15), and it evolves over time (see Section 3.2.3 for more on challenges in identity formation). The use of a CoP framework is therefore well suited here because of the interrelationships it holds between meaning making, identity negotiation and re-negotiation, community belonging and the practices of members, as these are core in teacher education practices and teacher development (Riordan 2018).

Moreover, Miller (2009: 174) has pointed out that within TESOL there seems to be a serious hiatus between language teacher education courses and the lived experiences of teachers. From this, she has argued for a shift in language teacher education to critical sociocultural reflection which takes account of identity and related issues of individuals in specific contexts, and the role of discourse in shaping experience (ibid.: 178). This suggests that there is much to be gained from collaborative RP with peers in a TESOL CoP setting as it can provide vital opportunities for teachers at both the early and the later stages of their professional careers to explore issues pertaining to teacher identity and the processes involved in teacher identity formation. For instance, they can be asked to reflect on the relationship between their personal identity and sociolinguistic identities and their teacher identity, given that conflicts can arise between these (Farrell 2017). They can also be encouraged to reflect on the types of challenges they may have encountered in developing a strong and confident sense of teacher identity, to anticipate which aspects of their personal identity may change as they grow professionally, and to reflect at a deeper, more critical level on how teacher identity is shaped by broader social, political and cultural influences and constraints outside the classroom. An interesting comparison made in our data is between the identities of the MA TESOL novice teachers and the PhD TESOL students who have more classroom experience. Further interesting avenues which will be explored in later chapters are the ways in which identity can change depending on audience/community member, for example, how it is shaped and manifested in interactions with a lecturer, a peer tutor and peers.

The next benefit we consider is the vital role that engaging in RP in CoPs can play in developing critical thinking amongst teachers. Kagan (1990) has concluded that critical reflective practice which involves possible revised thinking and action is the most valuable. This is supported by Farrell (2016b: 121), who has argued that critical reflection is essential because it moves the teacher beyond practice and links practice more closely with the broader moral, political and social issues that impact on a teacher's practice both inside and beyond the classroom, as well as affective issues. Such a critical focus should also involve teachers reflecting on the moral values and judgements that underlie practice in different teaching contexts and settings. This can help them to engage in a more critically oriented pedagogy, which can be empowering both for practitioners and those they teach (Kumaradivelu 1999). This suggests there is much to be gained from RP with a critical awareness-raising focus on ELTE programmes for practitioners at different stages of their professional careers, as a means to helping them to develop a more critically informed and critically oriented pedagogical approach. This critical approach also links in with the CoP framework in terms of driving new knowledge and making change (Wenger 1998).

Collaborative RP in CoPs guided by teacher educators can therefore provide student teachers with the necessary prompts and scaffolding to inspire a deep level of critical reflective practice whereby they can be encouraged to explore and challenge larger discourses of teaching and learning with a view to transforming existing norms and practices. In their previous exploration of RP in student teacher discourse, which drew on multiple RP modes, Farr and Riordan (2015) and Riordan (2018) found that different modes of communication (on-line synchronous, on-line asynchronous, and face-to-face versus written) lend themselves to various levels and topics of reflection. Their work has also revealed that the reflections of student teachers tend to be largely descriptive in nature and lack critical depth (see also McGarr and McCormak 2014), but that scaffolding and collaborative dialogue within a CoP setting can facilitate the move towards deeper levels of critical thought. The final area worth exploring is multimodal RP.

3.3.3 MULTIMODAL RP IN COPS

The practical merits of using multimedia for reflective purposes within CoPs have become more widely established in the academic literature due to the growing body of research in this area (Garrison et al. 2000; Kamhi-Stein 2000; Riordan 2018; Romano 2008; Schlager et al. 2009). This has led to an increased awareness in teacher education circles that 'multimedia holds potential for improvement in pedagogical practice by providing teachers with opportunities to reflect recursively and collaboratively on strategies useful in classroom discourse, and that this is likely to extend to many other areas' (Pryor and Bitter 2008: 2678). On-line CoPs have proven a particularly effective means of encouraging learning amongst novice and experienced teachers via peer mentoring and reflective practice. Riordan (2012), for instance, has shown that reflection and collaboration of this nature can provide a valuable support system for student and early career teachers because, as Romano (2008: 53) notes 'like other classroom instructors, they work independently for most of the day and have few opportunities to converse and collaborate with other teachers in the institutional setting'. This has corroborated earlier research by Stacey (1999) undertaken amongst postgraduate students on an MBA programme of study, which found that on-line engagement with peers fostered trust and cooperation amongst the participants. Both studies also concluded that this was important for the maintenance of the CoP because it provided a context for learning. Multimembership in various CoPs is also thought to contribute positively to teacher identity formation as it can encourage members to reflect on their identities in varied communities and share their knowledge across communities, which is known as 'brokering' (Wenger 1998).

While it is now widely accepted that on-line asynchronous tools can serve as an effective means of facilitating social learning and reflective practice (Farr and Riordan 2012; McLoughlin and Mynard 2009; Riordan 2018; Sert and Asik 2019; Szabo and Schwartz 2011), it is thought that on-line synchronous tools do not appear to lend themselves as well to RP (Riordan 2018). However, face-to-face modes can and do facilitate RP because, as noted previously, reflections amongst members of a professional community may be scaffolded by peers or by more experienced others, as is commonly the case on teacher education programmes (Farr and Riordan 2017; Riordan 2018; Riordan and Farr 2015). The importance of scaffolding of this kind has been underscored in the research literature. For instance, Lucas and Fleming (2011) compared the use of traditional professional journals and blogs for RP purposes by a community of students on a Bachelors of Sport and Recreation (BSR). The study revealed that there were no apparent differences between the two modes in terms of frequency of entries, structure of writing, levels of reflection and the language used. More notably, in both modes, the students were found to be mainly describing rather than critically reflecting on events. From this, the main conclusion reached by the researchers was that work on reflection needs to be initiated to ensure that students are scaffolded in how to reflect (Lucas and Fleming 2011). It has also been noted that electronic portfolios 'can be harnessed in teacher education programs to support the intermediate steps of learning, as well as to promote teaching and learning through reflective practices' (Firdyiwek and Scida 2014: 117). In previous research, we (Farr and Riordan 2017) have used blogs and electronic portfolios for experienced TESOL teachers enrolled in a structured PhD programme, and novice TESOL teachers on our MA in TESOL programme, in order to reflect on and make connections between theory and practice. Regarding the portfolios, we found evidence of language relating to professional development and formal education, which suggests that portfolios are conducive to discussing these themes. What was notable was that in comparison to the blogs data, the portfolios showed 'a more formal account of individual professional development options as a pathway to improved practices' (Farr and Riordan 2017: 23), although the novice portfolios reflected more learning with less experience, resulting from the differences in teaching experience between our two groups. We also found, however, that there was a tendency for more retrospective reflections in our blogs and portfolios, and as educators and established members of the CoP, we may need to consider the inclusion of more tasks for the teachers to promote, and indeed scaffold, future-oriented reflection. Similarly, Oakley et al. (2014: 39) used electronic portfolios with pre-service teachers on an MA in Early Childhood and Primary Education where they found that most of the teachers reached medium levels of reflection in their portfolios, and that more scaffolding, lecturer involvement and sharing and collaborating could give rise to improved results.

The findings above have corroborated earlier research by Murugaiah et al. (2010) which examined the formation of a CoP through blogging. This study featured three CoPs made up of either English, maths or science teachers. The CoP featuring English teachers held several face-to-face sessions with a view to building solidarity. The participants were also required to reflect on a good and a bad lesson for their blogging task and to engage in a discussion forum to comment on the posts. The study showed that although the postings were minimal initially, with effective moderation, the teachers began to post more frequently. The authors found that the teachers demonstrated the skills necessary for technology instruction, and that the activities the teachers were involved in allowed them to build on those skills. Furthermore, as well as creating a forum for the participants to share lessons, it also provided a safe environment for the teachers to express tensions and emotions, voice their feelings and, ultimately, to bond as a community, thereby serving an important affective role. This suggests that RP with peers via blogs and discussions within a CoP can serve multiple roles and bring a wide range of benefits for practitioners, as was also noted earlier in the case of face-to-face group discussions amongst teachers.

This chapter has explored key concepts and underlying principles concerning RP as a process alongside related approaches and models. It then critically appraised the benefits that can be gained for teachers at different stages of their professional development, from engaging in individual and collaborative RP within communities of practice and multimodal environments.

3.4 TASKS

1. Use Farrell's (2018) model outlined in Section 3.2.2 to begin your reflective journey. See http://www.sltejournal.com/article_68090_805b468ff06a6aef717be5a49f874c4e.pdf.

   Take notes on the following and discuss them with a peer:
   - teaching philosophy;
   - teaching principles;
   - pedagogical theory;
   - classroom practice;
   - beyond practice.

2. Share your teaching portfolios with a peer, or have a look on-line for some sample teaching portfolios. Read three to four extracts of the portfolio and examine the discourse in terms of Jay and Johnson's (2002) framework outlined in Section 3.2.2. Try to find examples of each level of reflection: descriptive, comparative and critical.

4

A DATA-LED APPROACH TO EXPLORING SOCIAL INTERACTIONS IN AN ENGLISH LANGUAGE TEACHER EDUCATION COMMUNITY

4.1 INTRODUCTION

In this chapter we will outline how corpus linguistics (CL) and discourse analysis (DA) have been used in a complementary and integrated way in the research reported on in this book to explore the social interactions of student teachers in an ELTE setting, as represented by TEC. From this, in Chapters 5, 6 and 7 which follow, we will provide an empirically based account of student teacher learning and professional growth from within the RP and CoP research paradigms. As a useful starting point, we consider how CADS can facilitate and enhance linguistic investigation before highlighting the particular benefits this approach can bring for research which seeks to expand our knowledge of the processes and benefits of RP undertaken within an ELTE environment. From this, we set out the specific aims of the research reported on, and the corpus-based methods used to address these. This is followed by a detailed description of TEC and the various face-to-face and on-line modes represented, which will provide key contextual information to help support the research findings. The final section of this chapter outlines the procedures used for the initial CL analyses, which were undertaken to establish student teacher participation levels across the various modes as a starting point to gauging their role and effectiveness; and to identify main themes for more qualitative analyses, as included in Chapters 5, 6 and 7 which follow. Accordingly, this chapter serves to highlight the ways in which the use of a data-led approach can shed light on processes and practices that lie at the heart of the ELTE CoP, which have only just begun to be chartered empirically (Farr and Riordan 2015; Mann and Walsh 2017; Riordan 2018).

4.2 RESEARCH APPROACH

Corpus linguistics and discourse analysis are research approaches which have developed independently in many language-related disciplines over the past fifty years or so; however, more recently, there has been a growing trend towards their combined use for the added benefits this can bring for linguistic investigation (Ädel and Reppen 2008; Evison 2013; Murphy 2010; O'Keeffe and Farr 2003; Thornbury 2010; Walsh et al. 2011). Corpus-based research was initially used mainly for quantitative research involving large quantities of data with specific attention given to high frequency linguistic items and recurring lexical patterns (Lindquist 2009). Quantitative CL approaches have been most appropriately applied to detailed linguistic analysis and the production of large reference works such as dictionaries and grammars (Biber et al. 1999; Carter and McCarthy 2006). However, there has been a growing trend for the use of smaller corpora in more qualitative linguistic research featuring discourse or conversation analysis (Farr 2010; Murphy 2015; Walsh et al. 2011), which is the approach drawn on by the present authors.

This combined approach has made it possible to achieve a more balanced two-pronged data analysis in order to address the historic limitations of using either CL or DA in isolation. For instance, corpus data is, by its very nature, decontextualised, which makes emic interpretations notoriously difficult to defend while traditional DA approaches have lacked a statistical basis, which has made it difficult for researchers to generalise the findings. McCarthy and Handford (2004: 168), and others since (Murphy 2015; Walsh 2006, 2011), have argued convincingly for the complementarity of quantitative approaches from CL and qualitative DA approaches in order to achieve enhanced descriptions of language use that could not otherwise be found. The merits of this approach have been recognised for some time in a wide range of contexts and domains including in forensic linguistics (Cotterill 2000), the workplace (Koester 2006), political discourse (Ädel 2010), media talk (O'Keeffe 2006; O'Sullivan 2015) and in research in third level education (Biber 2006; Evison 2013; Murphy 2015; Riordan 2018; Tao 2003; Walsh et al. 2011).

In this chapter we will set out how this approach was used by the present authors to explore the processes by which student teachers learn and develop profession-ally through collaborative dialogue and reflection within an ELTE community. This involved the use of CL in a mainly quantitative way in conjunction with more qualitative frameworks from DA, pragmatics, education and teacher education. For instance, CL methods and electronic tools from Wordsmith Tools (Scott 2008) were used, including frequency lists and keywords, to identify lexical features and patterning in the discursive practices observed in various face-to-face and on-line modes. These preliminary CL findings provided an exploratory platform from which to investigate the data more qualitatively using clusters and concordances together with frameworks from DA in order to test emergent hypotheses and achieve a more finely nuanced understanding of the data. A further software pro-gramme used in the data analysis was Linguistic Inquiry and Word Count (LIWC). This approach, designed originally by Pennebaker et al. (2007), allowed for a focus across texts on emotional, cognitive and structural components where this was deemed useful and relevant (see Chapter 7). Given the complexities encoded in the data, the use of a CADS type approach of the kind outlined was considered suit-able and likely to prove fruitful, as the analyses presented in Chapters 5, 6 and 7 of this book will provide evidence to support. To gain a better understanding of the focus and scope of the research, in the following section, we set out the main aims it sought to address.

4.3 RESEARCH AIMS

The research reported on in this book has three main aims:

1. To identify and map the linguistic, interactional and discourse features of social and collaborative learning in an ELTE CoP.
2. To explore what these features might tell us about the processes by which student teachers are socialised into the CoP, and develop professionally.
3. To offer some insights as to the implications of the findings for future directions in ELTE.

With these considerations in mind, in the following section a detailed description of TEC is provided together with the rationale for decisions taken in relation to its design.

4.4 TEACHER EDUCATION CORPUS

TEC represents the social interactions of student teachers engaging with peers, TP supervisors, lecturers and peer tutors. The student teachers represented two distinct groupings: they were either novices on a pre-service MA in TESOL programme or student teachers with a minimum of three years teaching experience on a PhD in TESOL programme. A total of sixty student teachers participated in the research, alongside four TP supervisors, three lecturers and one peer tutor. Of the student teachers involved, fifty-one were novices and nine were in the experienced category. TEC is therefore a specialised corpus comprising locally sourced data from a third level ELTE context. In terms of size, TEC is a relatively small corpus of circa 450,000 words sourced from a range of face-to-face and on-line modes of communication. In overall terms, the novice teacher data accounts for circa 70 per cent of the total data collected and the experienced teachers the remaining 30 per cent. The data was generated from student-performed academic tasks undertaken in various modes made available to student teachers during their programme of study, and it was collected over a ten year period between 2008 and 2018. The discussions and tasks represented in the data were designed to encourage the participating teachers to reflect on their classroom practice and related experiences, to share dialogue with one another, and to make connections between theory and practice, which is considered vital for professional development (Akbari 2007; Farr and Riordan 2015). In this way, the researchers sought to address a main criticism of historic RP approaches, which is that they have tended to remain confined to matters of techniques and procedures and to lack theoretical discussions, as was highlighted in Chapter 3. Tasks and activities were therefore designed to relate to both theoretical and practical questions of relevance to the teaching and learning of English as a foreign and second language, and to educational practices and processes more widely.

In designing a corpus that featured both face-to-face and on-line data, the researchers also sought to address the historic imbalance in RP practices and research in favour of written reflection to the detriment of the spoken form, as was under-scored also in the discussion in Chapter 3. Moreover, this approach created opportunities to explore RP processes across a range of modes reflecting distinct participant paradigms and further key variables, to gain a more finely nuanced understanding of the role/s and contribution these might make to student teacher socialisation and learning. In terms of the practical compilation of the corpus, similar guidelines and criteria were used as those set out by Farr et al. (2004) in relation to the Limerick Corpus of Irish English (LCIE) (see http://hdl.handle.net/10344/4712 for details of transcription conventions).

Figure 4.1 provides an overview of TEC in terms of the primary data represented, the various face-to-face and on-line modes from which it was sourced, and the amount of data in each case, and overall. A detailed account is provided subsequently of each data type and the various sub-sets. As indicated, the data from face-to-face contexts in TEC amounts to circa 250,000 words, representing 55 per cent of the

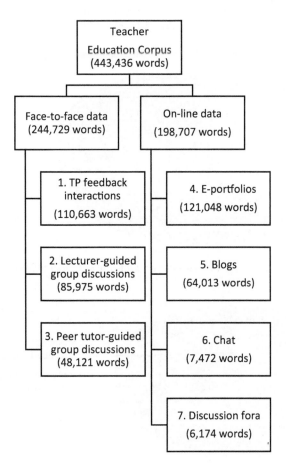

Figure 4.1   Overview of the Teacher Education Corpus

corpus. This compares with circa 200,000 words for the data from on-line sources, which represents the remaining 45 per cent.

Accordingly, as Chart 4.1 illustrates, TEC reflects a slight bias towards the face-to-face data. In order to facilitate comparative analyses, the research findings presented in the analysis chapters which follow are normalised to words per million, where relevant.

The face-to-face data was sourced from three distinct modes, each of which corresponds to a sub-corpus in TEC, that is: (1) TP feedback interactions, (2) lecturer-guided group discussions and (3) peer tutor-guided group discussions. This provided circa 111,000, 86,000 and 48,000 words of data which represented 45 per cent, 35 per cent and 20 per cent of the total face-to-face data in each case. Accordingly, as Chart 4.2 illustrates, the TP feedback interactions provided the largest source of data followed by the lecturer-guided group discussions and the peer tutor-guided group discussions.

By comparison, the on-line data was sourced from four modes, each of which also corresponds to a sub-corpus in TEC, that is: (1) e-portfolios, (2) blogs, (3) chat and (4) discussion fora. This generated circa 121,000, 64,000, 7,000 and 6,000 words in

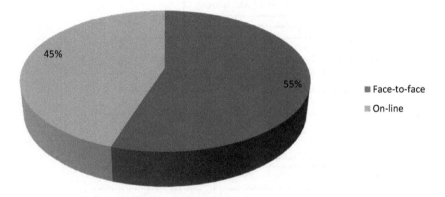

Chart 4.1   Face-to-face and on-line data in TEC (%)

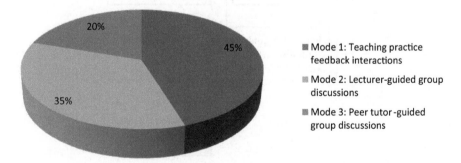

Chart 4.2   Face-to-face data in TEC by mode (%)

each case representing 61 per cent, 32 per cent, 4 per cent and 3 per cent of the total on-line data, as Chart 4.3 illustrates. Accordingly, a significantly larger amount of data was sourced from the e-portfolios and the blogs than chat and the discussion fora.

To summarise, Chart 4.4 illustrates the amount of data sourced from each of the modes represented in TEC in percentage terms in relation to the total corpus data.

As indicated, the on-line portfolios and the face-to-face TP interactions constitute the largest sources of data at 27 per cent and 25 per cent in each case. This is followed by the face-to-face lecturer-guided discussions, the on-line blogs, and the face-to-face

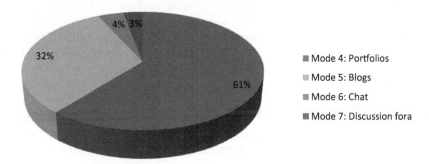

Chart 4.3   On-line data in TEC by mode (%)

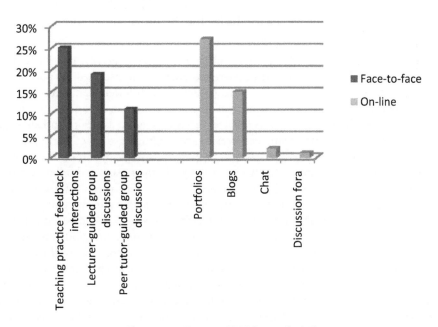

Chart 4.4   Data in TEC by mode (%)

peer tutor-guided discussions. Finally, chat and the discussion fora represent the two smallest sources of data at 2 per cent and 1 per cent in each case. From this overview of TEC, we proceed to a detailed description of the related sub-corpora, each of which corresponds to a distinct communication mode. At this stage, we also highlight key variables which provide important contextual information, and the data collection method in each case.

4.5 TEC MODES AND DATA COLLECTION METHODS

TEC comprises data sourced from a wide and varied range of modes, which need to be understood in terms of the key contextual variables at play in each case. These variables will be pivotal in the later analyses to help interpret the research findings on the basis of their potential influence, and include: the participant paradigm, whether participation was voluntary/obligatory and synchronous/asynchronous in nature, the types of tasks involved, and the extent to which the tasks were structured/semi-structured, and assessed/unassessed. A further factor considered was the representativeness of the data and whether any bias was reflected in favour of either student teacher grouping. This was of relevance only in those modes where the data related to both the novices and the experienced student teachers. Accordingly, in the following account, the amount of data representing each grouping will be signalled in percentage terms where relevant, as in the data analyses which follow.

4.5.1 MODE 1: FACE-TO-FACE TEACHING PRACTICE FEEDBACK INTERACTIONS

Mode 1 comprises data sourced from post-observation face-to-face TP feedback interactions between individual novice student teachers on an MA in TESOL programme and a TP supervisor, which were recorded and transcribed. As part of the MA programme of study, novice student teachers with fewer than three years of teaching experience (the vast majority of students) are required to take an elective module in Teaching Practice. This involves teaching English as a Foreign Language (EFL) lessons for one/two hours per week to multicultural groups of learners at the university from a variety of international backgrounds (typically Erasmus exchange students). The lessons are routinely observed by TP supervisors and followed a day or so later by one-to-one reflective feedback meetings. To prepare for these, the novice teachers are asked to reflect on the lesson they taught after watching a video recording of it. Although it was intended that these meetings would be student-led, the TP feedback interactions were, in most cases, structured and guided by the TP supervisors. Accordingly, the data from the TP feedback represents dyadic interaction between individual TP supervisors and novice student teachers that were structured around topics and issues relating to individual teaching practice lessons. They were an obligatory component of the TP module and therefore assessed. Table 4.1 summarises the variables relating to this mode and the related abbreviated forms

Table 4.1   Mode 1: Face-to-face teaching practice feedback interactions

Participant paradigm	Nature of participation		Task type			
	Voluntary (V)	Obligatory (O)	Structured (S)	Semi-structured (ST)	Assessed (A)	Unassessed (UA)
1 Novice student teacher and TP supervisor	√		√		√	

that are used for ease of reference in the data analyses in this, and subsequent, chapters.

4.5.2 MODE 2: FACE-TO-FACE LECTURER-GUIDED GROUP DISCUSSIONS

Mode 2 features data sourced from face-to-face group discussions that were guided by a lecturer (L) and featured either novice student teachers (NSTs) on an MA programme, or experienced student teachers (ESTs), who are taking a PhD in TESOL programme of study. These discussions took place in tutorial classes over the course of an academic semester and were recorded and transcribed. For the NSTs, these discussions formed part of a 'Preparation for Teaching Practice' module, which was an obligatory component of the programme and assessed. They were structured around tasks that involved preparing for, and reflecting on, teaching practice and were all face-to-face. Similarly, in the case of the ESTs, the discussions formed an obligatory and assessed part of their programme of study and were structured around tasks relating to observation, feedback and reflective practice. In overall terms, 85 per cent of the data from this mode comes from the discussions with the ESTs and the remaining 15 per cent from those with NSTs. Table 4.2 summarises the variables relating to each of the sub-data sets in this mode.

Table 4.2   Mode 2: Face-to-face lecturer-guided group discussions

Participant paradigm	Nature of participation		Task type			
	Voluntary (V)	Obligatory (O)	Structured (S)	Semi-structured (ST)	Assessed (A)	Unassessed (UA)
Novice student teachers and lecturer		√	√		√	
Experienced student teachers and lecturer		√	√		√	

Table 4.3   Mode 3: Face-to-face peer tutor-guided group discussions

Participant paradigm	Nature of participation		Task type			
	Voluntary (V)	Obligatory (O)	Structured (S)	Semi-structured (ST)	Assessed (A)	Unassessed (UA)
Novice student teachers and peer tutor	√			√		√

4.5.3 MODE 3: FACE-TO-FACE PEER TUTOR-GUIDED GROUP DISCUSSIONS

Mode 3 features data sourced from face-to-face group discussions with NSTs that were guided by a peer tutor (PT) and recorded and transcribed. These took place on a voluntary basis and were reflective in nature. Discussions were centred on teaching approaches and methods with questions and tasks set by the peer tutor; however, participants were encouraged to raise any further topics or issues of interest to them including their experiences on the MA TESOL programme. The data for this mode therefore represents voluntary, unassessed and reflected semi-structured tasks in context. Table 4.3 summarises the variables relating to this mode.

4.5.4 MODE 4: ON-LINE PORTFOLIOS

Mode 4 features data sourced from the individual reflective writing of student teachers (novice and experienced) in e-portfolios compiled using Google Sites. For the NSTs undertaking teaching practice, there was a requirement to complete weekly lesson plans, classroom observations, weekly reflections, tutor feedback forms, as well as writing a final overall reflection on teaching and learning. The ESTs, on the other hand, were required to create their own e-portfolio as part of a module based around reflective practice. This included a section in which they were required to write about their teaching philosophy in addition to two areas which they identified as a focus for professional development. These formed the basis of their later reflections and a continuous professional development plan. The data from the on-line portfolios was generated therefore from reflective tasks which were obligatory, assessed and structured in nature. In overall terms, 70 per cent of this written discourse comes from the NSTs and 30 per cent from the ESTs. Table 4.4 summarises the variables relating to each of the sub-data sets in this mode.

4.5.5 MODE 5: ON-LINE BLOGS

Mode 5 features data sourced from three types of reflective blogs: (1) individual blogs written by NSTs as a requirement for the TP module, which were assessed and structured around specific aspects of teaching; (2) individual blogs written by NSTs

Table 4.4   Mode 4: On-line portfolios

Participant paradigm	Nature of participation		Task type			
	Voluntary (V)	Obligatory (O)	Structured (S)	Semi-structured (ST)	Assessed (A)	Unassessed (UA)
Novice student teachers		√	√		√	
Experienced student teachers		√	√		√	

Table 4.5   Mode 5: On-line blogs

Participant paradigm	Nature of participation		Task type			
	Voluntary (V)	Obligatory (O)	Structured (S)	Semi-structured (ST)	Assessed (A)	Unassessed (UA)
Novice student teachers		√	√		√	
Novice student teachers	√			√		√
Experienced student teachers		√		√	√	

which were voluntary, unassessed and more loosely structured around teaching and learning; and (3) collaborative blogs written by ESTs that were obligatory and assessed and based more loosely on tasks designed to encourage them to share and reflect on their teaching experiences. The method used for the collaborative group blogs was to encourage one student teacher to initiate a reflective blog post about a topic of their choice and to ask the remaining students to reply, with students taking turns at initiating posts. The data from this sub-corpus therefore reflects the blogs of student teachers in each grouping which were structured to varying degrees around prescribed tasks. The NSTs provided 80 per cent of the data in this mode and 20 per cent came from the ESTs. Table 4.5 summarises the variables for each of the three sub-data sets in this mode.

4.5.6 MODE 6: ON-LINE CHAT

Mode 6 features data sourced from on-line chat between the novice student teachers and a peer tutor, which was voluntary, unassessed and synchronous in nature. The discussions were loosely structured around questions and tasks designed by the PT, which related to different aspects of language teaching with a particular focus on the teaching of grammar. However, participants were also encouraged to raise any topics, issues or concerns they might have relating to the MA programme and teaching in general. Table 4.6 summarises the variables relating to this mode.

Table 4.6   Mode 6: On-line synchronous chat

Participant paradigm	Nature of participation		Task type			
	Voluntary (V)	Obligatory (O)	Structured (S)	Semi-structured (ST)	Assessed (A)	Unassessed (UA)
Novice student teachers with peer tutor	√			√		√

4.5.7 MODE 7: ON-LINE DISCUSSION FORA

Mode 7 features data sourced from on-line discussion fora featuring novice student teachers and a peer tutor. These were voluntary, unassessed and asynchronous in nature. Discussions in this mode were also loosely structured, and in this case, centred on questions designed by the PT that focused on language teaching methods and underlying sociocultural dimensions. As was the case for the chat mode, in the discussion fora, NSTs were also encouraged to explore further areas of interest to them on their programme of study. Table 4.7 summarises the variables relating to this mode.

From this detailed description of the various TEC modes and the related sub-corpora, we turn to the findings for the preliminary corpus linguistic analyses. As highlighted previously, the first layer of CL analysis was undertaken to establish student teacher participation levels across modes as a starting point to evaluating their role and effectiveness, and to accurately position and interpret the research findings.

4.6 STUDENT TEACHER PARTICIPATION

Recording and transcribing the spoken discourse data made it possible to measure and compare student teacher participation in terms of average word count across the various modes, and to make comparisons between the NST and EST groupings. This allowed us to gauge the extent to which each context/mode engaged the student teachers and engendered their trust and a supportive learning environment. It was

Table 4.7   Mode 7: On-line asynchronous discussion fora

Participant paradigm	Nature of participation		Task type			
	Voluntary (V)	Obligatory (O)	Structured (S)	Semi-structured (ST)	Assessed (A)	Unassessed (UA)
Novice student teachers with peer tutor	√			√		√

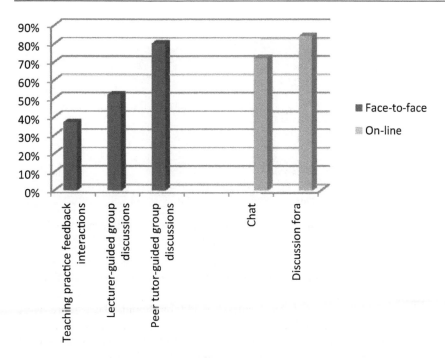

Chart 4.5   Average participation levels of student teachers across modes (%)

envisaged that this would provide early indications also of the contribution made by the student teachers to the building and maintenance of the ELTE CoP. Moreover, it afforded opportunities to explore the influence of key variables on student teacher participation. It should be noted at this point that participation levels were not measured in the case of the on-line portfolios and the blogs, which mainly featured the individual reflective writing of the student teachers. We begin with an overview of the findings for all of the remaining modes in terms of the average contribution made by the student teachers relative to other participants (lecturers, supervisors, peer tutors) in each case, as illustrated in Chart 4.5 in percentage terms.

As indicated, there was variability in the participation levels observed across the various face-to-face and on-line modes. In overall terms, student teacher participation was highest in the on-line discussion fora at 84 per cent, followed by the peer tutor-guided group discussions and chat at 80 per cent and 72 per cent in each case. By contrast, they were lowest in the TP feedback interactions at 37 per cent followed by the lecturer-guided group discussions at 52 per cent. The most salient finding in this area therefore is the consistently higher levels of student teacher participation in those modes where discussions were guided by a peer tutor by comparison with the significantly lower participation levels in modes featuring interactions with a lecturer or a TP supervisor.

This may have been due to the fact that the peer tutor-guided interactions in face-to-face and on-line modes alike were voluntary and unassessed, whereas the

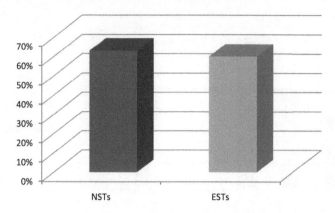

Chart 4.6   Participation levels of novice and experienced student teachers in TEC

lecturer-guided discussions were obligatory in nature and assessed. The lower levels of participation levels in the lecturer-guided discussions may also be attributable to the fact that in the preparation for TP context where 15 per cent of the data was sourced, it would be expected that lecturers would, or should, play a more overt guiding role. Meanwhile the less obvious variability in the participation levels in the on-line discussion fora and chat at 84 per cent and 72 per cent, and the level of 80 per cent recorded for the face-to-face equivalent, would also seem to suggest that for the novices, mode of communication was a less important influence than participant paradigm. These findings underscore the importance of the presence of the peer tutor in terms of encouraging student teacher participation, as highlighted in earlier research conducted in ELTE by Farr and Riordan (2015), and as confirmed more recently by Riordan (2018) in research conducted in a similar context.

Meanwhile, when broad comparisons were made between the average participation levels of NSTs and ESTs across the various modes, only a negligible discrepancy was observed with 60 per cent recorded for the former grouping, by comparison with 63 per cent for the latter, as Chart 4.6 illustrates.

By contrast, where comparisons could be made within a particular mode between the average participation levels for each student teacher grouping, as in the case of the lecturer-guided group discussions, a higher level of variability was observed. Hence, average participation levels of 63.5 per cent were recorded for the ESTs by comparison with 28.5 per cent for the NSTs, as Chart 4.7 reveals. This suggests that novice/experienced status also influenced the extent to which the student teachers participated in this mode. One possible explanation for the lower participation level of the novice student teachers in this case, which correlates with the conclusions reached by Copland (2012) in earlier research in this area, is that it reflects a lack of self-confidence on their part in relation to the legitimacy of their participation in the CoP as new recruits. Conversely, the higher level of participation of the ESTs may reflect a more confident and established sense of teacher identity on their part and that they perceive themselves as legitimate members of the teaching community. This

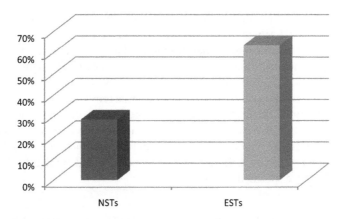

Chart 4.7   Participation levels of novice and experienced student teachers in lecturer-guided group discussions

is a hypothesis which will be further investigated in Chapter 6 of this book where the analysis focuses on how teacher identity is evoked and constructed.

To summarise, the findings for the first layer of CL analysis suggest that some of modes featured in TEC were more conducive to student teacher participation than others, and that this might be linked to several contextual variables. This included the participant paradigm in operation in each case, whether assessment was involved, the focus and nature of the tasks and the novice/experienced student teacher status of the participants. These types of influences seem more likely to have impacted on the participation of the NSTs than that of the ESTs, given that the levels recorded for the latter cohort remained more consistent overall, than those observed for the former grouping. Having gained a more complete picture of the TEC data and key contextual variables, we proceed to the second layer of CL analysis which was undertaken to help identify main themes for further quantitative and qualitative analyses in line with the research aims. The following section outlines the CL methods used for this purpose and presents the research findings.

4.7 IDENTIFYING MAIN ANALYTICAL THEMES

The second layer of CL analysis began with keyword searches in TEC relative to reference corpora using WordSmith Tools (Scott 2008). Keywords help to establish areas of lexical saliency and distinctiveness in one data set relative to others. For this purpose, the Limerick Corpus of Irish English (LCIE) representing circa one million words of conversational English, and the Limerick-Belfast Corpus of Academic English (LIBELCASE) representing circa one and a half million words of third level institutional discourse were chosen as reference corpora representing casual/informal (LCIE) or academic/formal (LIBELCASE) spoken Irish English. This made it possible for interesting comparative analyses to be made and for the TEC findings to be more accurately positioned in terms of their significance. Table 4.8 illustrates the top 100 keywords from TEC with reference to LCIE and LIBELCASE as reference corpora.

On the basis of an intuitive reading of the data, these items were classified into three areas of lexical saliency that were considered pertinent to the research aims and therefore worth exploring further by empirical means, that is: (1) metalanguage items relating to the theme of education, (2) items associated with cognitive processes and evaluation and (3) personal pronominal references. As Table 4.8 indicates, in the keywords list referenced against LCIE, thirty separate references were recorded in the first category, seven in the second, and three in the third. Comparative analysis made with LIBELCASE revealed twenty-three individual items associated with educational processes, five related to cognition/evaluation and two instances of personal pronoun use, as illustrated in Table 4.8. These keywords are set out and highlighted in Table 4.9 for each of the three specified categories.

Table 4.8   Top 100 keywords from TEC with reference to LCIE and LIBEL CASE

Keywords A (LCIE)				Keywords B (LIBELCASE)			
1	STUDENTS	51	THEIR	1	AND	51	GIVE
2	LESSON	52	TP	2	OF	52	PRACTICE
3	TEACHING	53	FUTURE	3	THAT	53	BACK
4	CLASS	54	MM	4	A	54	THINK
5	MHMM	55	WHICH	5	I	55	DID
6	MMHM	56	OVERALL	6	THIS	56	HERE
7	LEARNING	57	AIMS	7	STUDENTS	57	EM
8	TEACHER	58	WORDS	8	MY	58	THEY'RE
9	I	59	EXERCISE	9	ON	59	GRAMMAR
10	PRACTICE	60	QUITE	10	WHAT	60	FELT
11	PLAN	61	LEARNED	11	WERE	61	LEARNING
12	ALSO	62	BECAUSE	12	CLASS	62	STILL
13	MY	63	TOPIC	13	THERE	63	CLASSROOM
14	LANGUAGE	64	ASPECTS	14	WELL	64	FEEDBACK
15	STUDENT	65	TASK	15	IT'S	65	PLAN
16	TO	66	REFLECTIVE	16	TEACHING	66	HER
17	FEEL	67	KNOWLEDGE	17	ONE	67	OVER
18	CLASSROOM	68	DIFFICULT	18	LESSON	68	POINT
19	MORE	69	LEARNERS	19	THEN	69	TEACH
20	AS	70	THINK	20	#	70	EXAMPLE
21	TEACH	71	ACTIVITIES	21	REALLY	71	REFLECTION
22	OK	72	IMPORTANT	22	DON'T	72	STUDENT
23	FELT	73	THEORY	23	AM	73	CLASSES
24	GRAMMAR	74	PERSONAL	24	UP	74	EHM
25	UH	75	USING	25	LANGUAGE	75	WASN'T
26	FOCUS	76	LESSONS	26	MHMM	76	CAN'T
27	SKILLS	77	DIDN'T	27	YOU'RE	77	EXPERIENCE
28	OF	78	ACHIEVE	28	GOING	78	HAD
29	FEEDBACK	79	IMPROVE	29	YEAH	79	START
30	EXPERIENCE	80	PRONUNCIATION	30	I'M	80	DOES
31	TEACHERS	81	OBSERVED	31	MMHM	81	ENOUGH

(Continued)

Table 4.8   Continued

Keywords A (LCIE)				Keywords B (LIBELCASE)			
32	LEVEL	82	WRITING	32	WILL	82	I'VE
33	LEARN	83	EACH	33	THAT'S	83	UNDERSTAND
34	REFLECTION	84	WITH	34	THINGS	84	INSTRUCTIONS
35	CLASSES	85	SOMETIMES	35	WAS	85	THERE'S
36	THIS	86	OBSERVER	36	DIDN'T	86	MYSELF
37	THE	87	DEVELOP	37	DOING	87	AIMS
38	TAUGHT	88	INTERMEDIATE	38	TEACHER	88	MM
39	SEMESTER	89	USEFUL	39	WORK	89	VOCABULARY
40	EHM	90	HOWEVER	40	KIND	90	TAUGHT
41	MATERIALS	91	PLEASED	41	OK	91	SEMESTER
42	VOCABULARY	92	MATERIAL	42	S	92	LAUGHING
43	INSTRUCTIONS	93	PORTFOLIO	43	THEM	93	FOCUS
44	DIFFERENT	94	ADVANCED	44	RIGHT	94	TP
45	ACTIVITY	95	SOME	45	T	95	MATERIALS
46	GROUP	96	INTERACTION	46	FEEL	96	LEARN
47	INTERESTING	97	SELF	47	HE	97	LIKE
48	QUESTIONS	98	THEM	48	TEACHERS	98	YEARS
49	ENGLISH	99	AGREE	49	O	99	LESSONS
50	USE	100	LEXIS	50	ME	100	I'D

From the preliminary findings and classifications in Table 4.9, the following three areas were identified as main themes meriting further quantitative and qualitative investigation:

1. Metalanguage and topic: which were considered likely to be closely related, and worth exploring as evidence of shared repertoire and student teacher socialisation into the ELTE CoP (in Chapter 5).
2. Personal pronoun use: to be investigated as evidence of teacher identity formation and expression (in Chapter 6).
3. Cognitive/evaluative expression: to be explored in order to gain insight into teacher beliefs and teacher cognition as indicative of the development of reflective teachers (in Chapter 7).

Guided by these data-based hypotheses, the further analyses reported on in this book are themed and structured as follows: Chapter 5 will explore how metalanguage and topic are manifested and articulated in the student teachers' discursive practices and what this might tell us about their socialisation into the ELTE CoP and the shared values, norms and practices of this teaching community. Chapter 6 will demonstrate how teacher identity is evoked and indexed through personal pronoun referencing to uncover the processes involved in teacher identity formation and expression, and Chapter 7 will uncover how student teachers express, share and co-construct beliefs and understandings and offer insights as to what this might reveal about their journey towards becoming reflective practitioners.

Table 4.9   Classification of top 100 TEC keywords across three main categories

Keywords (LCIE)			Keywords (LIBELCASE)		
Metalanguage	Cognition	Reference	Metalanguage	Cognition	Reference
STUDENTS	FEEL	I	I	FEEL	I
LESSON	REFLECTION	SELF	STUDENTS	THINK	ME
TEACHING	INTERESTING	THEM	CLASS	REFLECTION	
CLASS	IMPROVE		TEACHING	UNDERSTAND	
LEARNING	DEVELOP		LESSON	LIKE	
TEACHER	USEFUL		LANGUAGE		
PRACTICE	AGREE		TEACHER		
PLAN			WORK		
LANGUAGE			FEEL		
CLASSROOM			ME		
TEACH			PRACTICE		
GRAMMAR			THINK		
FEEDBACK			GRAMMAR		
EXPERIENCE			LEARNING		
LEVEL			CLASSROOM		
LEARN			FEEDBACK		
CLASSES			PLAN		
SEMESTER			TEACH		
MATERIALS			REFLECTION		
INSTRUCTIONS			STUDENT		
ACTIVITY			UNDERSTAND		
GROUP			INSTRUCTIONS		
QUESTIONS			AIMS		
ENGLISH			VOCABULARY		
PRONUNCIATION			SEMESTER		
OBSERVED			TP		
WRITING			MATERIALS		
OBSERVER			LEARN		
INTERMEDIATE			LIKE		
PORTFOLIO			LESSONS		
ADVANCED					

4.8 SUMMARY

In this chapter, we have made the case for a data-led approach to linguistic investigation and outlined the tools and methods that were used to achieve this for the purposes of the research in this book. From this, we have presented and rationalised the specific CADS approach used to achieve a more accurate and finely nuanced understanding of how student teachers learn and grow professionally from within the RP and CoP research paradigms. A detailed account was provided subsequently of TEC, which constitutes the primary data used, and the various face-to-face and on-line modes represented, as well as key variables considered vital to the data analyses. The findings of preliminary corpus analyses were also presented in this chapter, as well as the methods used, from which valuable insights were gained into student teacher participation across the various modes as evidence of their engagement in the ELTE CoP. As well as providing key contextual information which will be drawn on in later chapters to interpret and support the main research findings, these initial layers of corpus-based analysis offered early indications of the role and effectiveness of different modes and the impact of key underlying influences, notably participant paradigm and novice/experienced student teacher status. Finally, in line with the data-led approach argued for throughout this book, CL methods were used to identify main themes for further quantitative and qualitative analyses, as reported on in Chapters 5, 6 and 7 where we endeavour to complete the picture we are building of the nature and role of social interactions within an ELTE community.

5

SOCIALISATION INTO THE ENGLISH LANGUAGE TEACHER EDUCATION COMMUNITY OF PRACTICE

5.1 INTRODUCTION

In this chapter, it is our intention to provide a snapshot of the ways in which student teachers are socialised into the ELTE teaching community, drawing on data from the TEC corpus (see Chapter 4 for a detailed account of TEC). This will be approached by exploring the shared repertoire of members of the ELTE community, which is one of the three core elements of the CoP framework. The initial focus of the analysis will be on metalanguage that is of relevance to English language teaching, and this, in turn, will serve as a platform from which to explore topics that are of interest and concern to CoP members. From there, we can gain a sense of how student teachers at the novice and more experienced stages of professional development articulate their professional knowledge and show engagement in ELT, which Freeman (2016) has suggested is likely to differ according to either the peripheral or full membership role they assume in the CoP (see Chapter 2).

As well as enhancing our understanding of the fabric of the ELTE community, the analysis also seeks to demonstrate how student teacher socialisation and learning can be facilitated and fostered through social interaction with peers and more expert teachers and mentors across varied modes of communication. This is important to provide empirical evidence to support arguments made in this book and elsewhere for a holistic approach to ELTE. From the findings that emerge, it is also possible to evaluate the contribution made by distinct modes to the socialisation process, which is a further area where empirical research has previously been lacking (Mann and Walsh 2017). Accordingly, the analysis in this chapter sets out to add to our knowledge of the shared repertoire of the ELTE community manifested at the levels of metalanguage and topic, as evidence of student teacher socialisation and how best this can be achieved. In line with the educational philosophy reflected in this book, at the end of this chapter we suggest two follow-up tasks to allow for further investigation by the reader of the themes explored. The discussion begins by investigating the concept of shared repertoire, which is central to the CoP framework and to the analysis in this chapter.

5.2 SHARED REPERTOIRE

Lave and Wenger (1991) conceptualised shared repertoire as the common resources that create, maintain and reinforce a community of practice. The CoP can evolve naturally because of the members' shared common interest in a particular domain or area, or it can be created deliberately with the goal of gaining knowledge related to a specific field. It is through the process of sharing information and experiences with the group that members learn from each other and have the opportunity to develop personally and professionally (Lave and Wenger 1991: 95). These resources may be verbal and non-verbal, literal and symbolic, and are seen as 'the cumulative result of internal negotiation between members of the CoP' (ibid.). As Lave and Wenger state, the repertoire of a CoP includes 'routines, words, tools, ways of doing this, stories, gestures, symbols, genres, actions' (1991: 95), which suggests a wide range of indicators. As the discussion in Chapter 2 highlighted, theorists working in the L2 teacher education context have attempted to conceptualise the shared knowledge base of the L2 teaching community as a guide to deciding the content and focus of L2 teacher education programmes. From this, a number of practical frameworks have emerged including the PACK model, as proposed by Shulman (1986), which has pedagogical and content knowledge as its core components; TPACK, which is a revised model of the former and designed to take account also of technological knowledge, as introduced by Mishra and Koehler (2006); and Freeman's (2016) Design Theory, which places an additional emphasis on tools and their appropriate use in different contexts. Freeman's model also makes a key distinction between the inappropriate expression of knowledge by new recruits to the L2 teacher CoP by which it becomes clear that they are partial rather than fully fledged members, which he refers to as 'articulation', by comparison with the more expert and appropriate expression of knowledge by more established members, referred to as 'expression'. In the analysis which follows, these hypotheses will be explored empirically as we uncover the nature of the metalanguage used by the student teachers and the topics they discuss, which are likely to be indicators of the extent of their shared professional knowledge in these key areas.

Previous CADS research has been undertaken within the CoP research paradigm in the applied linguistic and teacher education fields to investigate what constitutes shared repertoire and how it is manifested. This includes a study by Cutting (2000) which explored topics of interest and concern to post-graduate students on MA in Applied Linguistics programme and Vaughan's (2010) research which explored shared repertoire in the context of the professional talk of TESOL teachers during staffroom meetings. More recently, research undertaken by Farr and Riordan (2015), and Riordan (2018), has started to map the knowledge base, beliefs and practices of new and more established members of the ELTE CoP as evidence of their membership of the TESOL CoP. These studies have benefited from the increasing availability of locally sourced corpora designed for local applications. The progress made in this area has helped to bring a more bottom-up perspective to the previous, mainly theoretical, discussions in the CoP. However, our understanding of the processes by which student teachers become socialised into the CoP in terms of its knowledge base, norms, beliefs and practices remains incomplete. The availability of context specific educational corpora, such as TEC, which features the social interactions of student teachers at different stages of their professional development, creates new and exciting opportunities therefore to expand our knowledge in this area, as well as offering potential fruitful outcomes that can help to inform future directions in ELTE in the local context, and more widely. With these considerations in mind, we proceed to a review of the key concepts of metalanguage and topic as the specified areas of focus for the analysis in this chapter.

5.2.1 METALANGUAGE

In their initial teacher education, most prospective teachers are introduced to the professional terms around which their future pedagogical practices revolve, referred to in this book as metalanguage. As this is a term that is commonly used in several linguistic fields but not always in the same way, we begin by establishing a working definition for the present purposes. From a narrow linguistic perspective, meta-language equates with the terminology used to formally label and classify parts of speech (Berry 2005: 20). This contrasts with the broader definition of 'language about language', which is widely accepted in the applied linguistic field (Andrews 2001). In teacher education, metalanguage has also been used in a more general sense to refer to the language knowledge of language teachers (for example, Andrews 1999; Borg 1999; Lock and Tsui 2000). Steel and Alderson (1995: 92) have argued that what is meant by knowledge about language needs to be explored but that it typically includes a knowledge of and an ability to use metalanguage appropriately. In L2 educational contexts, metalanguage is also commonly used to refer to the language of pedagogic grammars (Berry 2005). Lock and Tsui (2000: 24) have observed that teachers, course books and learners inevitably tend to talk about those aspects of grammar that they have a shared metalanguage to talk about. This suggests that the use of metalanguage by language teachers may also provide insights into their language awareness and subject expertise more widely. It further leads to an expectation and requirement that L2 teachers acquire a knowledge of metalanguage as part of their broader knowledge about language (KaL) and linguistic theory given the assumed link between knowledge of formal aspects of language and teaching performance (Andrews 2001).

The use of metalanguage by teachers is therefore likely to be intricately intertwined with subject content and topics of professional and educational concern. In this regard, the use of the term has been extended in educational circles to refer to general pedagogical matters (Carter 1995), and to theoretical aspects relating to language pedagogy and education more widely (Dakowska 1993; Widdowson 1997). Accordingly, metalanguage has a potentially wide scope of reference which can include terminology relating to linguistic knowledge and language systems (for example, *verb*, *tense*) and language use (for example, *dialect*, *proficiency*), terms associated more broadly with educational theory and practice (for example, *sociocultural theory*, *scaffolding*), references made to pedagogical tools and materials (*course book*, *slides*, *corpora*, *exams*), and contexts of learning (*school*, *classroom*, *advanced group*, *EFL*). In the present analysis, we therefore use the term metalanguage in its broadest sense to refer to all lexical items that relate to the professional knowledge base, norms and practices of English language teachers, which, when viewed together, can provide a lens through which to explore student teacher socialisation into the CoP. The specific classification system used in the present analysis to explore the use of metalanguage by student teachers is set out and further rationalised below before the related corpus findings are presented.

5.2.2 TOPIC

A key assumption made in the present analysis, in line with the conclusions reached by Farr and Riordan (2015), is that the use of metalanguage in a student teacher environment is likely to signal topics that are familiar and of shared professional interest to the members of the ELTE community. Keenan and Schieffelin (1976: 338) originally proposed the notion of discourse topic which they defined as 'the proposition (or set of propositions) about which the speaker is either providing or requesting new information'. However, the question of what constitutes a topic has remained taxing for researchers. For instance, while the aforementioned authors argue that topic must be seen to operate over a series of utterances, Brown and Yule (1983: 75) maintain that it must be based on a reasonable judgement of 'what is being talked about', which is the approach adopted by the present authors in this book. Despite the difficulties in conceptualisation which remain, research has been conducted that has explored topic as a mode of analysis, although this has mostly been undertaken in the context of casual conversation (for example, see Coates 1996; Myers 1998; Pilkington 1998).

Corpus-based researchers have successfully demonstrated that there are certain institutionalised forms of discourse in which topic is more readily identifiable as it needs to be openly addressed, as, for example, in media talk (O'Keeffe 2006) and in teachers' staffroom discussions (Vaughan 2010). This is also likely to be the case in third level educational contexts, which typically feature lectures framed around themes and topics relating to a prescribed curriculum followed by tutorials in which tutors set related discussion tasks and students are expected to keep their contributions relevant. Similarly, in the context of third level TP feedback encounters, there is an expectation that the range of topics discussed will centre primarily on pedagogical issues and concerns, as Farr's (2011) research has demonstrated. However, as in the case of the ELTE data featured in this book, third level students may also be offered opportunities to engage in discussions and reflective writing of a less structured and freer nature, whereby the nature of any topics raised is less predictable. Given that TEC features a variety of face-to-face and on-line modes in which discussions and tasks were guided and structured to varying degrees, this offers the scope for an interesting comparative analysis of topic across the data sets, taking this consideration into account as well as further contextual variables as were highlighted in Chapter 4, including: data type and mode, participant paradigm, participation levels, novice/experienced student teacher status, whether tasks were voluntary/ obligatory, assessed/unassessed and the synchronous/asynchronous nature of the communication.

Accordingly, in the analysis which follows, we explore topic as evidence of student teacher socialisation and engagement in the ELTE CoP, as manifested in the discursive practices of novice/experienced student teachers across a range of modes of communication. As will be demonstrated, this will be achieved by investigating longer stretches of discourse using more qualitative DA approaches, with the focus of the analysis guided by the initial CL findings for metalanguage, as was rationalised in Chapter 4. From this, further comparative analyses will be made to gauge the role and value of particular modes in terms of providing an effective and safe forum for student teachers to articulate their knowledge, practices, beliefs and concerns as part of the socialisation process. Having reviewed the existing research literature and established the scope and focus of the present analysis, we proceed to the first layer of corpus analysis and the findings which relate to metalanguage use.

5.3 METALANGUAGE IN TEC

The starting point of the investigation into metalanguage use was to generate a frequency list for TEC using the wordlist function of WordSmith Tools (Scott 2008). From the top 1000 words listed, all items considered of relevance to the business of teaching English were identified, as Table 5.1 illustrates, alongside the word rank (N) and frequency in each case.

Table 5.1   Metalanguage in the top 1000 words in TEC

N	Word	Freq.	N	Word	Freq.	N	Word	Freq.
19	STUDENTS	3107	421	RESEARCH	125	713	LEVELS	63
32	TEACHING	2488	423	PORTFOLIO	124	723	TEST	63
34	LESSON	2048	435	PROFESSIONAL	118	733	SENTENCES	62
41	CLASS	1914	442	ROLE	116	741	PRESENTATION	61
74	LEARNING	959	443	TIMING	116	743	SUBJECT	61
76	TEACHER	931	444	DICTIONARY	115	750	SONG	60
78	LANGUAGE	909	452	MODULE	112	765	GTM	58
101	PLAN	677	461	MANAGEMENT	109	766	MA	58
103	PRACTICE	669	462	STYLE	109	768	ONLINE	58
132	ENGLISH	527	464	CAREER	108	769	PREPARATION	58
137	LEVEL	509	465	STRATEGIES	108	774	TTT	58
155	CLASSROOM	452	469	CULTURAL	105	782	MUSIC	57
157	WORDS	444	470	LEXIS	105	788	GAMES	56
158	FEEDBACK	443	474	MONITORING	104	793	CHILDREN	55
168	QUESTIONS	414	475	OUTCOMES	104	795	DICTIONARIES	55
171	GROUP	402	481	RAPPORT	103	796	EVALUATION	55
185	GRAMMAR	360	482	ROOM	103	799	GRADE	55
200	SKILLS	332	483	STUDY	103	801	PAGE	55
204	WRITING	321	492	EXPERIENCED	100	803	CORPUS	54
222	SEMESTER	287	495	THEME	100	805	LANGUAGES	54
227	VOCABULARY	275	497	EXPLANATIONS	99	812	VARIETY	54
230	MATERIALS	273	500	TECHNIQUES	99	814	BLOG	53
242	BOOK	260	503	OBJECTIVES	98	815	BRAIN	53
245	INSTRUCTIONS	257	508	OBSERVATION	97	823	ABILITY	52
254	EXERCISE	245	510	CORRECTION	96	825	COLLEAGUES	52
259	ACTIVITY	241	511	CULTURE	96	849	RELATIONSHIP	51
260	AIMS	240	516	PAIRS	95	850	ATMOSPHERE	50

(*Continued*)

Table 5.1   Continued

N	Word	Freq.	N	Word	Freq.	N	Word	Freq.
265	READING	231	530	METHODS	92	854	LINGUISTICS	50
276	LISTENING	219	533	DEGREE	91	860	AMERICAN	49
282	BOARD	214	535	EFL	91	865	PARTICIPATION	49
283	SPEAKING	214	550	NATIVE	89	867	PROGRAM	49
287	SCHOOL	205	579	ELICITATION	84	883	COMMUNICATION	47
288	KNOWLEDGE	204	583	UPPER	84	884	ENGAGEMENT	47
296	TERMS	198	601	IRISH	80	904	COMMUNITY	45
297	THEORY	197	602	SUPERVISOR	80	909	LIMERICK	45
310	TP	189	618	HOMEWORK	77	917	ACADEMIC	44
311	TASK	188	620	MISTAKES	77	933	COMPREHENSION	43
315	TOPIC	186	624	FRENCH	76	934	CONDITIONAL	43
339	UNIVERSITY	165	644	AGE	71	942	PHRASAL	43
345	OBSERVED	162	653	TEXT	71	944	SAUDI	43
346	PRONUNCIATION	162	659	COLLEGE	70	948	WEBSITE	43
356	ADVANCED	155	663	IRELAND	70	950	ARTICLE	42
363	APPROACH	152	668	STT	69	955	IDENTITY	42
371	VIDEO	148	690	VERBS	66	975	VALIDATION	41
372	ESL	147	694	JOB	65	976	AIDS	40
373	TECHNOLOGY	147	697	PHD	65	984	PHILOSOPHY	40
393	OBSERVER	137	699	RULES	65	987	SENTENCE	40
394	PROBLEMS	137	700	SPANISH	65	988	STRATEGY	40
397	INTERACTION	136	701	SPEECH	65	990	ADULTS	39
418	EAP	126	702	SYSTEMS	65	998	LINGUISTIC	39
419	EDUCATION	125	710	TRAINING	64	999	MODULES	39

From an intuitive reading of the data, these items were then coded thematically and tabulated using a classification system designed by the present authors which sought to take account of the various components that constitute the professional knowledge base of the L2 CoP, as conceptualised in Freeman's (2016) Design Theory, and TPACK (Mishra and Koehler 2006). Informed by these approaches, a framework was devised that features the following five core elements of shared professional knowledge: (1) knowledge of the professional CoP, (2) knowledge of educational theory and practice, (3) knowledge of linguistics and language as subject content, (4) knowledge of pedagogical tools and materials; and (5) knowledge of learning contexts; this latter type incorporates institutional, geographic and learner-related contexts. Metalanguage use was classified across these five categories which are set out in Table 5.2 alongside examples found in the TEC data.

5.3.1 DISTRIBUTION OF METALANGUAGE IN TEC

As Chart 5.1 illustrates, of the 154 separate metalanguage items that were identified in TEC, seventy-eight were associated with educational theory/practice, twenty-six with

Table 5.2   Sub-categories of metalanguage in TEC

Metalanguage sub-categories	Examples
1. Professional CoP	*Community, colleagues, profession, career, job, supervisor, training*
2. Educational theory/practice	*Education, methods, testing, elicitation, theory, grades, students*
3. Linguistics/language	*Grammar, verbs, sentences, tense, linguistic, pronunciation, lexis, variety*
4. Pedagogical tools/materials	*Board, dictionary, book, materials, text, corpus, games, songs, video, blog*
5. Learning contexts	*Classroom, school, Saudi, Spanish, Limerick, Ireland, EFL, advanced*

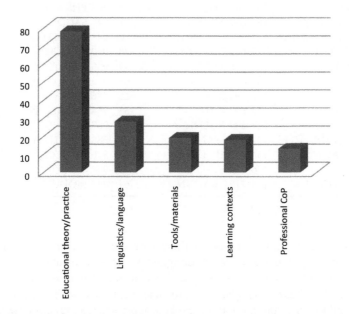

Chart 5.1   Distribution of metalanguage across sub-categories in TEC

linguistics/language teaching, nineteen with pedagogical tools/materials, eighteen with learning contexts, and thirteen with the professional CoP.

As indicated, almost half of the items recorded related to education theory and practice while the second largest grouping, representing about one sixth in overall terms, featured items associated with linguistics/language. Slightly fewer items were related to pedagogical tools/materials, and with learning contexts, while the lowest number of individual items was recorded for the professional CoP sub-category. These distribution patterns must be understood in terms of several possible influences. The first is the overall bias in the TEC data (60 per cent / 30 per cent) in favour of the NSTs, as highlighted in Chapter 4. It is plausible to assume, for instance, that student teachers in both groupings would be familiar with educational theory/ practice to varying degrees, but that the NSTs would be considerably less aware than the ESTs of linguistic/language-related items given their specialised use. In a similar vein, the relatively low number of metalanguage items recorded for the professional CoP sub-category suggests that the NSTs had yet to acquire a fully developed sense of the teaching community they were entering, and their own teacher role and identity within it. These findings are consistent with Freeman's conceptualisation of peripheral/full membership of the CoP on the basis of shared knowledge and how it is evoked (2016: 243).

From this, distribution patterns were explored comparatively for the face-to-face/ on-line data to gauge the influence of both types of communication on metalanguage usage using similar methods as previously. From the frequency lists generated for each data type, all metalanguage items in the top 1000 words in each list were classified. As Chart 5.2 illustrates, a significantly higher level of metalanguage use was observed in the on-line data set by comparison with the face-to-face equivalent, with 136 items recorded for the former, and eighty-nine for the latter. This was despite the slight bias (55 per cent / 45 per cent) reflected in TEC in favour of the face-to face data, and the overall bias in TEC towards the novices, which once again was more obvious in the face-to-face data. This further underscores the higher level of metalanguage use found in the on-line data.

This is consistent with the findings from Biber's linguistic analysis of third level discourse, as highlighted in Chapter 1, which found that metalanguage was used with greater frequency and variety in written rather than spoken academic registers. This was attributed to factors pertaining to real time communication (Biber 2006: 36–46). Similarly, Riordan's (2018) study of student teacher discourse recorded a higher level of lexical density in the discursive practices of student teachers in on-line asynchronous modes than in their face-to-face verbalisations, which, again, was attributed to the greater time and space afforded to the participants to articulate their thoughts in the former type of communication.

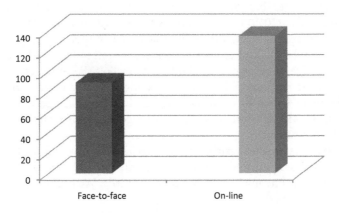

Chart 5.2   Distribution of metalanguage in face-to face and on-line modes in TEC

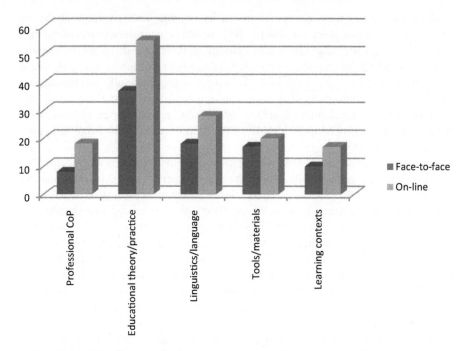

Chart 5.3   Distribution of metalanguage across sub-categories in face-to-face and on-line modes in TEC

To more accurately gauge the influence of face-to-face/on-line communication on metalanguage use, distribution was mapped across the specified sub-categories for the various modes featuring in each data type. As Chart 5.3 illustrates, in all of the five specified sub-categories, higher levels of metalanguage use were recorded in the on-line data than were found in the face-to-face type. These findings confirm that, broadly speaking, communicative medium was a key influence on the student teachers' metalanguage use. These findings correlate with the conclusions reached by Biber (2006), and Riordan (2018) more recently, whereby written academic registers were found to reflect lexically richer discursive practices than spoken academic registers. Interestingly, similar patterns of distribution were found in the face-to-face/on-line data across the five sub-categories as for TEC as a whole. For instance, in each data set, most of the items found related to a knowledge of educational theory/practice, followed by items linked to linguistic/language knowledge. In each sub-category, there were also noticeably fewer items in the pedagogical tools/materials and professional CoP sub-categories.

This suggests that further variables were likely to be at play and worth exploring. Accordingly, analyses were undertaken subsequently to establish distribution in each face-to-face and on-line mode with comparisons made. We begin with the findings for the face-to-face modes.

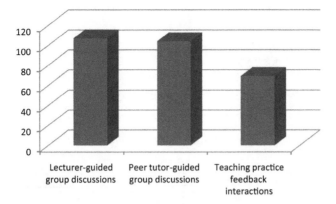

Chart 5.4   Distribution of metalanguage across face-to-face modes in TEC

5.3.2 DISTRIBUTION OF METALANGUAGE IN FACE-TO-FACE MODES IN TEC

As outlined in Chapter 4 previously, the face-to-face data in TEC was sourced from three modes: (1) TP feedback encounters featuring an individual novice student teacher (NST) and a TP supervisor (TPS), (2) lecturer-guided group discussions featuring NSTs/ESTs and (3) peer tutor-guided group discussions with NSTs. As Chart 5.4 illustrates, metalanguage use was similar in the lecturer-guided and peer tutor-guided group discussions, with 107 items recorded in the former and 104 items in the latter. This compares with sixty-nine in the TP feedback interactions, which is somewhat fewer.

These trends were then explored more qualitatively subsequently to establish the precise nature of metalanguage use in each of the three spoken modes. The findings are presented in Chart 5.5 and discussed subsequently for each mode, with comparisons made.

Mode 1: Distribution of Metalanguage in TP Feedback
The TP feedback interactions featured discussions that were focused on EFL lessons taught by NSTs and observed by a TP supervisor. As Chart 5.6 illustrates, of the total number of sixty-nine metalanguage items recorded in this context, an equal number of twenty-six related to educational theory/practice and linguistics/language. A further nine items were associated with learning contexts, seven with tools/materials, and only one with the professional CoP.

Accordingly, items relating to linguistics/language, that is, subject content, featured more significantly in this sub-corpus by comparison with TEC as a whole, for example *pronunciation, vocabulary, tense, modal* and *verb.* Also recorded were items relating to educational theory/practice, for example *monitoring, questioning, nomination,* and references to tools/materials, for example, *book, board, pictures and tape,* and to learning contexts, particularly specific first language (L1) groupings, for example, *German, French, Spanish and Chinese.* Given that talk in this context was focused on

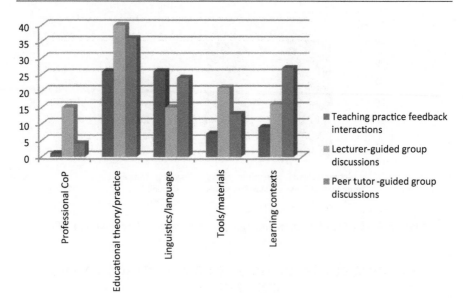

Chart 5.5   Distribution of metalanguage across sub-categories in face-to-face modes in TEC

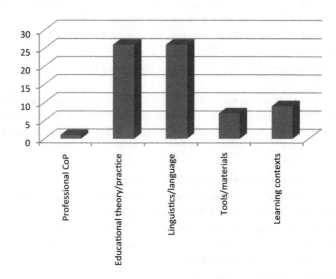

Chart 5.6   Distribution of metalanguage across sub-categories in teaching practice feedback interactions

reviewing EFL lessons based on prescribed materials and planned with multicultural learner groups in mind, these findings were in keeping. Interestingly, only the item *profession* was recorded in the CoP sub-category. This suggests that the focus of talk was on individual student teacher performance rather than on professional norms and practices in this educational domain in general. This may be due to the novice status of those being supervised, who may not be perceived to be 'ready' at this stage to generalise their experiences. From the findings for the TP feedback data, we turn to the outcomes for the face-to-face lecturer-guided group discussions featuring either NSTs or ESTs.

Mode 2: Distribution of Metalanguage in Lecturer-Guided Group Discussions
The discussions involving the NSTs were sourced from preparation for TP classes and structured around lesson planning rather than on individual teacher performance, while those featuring the ESTs centred on modules they had studied relating to observation, feedback and reflective practice. Participants in both groupings were also encouraged to make links between pedagogical theory and their own teaching should they so wish and to use the space provided for reflection on different aspects of teaching. As Chart 5.7 illustrates, of the total number of 107 items identified for this mode, forty were associated with educational theory/practice, twenty-one with tools/materials, sixteen with learning contexts, and fifteen were related equally to the linguistic/language and the CoP sub-categories. Accordingly, a different pattern of metalanguage distribution was recorded for this context with significantly more references to tools/materials, learning contexts and the professional CoP than for the TP feedback interactions.

These findings must be positioned first in relation to the data type, which, in this case, reflected a very strong bias (85 per cent / 15 per cent) in favour of the ESTs, who had come to the programme with a minimum of three years teaching experience. From this, they could be expected to have acquired a good working knowledge of the needs of different learner groups, and to be well-informed about existing and emergent language teaching resources and materials. As some in the group had

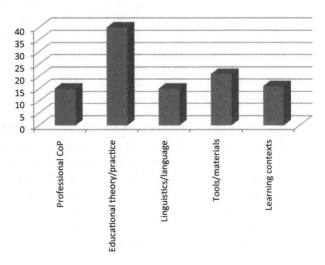

Chart 5.7   Distribution of metalanguage across sub-categories in lecturer-guided group discussions

also opted to take a module in materials' development as part of their programme of study, this would have afforded them further opportunities to become familiar with more recent language learning technologies and their applications in the L2 classroom. The NSTs, too, would have learned about tools/materials designed for language teaching on core modules and electives during their programme of study, as well as from teaching practice. Moreover, it would be expected that discussions in the preparation for TP context around the design of lessons would have a strong focus of this kind.

These factors may explain the larger range of items found in this mode that related to tools and resources, with both traditional tools and new technologies mentioned, for example, *song, games, video, internet corpus* and *blogs*, and the more extensive references to learning contexts, for example, *secondary, advanced, intermediate, Saudi* and *Indonesia*. Of note also, in this context were items that suggest a knowledge of the sociolinguistic dimensions of teaching and learning English, for example, *dialect, variety, standard* and *Englishes*. This may also indicate an awareness of changing norms surrounding the target models of English taught. This seems more likely in the case of the ESTs than the NSTs in the light of recent research carried out by Farr and Farrell (2017) which revealed that inexperienced TESOL teachers tend to be more preoccupied with the practical aspects of teaching than with normative or ideological considerations. A further striking feature of the metalanguage used in this context was that it featured more items relating to CoP than found in the TP feedback data, for example, *colleagues, peers, collaboration, community* and *career*. Again, this may be due to the bias in the data in favour of the ESTs, who could be expected to have developed a strong sense of being part of a professional community with shared practices and norms.

In general, the findings for metalanguage use in this spoken mode suggest that face-to-face group discussions guided by a lecturer can provide a useful forum for student teachers to explore, and gain insight into, different aspects of teaching to enhance their practical knowledge base. They would also seem to offer a suitable platform for more critically oriented discussion and awareness-raising in relation to the ideologies underpinning the use and teaching of English, especially for ESTs. Comparisons were made subsequently with metalanguage use in the face-to-face group discussions featuring only NSTs and a peer tutor.

Mode 3: Distribution of Metalanguage in Peer Tutor-Guided Group Discussions
The focus of talk in this context was on different teaching approaches and methods with questions set by the peer tutor. Participants were also encouraged to use the space to discuss their experiences on their teacher education programme, should they so wish. As Chart 5.8 illustrates, of the total of 104 metalanguage items found in this context, thirty-six related to educational theory/practice, twenty-seven to learning contexts, twenty-four were associated with linguistic/ language knowledge, thirteen with tools/materials, and four with the professional CoP.

The data in Chart 5.8 indicates that although the overall number of separate metalanguage items found was similar to that recorded for the lecturer-guided

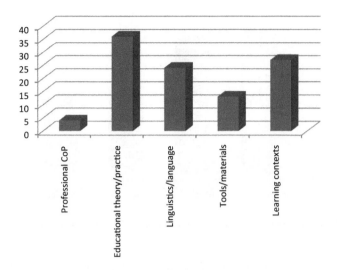

Chart 5.8   Distribution of metalanguage in peer tutor-guided group discussions

discussions, distribution patterns across the five specified sub-categories varied between these two modes. Of interest in this context is the substantially lower number of items in the CoP sub-category, and conversely, the higher number of items relating to linguistics/language, for example, *grammar, pronunciation, vocabulary, idioms*; and learning contexts, for example, *advanced, intermediate, Spanish, Chinese.* As in the lecturer-guided group discussions, this would suggest a strong interest in the language systems of English, as well as the language content of lessons, and language use more widely, and that this mode provided a suitable forum for discussions of this nature. Accordingly, this mode seems to have provided the NSTs with a useful and non-threatening space to enhance their language aware-ness and to strengthen their formal knowledge of English, as well as offering them opportunities to explore the diverse needs and abilities of English language learners. The earlier analysis of participation levels would seem to confirm this as it revealed that the presence of a peer tutor rather than a lecturer encouraged higher levels of engagement.

In this context, references were also made to language theorists, for example, *Chomsky* and *Krashen*; and to linguistic concepts and hypotheses from SLA, for example, *fossilisation* and *interlanguage.* This suggests a burgeoning interest on the part of the NSTs in the processes involved in first and second language acquisition and language learning, and it also provides evidence of student teacher cognition and learning. Fewer references were made in this context to CoP than in the lecturer-guided discussions featuring the ESTs. Moreover, the items found, for example, *super-visor, mentor, observation,* evoke a sense of apprenticeship rather than fully fledged membership in the professional CoP. From this snapshot of the metalanguage use of the student teachers across the face-to-face modes, we turn next to the comparative findings for the on-line versions.

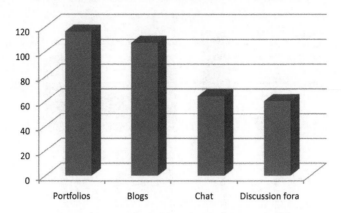

Chart 5.9   Distribution of metalanguage across on-line modes in TEC

5.3.3 DISTRIBUTION OF METALANGUAGE IN ON-LINE MODES IN TEC

The reader will recall that TEC also featured on-line data sourced from the following four modes: (1) e-portfolios comprised of the individual reflective writing of NSTs and ESTs, (2) blogs written by NSTs and ESTs, (3) chat and (4) discussion fora featuring only NSTs in interaction with a peer tutor. Using similar methods as previously, the analysis began by measuring the distribution of metalanguage use across these modes. Chart 5.9 illustrates the findings in this area for comparative purposes. As indicated, metalanguage use was most visible in the on-line portfolios where 116 separate items were found. This was followed by 107 items recorded for the blogs, sixty-four for chat mode, and sixty for the discussion fora. This indicates a noticeably higher use of metalanguage in the portfolios and the blogs than in chat and the discussion fora. Moreover, in overall terms, it reveals that metalanguage use was more salient in the portfolios than in any other mode featured in TEC.

To explore these trends more qualitatively, distribution patterns were mapped across the five specified sub-categories for each of the on-line modes. The findings are presented in Chart 5.10 for comparative purposes and further discussed subsequently for each on-line mode.

Mode 4: Distribution of Metalanguage in On-Line Portfolios
The on-line portfolios featured the individual reflective writing of NSTs and ESTs, which was structured around reflective tasks relating to different aspects of teaching including approaches, methods and techniques. However, the student teachers were also encouraged to self-select topics and issues that they wished to explore reflectively with a view to improving their own teaching. As Chart 5.11 illustrates, of the 116 metalanguage items recorded for this mode, forty-nine related to educational theory/practice, twenty-two to linguistics/language, twenty-one to learning contexts, fifteen to tools/materials, and only nine to the professional CoP. These trends

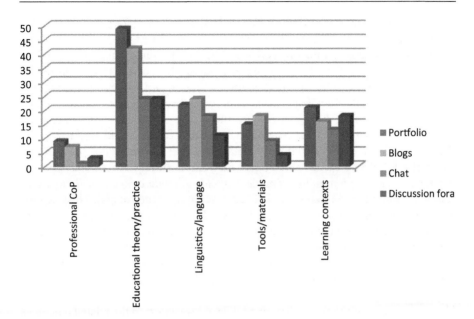

Chart 5.10   Distribution of metalanguage across sub-categories in on-line modes in TEC

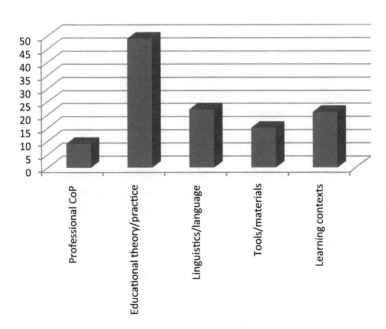

Chart 5.11   Distribution of metalanguage across sub-categories in on-line portfolios

were most similar therefore to those recorded for the face-to-face peer tutor-guided group discussions.

One likely explanation for this is that in both modes there was a strong bias in the data in favour of the NSTs. References made in this context to both historical and contemporary teaching approaches and methodologies, for example, *Grammar Translation Method, Audiolingualism, Communicative Language Teaching, Task-Based Teaching*, can be linked directly to the nature of the tasks set, which were structured and assessed. Items relating to associated concepts and acronyms were also recorded, for example, *inductive, deductive, PPP* (presentation, practice and production), *TT/ST* (teacher talk/student talk). Interestingly, some highly special-ised terms were also found, for example, *scaffolding, reinforcement, mediation*, sug-gesting a more mature interest in SLA processes and teacher role(s). This suggests that this mode may also have provided a useful forum for the student teachers to explore different aspects of teaching more critically. This finding supports Riordan's (2018) claim that the use of on-line diaries can help to foster a deeper level of reflec-tion amongst student teachers enabling them to progress from descriptive accounts to more critically oriented analyses of teaching. This is an area which we will revisit later in this chapter when the DA findings for topic are presented. From the findings for metalanguage use in the on-line portfolios, we turn next to the related outcomes for the blogs.

Mode 5: Distribution of Metalanguage in On-Line Blogs
We will begin by briefly recalling the nature of the blogs by the student teachers, which differed for both cohorts. For the novices, there were two types of individual blogs: those which featured as an obligatory component on a TP module, which were structured and assessed; and those which were voluntary, semi-structured and unassessed. Meanwhile the ESTs engaged only in collaborative reflective blogs; these were also assessed and an obligatory component of their programme of study but semi-structured in nature. The structured blogs centred on theoretical and practical aspects of language teaching while the unstructured blogs were initiated by student teachers and based on topics of their own choice. In all cases, participants were also encouraged to explore issues they might find interesting or useful relating to the busi-ness of teaching English.

As Chart 5.9 indicated previously, 107 separate items of metalanguage were recorded for the blogs. In overall terms, these numbers were second only to those recorded for the on-line portfolios, with similar trends observed as for the guided group discussions. This similarity may be due to some extent to the fact that in these modes, there was a bias in the data in favour of the NSTs. The findings further suggest that like the guided discussions and the e-portfolios, the blogs offered a useful platform for the student teachers in each cohort to articulate their practices. Meanwhile, as Chart 5.12 illustrates, when distribution patterns across the specified sub-categories were mapped, it was found that of the total number of items recorded, forty-two items related to educational theory/practice, twenty-four to linguistics/ language, eighteen to tools/materials, sixteen to learning contexts, and seven to the professional CoP. These patterns were most comparable to those found in the

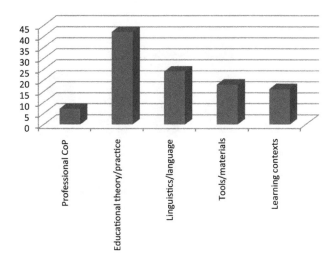

Chart 5.12   Distribution of metalanguage across sub-categories in on-line blogs

lecturer-guided discussions with a slightly higher number of items recorded for the linguistics/language sub-category.

Of note, in this context, were references made by student teachers in both groupings to *techniques, skills, management,* which suggest an interest in teacher roles and competencies. Terms associated with language testing and assessment were also found. Interestingly, general references featured in the blogs written by the NSTs, for example, *exam, grade, test,* whereas specific English language exams and testing bodies/systems were mentioned in those written by the ESTs, for example, *Cambridge IELTS* (International English Language Testing System). This suggests that the NSTs and ESTs alike were aware of general norms around testing in education but that only the ESTs had acquired the specialised knowledge in this area that is expected and required of fully fledged members of the TESOL CoP. From these findings for metalanguage use in the blogs, we make further comparative analyses with the chat data.

Mode 6: Distribution of Metalanguage in On-Line Chat
In this context, the NSTs interacted with each other and with a peer tutor in synchronous on-line chat that centred on different aspects of language teaching, particularly the teaching of grammar, as well as the content of the MA TESOL programme in general. They were also encouraged to self-select topics and issues of interest should they so wish, as in the portfolios and blogs. As Chart 5.9 illustrated previously, metalanguage use in chat was noticeably less visible than in any other mode in TEC with only sixty-five items found, which was comparable to the low number found also in the TP feedback data. A possible explanation for this finding is that the NSTs may have used chat mode to self-select topics more so than the other modes. As Chart 5.13 illustrates, distribution patterns in this context were similar to those found in TEC in general with twenty-four items associated with educational theory/practice, eighteen

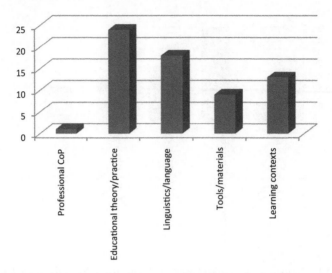

Chart 5.13   Distribution of metalanguage across sub-categories in on-line chat

with linguistics/language, thirteen with learning contexts, nine with tools/materials resources, and only one with the professional CoP.

Of interest in this context are highly specialised items relating to theorists of first and second language learning, for example, *Chomsky, Piaget, Vygotsky*. This suggests that this mode provided a useful forum for the NSTs to share and develop special-ised theoretical knowledge as a follow-up to lectures and tutorials. References made to *assignments, essays, research, articles* also suggest that NSTs used the mode to discuss the academic requirements of their programmes of study, and that they were becoming familiar with the wider academic community. Meanwhile, items such as *workload, deadlines* would seem to indicate that chat offered an outlet for the expres-sion of discontent and stress. The fact that only one item was found relating to CoP, namely *profession*, would offer further evidence to support the view that at this early stage of their professional development, the NSTs were only partial members of the TESOL CoP, with a superficial understanding of its workings. From these findings for metalanguage use in chat mode, we proceed to the outcomes in this area relating to the discussion fora.

Mode 7: Distribution of Metalanguage in On-Line Discussion Fora
The discussion fora featured the asynchronous talk of NSTs with a peer tutor. They were loosely structured around tasks and questions which related to sociocultural theories of second language teaching and learning as well as practical, cultural con-siderations. However, NSTs were encouraged to use the space to raise any issues of interest on their programme of study. As Chart 5.9 indicated previously, in overall terms, the lowest number of metalanguage items was recorded for this mode. This suggests that, like chat, it may have been used more than other modes as a forum for self-selected topics, or as an outlet for emotional expression. As Chart 5.14 illustrates,

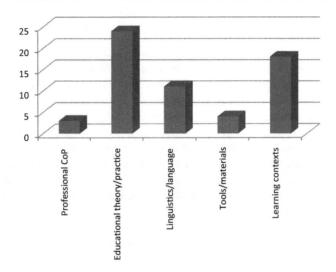

Chart 5.14   Distribution of metalanguage across sub-categories in on-line discussion fora

of the sixty items found in this context, twenty-four were associated with educational theory/practice, eighteen with learning contexts, eleven with linguistics/ language, four with tools/materials, and only three with the professional CoP. These trends were broadly similar to the distribution patterns found in TEC in general and most comparable with those recorded for chat mode, which offers further indications that these on-line contexts may have been used for somewhat similar purposes.

The trends also suggest a keen interest on the part of the NSTs in cultural aspects of teaching and learning, with items such as *culture, multiculturalism, diversity* recorded, as well as references made to a diverse range of learning contexts, for example, *school, university, Arabic, Chinese, Spanish, Dubai.* Acronyms were also identified, as are widely used in the TESOL world to denote areas of specialism, for example, *EAP* (English for Academic Purposes), *ESP* (English for Specific Purposes), as well as those used for international benchmarking in relation to learner proficiency levels, for example *CEFR* (Common European Framework of Reference). This suggests that this mode provided a useful forum for the NSTs to make links between language, culture and language teaching. The nature of the items recorded also evokes a developing awareness on their part of the international nature of the ELT educational domain, and the implications this carries for them as future practitioners, in terms of the career pathways this offers. In this sense, these references provide evidence of their socialisation into the global TESOL teaching community. From this detailed account of the metalanguage use of student teachers at different stages of their professional education across a range of modes of communication, we offer some suggestions as to what the findings might tell us about the shared lexical repertoire of the TESOL CoP and the contribution made by the distinct modes to the socialisation process.

5.4 DISCUSSION: METALANGUAGE

The analysis has revealed a wide and diverse range of metalanguage items in the discursive practices of NSTs and ESTs across a range of face-to-face and on-line modes of communication. Varying trends were observed both in terms of the number of separate items recorded in the various modes and as regards their nature. Moreover, there was variation in the patterns recorded for each student teacher grouping. In overall terms, a higher density of metalanguage use was observed in the on-line modes, with the on-line portfolios featuring the largest number of individual items. By contrast, the lowest number was recorded in chat, followed by the discussion fora and the face-to-face TP feedback interactions. This indicated that both medium and mode of communication were important determining influences. As the latter modes featured only NSTs, the NST/EST status of the participants was also seen to play a crucial underlying role for the patterns observed.

As for the type of metalanguage items recorded, references to education theory/ practice were most salient in the TEC data, followed by items linked to linguistics/ language. This provided evidence that both general pedagogical knowledge and subject specific expertise were being developed. Also visible were items associated with tools/materials, which suggested an interest in the mechanics of teaching, as would be expected of novice and early career teachers (Farr and Farrell 2017). References to learning contexts were also salient, which may be indicative of a newfound knowledge of diverse learner groups on the part of the NSTs, as well as a developing sense of awareness that they were becoming members of a global teaching community. Across the modes, acronyms were also found that are commonly used in the TESOL profession. These included references to learner proficiency levels, international examinations and specialised areas of teaching. This provided further evidence that the student teachers were becoming familiar with the norms and practices of their chosen profession. However, interestingly, items indexing the professional CoP were noticeably few, which would seem to suggest that the novices had yet to acquire a fully developed sense of the professional community they were entering, and their teacher identity within it, given the strong bias in the data in favour of this group. This is a hypothesis that is further explored in the discourse analysis of topic which follows, and in Chapter 6 where it is revisited as a main theme.

The mapping of metalanguage across modes was further useful in providing early indications of the role they might play in fostering student teacher socialisation and learning and, therefore, their effectiveness. For instance, the items recorded in the TP feedback context, in the guided group discussions and in chat and the discussion fora, suggested that these modes were conducive to awareness-raising in relation to subject knowledge and practical aspects of teaching, as well as offering opportunities for scaffolding by peers and teacher educators. Meanwhile, metalanguage use in the on-line portfolios, blogs and chat indicated that in these modes crucial links were being made between theory and practice. The portfolios also seemed to encourage a more critical type of pedagogical reflection. Interestingly, items found only in chat suggested that this mode may also have provided a safe space for the relief of stress associated with academic workload and assignments.

The analysis of metalanguage has been useful in shedding light on the professional terms and concepts that student teachers become familiar with as they develop theoretical knowledge and practical expertise in their subject area and in educational matters more generally. In so doing, it has also offered a lens into the shared lexical repertoire of this CoP. As Wenger (1998) and others since have argued (for example, see Morton and Gray 2010), metalanguage use shows engagement with a CoP as reifications (that is, shared jargon) between members. Moreover, Borg (2006) has posited that the development of professional discourse might play a role in cognitive change during teacher education. In this regard, the analysis has indicated some of the ways in which student teachers can be encouraged to articulate their practices and build and share knowledge, with the guided support of TP supervisors, lecturers, tutors and peers. Crucially, the findings for metalanguage have also provided early indications of the types of topics that are of shared professional interest and concern to new and established members of the ELTE CoP, which can be further explored by means of a more qualitative DA, as is the present intention. This second layer of analysis thereby offers the potential for deeper understandings to be brought to light concerning the shared knowledge, norms, beliefs and aspirations of the members of the CoP, how these are articulated by student teachers at different stages of their professional development, and the ways in which they can be fostered in a teacher education environment.

5.5 TOPIC IN TEC

The DA of topic began with the up-close exploration of the TEC data across the various modes using keyword searches and intensive intuitive reading. This was with the aim of identifying micro-topics relating to the five areas of professional competence specified in the classification system used previously to explore metalanguage use. The choice of this approach was influenced by Farrell's (2016a) successful use of thematic coding to investigate topics of interest to early career English as a Second Language (ESL) teachers in the Canadian secondary school context, for the purpose of reflective practice. Table 5.3 re-establishes these categories, and lists the related micro-topics identified for each.

As indicated, a total of thirty micro-topics were identified across the five main themes, although there was overlapping at times as the later DA will highlight. Of these, eight were indexed to the professional CoP, for example, *workload* and *teaching practice*. A further eight were associated with different aspects of linguistics/language, for example, *L2 theories/approaches* and *language teaching methodologies*. Five were related to educational theory/practice, for example, *learning theories/approaches* and *lesson planning*. Five were related to learning contexts, for example, *local* and *international*, and four were linked to tools/materials, as in: *course books* and *board use*. The findings suggest that a wide and varied range of topics were engaged in by the student teachers across the various modes. Interestingly, themes indexed to professional CoP and linguistics/language featured most saliently, which is encouraging as it suggests professional growth and an expanding expertise in the subject area.

As indicated, the student teachers showed a strong interest in different aspects of teaching and learning. Encouragingly, this included trying to make links between

Table 5.3   Overview of thematic categories and related micro-topics in TEC

Thematic categories	Micro-topics
1. Professional CoP	(1) Workload (2) Teaching practice (3) Observation (4) TP feedback (5) Professional norms (6) Professional relationships (7) Professional identity (8) Careers
2. Educational theory/practice	(1) Learning theories/approaches (2) Lesson planning (3) Classroom skills (4) Classroom management (5) Psychological challenges
3. Linguistics/ language	(1) L2 theories/approaches (2) Language teaching methodologies (3) Subject knowledge (4) Language lessons (5) Models of English (6) Grammar teaching (7) Pronunciation teaching (8) L2 teacher talk
4. Tools/materials	(1) Course books (2) Board use (3) Slides (4) Corpora
5. Learning contexts	(1) Local (2) International (3) Culturally related issues (4) Learner knowledge (5) Proficiency levels

educational and linguistic theory and their classroom practices in their interactions across the various modes, as extracts 5.1 and 5.2 from the peer-guided group discussions and their on-line chat reveal.

Extract 5.1 (Mode 3: Face-to-Face Peer Tutor-Guided Group Discussions)

```
NST 1: I have been trying to work out what Input plus one actually
       means when it comes to teaching the intermediates
NST 2: Yeah, it's hard to apply
```

Extract 5.2 (Mode 6: On-Line Chat)

```
NST 1: When I read about Vygotsky's idea of ZPD it made me think a
       lot more about how I pitch the lesson in terms of making it
       accessible but at the same time challenging for learners
NST 2: Yes, it's an important principle to help guide us when we
       chose the subject content of lessons
```

These exchanges highlight the benefits that can be gained by affording student teachers multiple and varied opportunities to co-construct theoretical knowledge and share practical expertise, which in these cases related to pitching subject content more accurately to the proficiency level of learners.

The challenges arising for NSTs from a lack of subject knowledge was a recurrent theme across the various modes. For instance, in extract 5.3, sourced from an on-line blog, we find a frank disclosure by one of the NSTs concerning her inability to teach grammar, which she links to her own poor knowledge in this area.

Extract 5.3 (Mode 5: On-Line Blogs)

```
NST: I feel I don't know grammar well enough to be able to teach it.
```

The NSTs also described the difficulties they experienced teaching grammar and pronunciation in their reflective writing in the on-line portfolios, and in the peer tutor-guided group discussions, as extracts 5.4 and 5.5 exemplify.

Extract 5.4 (Mode 4: On-Line Portfolios)

```
NST: I can't teach grammar but my team teacher helped me a lot
     because she told me I didn't need to know everything and that
     the teachers' book was actually really good because it gives
     the rules and examples so I use it now.
```

Extract 5.5 (Mode 3: Face-to-Face Peer Tutor-Guided Group Discussions)

```
NST 1: I know I'm avoiding teaching pronunciation and my TP supervi-
       sor said I should integrate it in the next lesson
NST 2: I think you'd be well able to do that if you focus on maybe
       one or two sounds
NST 1: Yeah I might have a go next week
NST 2: Yeah, see how you get on I mean it mightn't be such a big
       deal anyway
```

Farrell's research, as reported in Farr (2015), has suggested that the teaching of language systems is an area where novices from native English backgrounds typically lack confidence, often due to a prior lack of formal education in this area. These extracts reveal that both reflective portfolios and peer tutor-guided face-to-face discussions can provide a safe and supportive environment for novices to articulate these common fears wherein issues of face are likely to be at the fore, as well as creating opportunities for scaffolding by peers, which is vital for teacher learning. This highlights, once again, the important role that peers and peer tutors can play in the affective realm of student teacher learning. However, there was also evidence that some NSTs might have preferred the more private and intimate setting of TP feedback encounters to raise issues of this kind, possibly due to a fear of losing face in front of peers, as would seem to be the case in extract 5.6.

Extract 5.6 (Mode 1: Face-to-Face Teaching Practice Feedback Interactions)

```
NST: My worst nightmare is being asked a grammar question I can't
     answer
TPS: OK, but has this actually happened?
NST: Well no but it could
TPS: Right, so would it be useful to talk about some strategies you
     could use if this did happen?
NST: Yes that would definitely be a help
```

Moreover, as illustrated, interactions in this mode created opportunities for targeted scaffolding and shared learning between an established member of the CoP and a new recruit, which is considered vital for the socialisation and professional development of NSTs (Riordan 2018).

There were also several instances where the guided group discussions were seen to offer a useful forum for awareness-raising and scaffolding in relation to different aspects of professional development. For instance, in extract 5.7, the NSTs are exploring the benefits of the mentoring relationship with experienced teachers. Note how the lecturer's follow-up question gently probed the NST to reflect on and articulate the precise benefits of the observation for her own learning, which in this case was in the area of lesson planning.

Extract 5.7 (Mode 2: Face-to-Face Lecturer-Guided Group Discussions)

```
NST: I liked that we could watch them teach and then get to talk to
     them about the lesson afterward yeah it was helpful
L:   In what ways did you find it helpful?
NST: Well, I got the chance to ask why her why she was doing certain
     things and how she came to that decision so it helped me to
     understand more about how she planned her lessons
```

Similarly, in extract 5.8, the NSTs are being encouraged to reflect on the value of collaborative dialogue with mentors around teaching practice.

Extract 5.8 (Mode 3: Face-to-Face Peer Tutor-Guided Group Discussions)

```
PT:  What did you learn from your chat with the class teacher?
NST: Things like establishing good rapport with the students
     and getting the balance right between being friendly and
     professional
```

These findings support Farr and Farrell's account (2017), which highlighted the ways in which guided group discussions can be used to raise student teacher awareness of key aspects of classroom practice, including good classroom management practices. The guided group discussions also afforded opportunities for awareness-raising in relation to issues around teacher identity formation. In extract 5.9, the NSTs are discussing the tensions that can arise between personal and professional identity.

Extract 5.9 (Mode 2: Face-to-Face Lecturer-Guided Group Discussions)

```
NST 1: I felt I was being the muinteoir which I didn't want as it's
       not me
NST 2: Yeah I get you
L:     Can you tell everyone what that means?
```

Here, we note the first speaker's use of the Irish word for teacher, *muinteor*, as she describes the type of practitioner she does not want to be, as this is a term that carries negative connotations of being strict and unapproachable. From the response, it is clear there is a shared, cultural understanding between the two NSTs involved as both are speakers of Irish and native to Ireland. However, as cultural references of this kind would clearly pose a problem for NSTs from non-Irish backgrounds, the lecturer asks for further contextual information to ensure that the discussion is made accessible for all. This highlights the key mediating role that lecturers/tutors can play to enable student teachers from all backgrounds to engage in collaborative discussions with peers for the purpose of shared learning. This will become an increasingly important consideration on ELTE programmes in the context of the growing internationalisation of third level education. Accordingly, it carries implications for programme design in terms of the types of supports needed for international students.

At times, discussions also centred on the normative dimensions of English language teaching, as in extract 5.10 where the issue of suitable target models for the teaching of pronunciation was raised.

Extract 5.10 (Face-to-Face Lecturer-Guided Group Discussions)

```
NST 1: The accent [featured on the CD listening activity] was dif-
       ferent to how I would say it which made me think about what
       models of pronunciation we're supposed to teach
NST 2: Yeah I mean are we supposed to put on a British accent?
L:     Well historically British or American models would have
       been used that is now slowly changing in the light of World
       Englishes but restrictions remain in many contexts on the
       models we can teach and use
```

Borg (2003: 104) has observed that new recruits must conform to the expectations of the teaching community in order to enter it. Similarly, Farr (2010) has argued that it is essential for NSTs to be made aware of existing norms before they can begin to critique them. This suggests that over the course of their formal teacher education, NSTs should be offered opportunities to explore established norms and how they have shaped classroom practice before moving on to more critically oriented discussions of how these might be changing, and the implications this carries. Interestingly, the comments made by the NSTs in the previous exchange indicate that they lack understanding concerning the norms underlying the target models taught in the ELT classroom and the implications this might carry for their own practices. In this sense they reflect what Freeman (2016) has labelled articulation, whereby new recruits to the teaching CoP express views which mark them as peripheral rather than full and established members. What is further worth pointing out is that, in this example, it is clear that a learning gap has emerged, and with it an opportunity for student teacher learning. As illustrated, this is noticed and acted on by the lecturer, who highlights changing developments in this area. This exchange demonstrates how group discussions that are guided by a more expert other can be successfully exploited for awareness-raising and scaffolding.

Across the various modes, the student teachers in both groupings also showed an interest in discussing new technologies in language learning and their applications. In extract 5.11, from the lecturer-guided group discussions, the NSTs are tentatively exploring how corpora could be used with EFL learners and the practical challenges this might pose for teachers.

Extract 5.11 (Mode 2: Face-to-Face Lecturer-Guided Group Discussions)

```
NST 1: You can use a corpus and get them to look at collocations
NST 2: Yeah but it takes time and I'd really have to know what I
       was doing
```

Meanwhile, in extract 5.12 from the on-line portfolios, we find one of the ESTs reflecting more critically on the implications of various new technologies for language teaching. This finding supports Riordan's (2018) argument that on-line portfolios can be effective in encouraging a deeper and more critically oriented type of reflection.

Extract 5.12 (Mode 4: On-Line Portfolios)

```
Talking about the MOOCS [massive open online courses], blended
learning and on-line learning in general, I expect the process
of teaching/learning will be developed in a very short period
of time. Both lecturers and students in universities will make
use of the up to date technology. However, the idea of on-line
learning and technology will not eliminate the role of face-to-
face teaching and learning. It adds to facilitate the process of
teaching and learning, and it makes use of the variable technical
tools.
```

As the findings for metalanguage use suggested, the data from the discussion fora revealed that the NSTs were developing a growing interest in EFL learners and becoming more knowledgeable about their learning needs, as extract 5.13 illustrates. This can be seen to reflect an increased professional maturity on their part in the sense that the focus of their attention might be moving away from their own concerns to those of their learners.

Extract 5.13 (Mode 7: On-Line Discussion Fora)

```
NST: I look up the CEFR guidelines on-line to find out what they
     can and can't do which is good so we know what they need
```

Similarly, there was evidence to support the earlier indications that the NSTs were becoming more aware of the global TESOL profession and what this might mean for them in terms of future career opportunities, as well as some of the cultural implications involved, as extract 5.14 illustrates.

Extract 5.14 (Mode 7: On-Line Discussion Fora)

```
NST 1: So we'll all be running off to Dubai the minute we're
       finished
NST 2: Yeah but it's meant to be really strict and teachers have
       to be careful about dress otherwise learners might get
       offended
```

This suggests a newfound knowledge in the area of intercultural awareness, which is further indicative of their socialisation into the TESOL CoP. It also signals that the NSTs envisaged being part of the international TESOL teaching community in the not too distant future, thereby reflecting a developing sense of teacher identity and that they are assuming a less peripheral role in the CoP.

Student teacher engagement with the research literature and the wider academic community was also in evidence. For instance, in extract 5.15, which is sourced from the on-line blogs, we find one of the NSTs recalling a conference she had recently attended in which she heard a talk given by well-known, applied linguist Professor Michael McCarthy on the subject of spoken grammar. As well as revealing a burgeoning interest in linguistic theory, this extract also provides us with first-hand evidence of 'brokering' whereby knowledge gained by a community member in one context adds to the shared repertoire of the CoP (Wenger 1998).

Extract 5.15 (Mode 5: On-Line Blogs)

```
NST: During the weekend, I attended a conference in Dublin. It was
     really good. Mike McCarthy was the speaker. He told us a lot
     about spoken grammar and how different it is to written grammar.
     I was fascinated by what he said about 'chunks' in speech.
```

Further to these types of gains, it was clear that some of the modes also provided the NSTs with a safe space to 'let off steam', with disclosure of this kind more often taking place in on-line chat and on-line discussion fora, as extracts 5.16 and 5.17 exemplify.

Extract 5.16 (Mode 6: On-Line Chat)

```
NST: We're all complaining about workload as we're in the middle of
     assignments and deadlines are looming.
```

As illustrated, in the first case, it is the cumulative workload on the MA programme that is the cause of discontent, while, in the second, it is the unexpected amount of time and effort involved in teaching practice.

Extract 5.17 (Mode 7: On-Line Discussion Fora)

```
NST: Everyone is saying that the workload for TP is pretty over-
     whelming. I had no idea I would be spending so much time plan-
     ning lessons and finding good materials.
```

Research by Farr and Farrell (2017) in the area of student teacher reflective practice has shown that NSTs often find lesson planning an arduous task with many under-estimating the amount of time and effort involved. From the previous comments, there is a clear sense that the NSTs involved were challenged by the workload associ-ated with TP, and by the academic requirements of the MA programme in general. Interestingly, chat was found to be the most preferred environment for the expression of stress and frustration caused by workload and fast approaching deadlines. It was also used by the NSTs for emotional disclosures made in relation to the TP experi-ence. For instance, in extract 5.18, we find NSTs discussing the psychological impact of being supervised during TP.

Extract 5.18 (Mode 6: On-Line Chat)

```
NST 1: I felt so nervous being watched. It was actually so stressful
NST 2: I know what you mean but I was glad she was there in case I
       got stuck
```

The anxiety felt by NSTs during teaching practice has been well-documented (Farr 2011; Farr and Farrell 2017; Farrell 2016a; Riordan 2018; Walsh 2006). Farr (2011) has advised that although the presence of a TP supervisor in the classroom can be reassuring for some novices, others find it unduly stressful. Growing recognition of this problem has led to calls for safe spaces to be afforded to student and early career teachers so that they can express the fears and concerns that typically stem from a lack of confidence and professional expertise (Farr and Farrell 2017). Farrell (2016a) has argued that this can help them to rationalise and generalise their experiences as new recruits to the teaching profession as well as creating opportunities for teacher learning on the basis of individual and shared experiences. Chat would seem to offer a particularly suitable space for this purpose as it involves synchronous discus-sions whereby NSTs can provide each other with instantaneous mutual support. The on-line portfolios were also found to play an important role in the affective realm of communication by offering a more private space for NSTs to articulate the psycho-logical challenges they experienced in TP as a starting point to addressing them, as in extract 5.19 where one of the NSTs recounts the difficulties she experienced working with a peer during TP.

Extract 5.19 (Mode 4: On-Line Portfolios)

```
NST: Maybe it's because I'm more used to working on my own but I
     have to admit I found it hard to work with my team teacher. She
```

kept telling me what to do because she had more experience. I
know she was only trying to help but I felt it undermined me
and we actually fell out over it which was a bit of a nightmare

In this way, this mode allowed for personal disclosures of a more sensitive nature where issues of face were at stake. These findings highlight the importance of providing student teachers with multiple and varied modes of communication to help them to address the complex demands and challenges they face as part of their professional journey. In the following section, we summarise the main trends observed in the area of topic, and we offer some further suggestions as to their significance.

5.6 DISCUSSION: TOPIC

The analysis of topic has provided a wealth of insights concerning the theoretical knowledge base, practical expertise, and norms that form the fabric of the TESOL CoP and the processes by which new recruits are socialised into its workings. The broad findings to emerge are that group discussions that are guided by mentors in face-to-face and on-line modes can provide a useful platform for awareness-raising and scaffolding. This can encourage NSTs to explore practical issues and challenges of relevance and concern to all entrants to the CoP. These modes also create opportunities for NSTs and ESTs alike to make connections between theory and practice, which is vital for their professional growth, and to explore issues pertaining to their professional role and identity.

Meanwhile, on-line chat and reflective portfolios can play an effective role in the affective realm of communication by offering a non-face threatening environment for the release of stress brought on by the demands of teaching practice and workload. In particular, chat provides a vehicle for peers to offer and receive emotional support, which is crucial for the well-being and professional development of CoP members, especially where apprentices are concerned, as they typically lack confidence and feel daunted by their new professional role and responsibilities (Farrell 2016a). The more intimate setting of dyadic TP feedback encounters can further offer a suitable environment for frank disclosures in relation to individual teacher performance where issues of face are likely to be at the fore, as well as creating opportunities for targeted scaffolding by mentors. Finally, the use of on-line portfolios has been found to create opportunities for student teachers to reflect more deeply on topics of professional interest. This underscores the crucial role they can play in fostering critical reflective thinking, as the discussion in Chapter 7 will further explore.

The findings presented in this chapter are considered important because they provide a wealth of empirical evidence to support the theoretical and pedagogical arguments made by the authors of this book (see Chapters 2 and 3), as by others (for example, see Farrell 2016b; Mann and Walsh 2017), for a holistic approach to ELTE. This envisages student teachers being engaged in collaborative dialogue, reflection and shared learning in ways which have been demonstrated in order to facilitate their socialisation into the teaching community and to foster their ongoing professional growth as active and engaged community members.

5.7 SUMMARY

In this chapter, we have demonstrated how a CADS approach can be used to achieve a finely nuanced understanding of the processes involved in student teacher socialisation into the ELTE CoP. This was explored at the level of metalanguage and topic as evidence of shared repertoire. From this, a wealth of insights has been gained into the knowledge base, beliefs, norms, practices and concerns of new recruits and established members of the teaching community. The analysis has also illuminated the various mechanisms by which the socialisation of student teachers at different stages of their professional development can best be fostered as part of a holistic approach to ELTE, thereby strengthening theoretical arguments in favour of this approach. In Chapter 8 of this book we offer some further suggestions as to the implications of the findings revealed in this chapter and in the analyses in Chapters 6 and 7 which follow, in terms of informing future directions in teacher education.

5.8 TASKS

1. Metalanguage use. Explore your own use of metalanguage with peers using a similar corpus-based approach as featured in the research reported on in this chapter:
   - Record a twenty minute guided conversation with peers in your own institutional context, with the permission of the lecturer/tutor, and transcribe the data in order to compile a small, locally sourced corpus.
   - Using a freely available software package such as AntConc (http://www. laurenceanthony.net/software), generate a list of the top 1000 most frequent words.
   - Identify and categorise all metalanguage items drawing on the framework presented in this chapter. Complete Table 5.4 in terms of the number of individual items in each sub-category and examples.
   - What conclusions can be drawn from the findings in relation to your own socialisation into the TESOL CoP and that of peers?

Table 5.4

Sub-category	No. items	Examples
1. Professional CoP		
2. Educational theory/practice		
3. Linguistics/language		
4. Tools/materials		
5. Learning contexts		

2. Pedagogical challenges and strategies. Re-read some of the extracts from earlier in this chapter as specified in Table 5.5, and:
   - Identify and reflect on the main challenge in each case.
   - Identify the strategy offered to help address the challenge in each case.
   - Propose a further strategy for each challenge.

Table 5.5

Challenge	Specified strategy	Your strategy
Extract 5.2:		
Extract 5.5:		
Extract 5.6:		
Extract 5.7:		
Extract 5.9:		
Extract 5.11:		
Extract 5.13:		
Extract 5.15:		

6

LANGUAGE TEACHER IDENTITY

6.1 INTRODUCTION

In Chapter 2, the complexity of the position of the teacher, their beliefs, attitudes and cognitions was discussed in the context of changing teaching methodologies over the last forty to fifty years. Inevitably, with this acknowledgement and perspective of the teacher in the complex social environment of the classroom, teacher identity became an important component in helping to understand language teaching (Pennington and Richards 2016: 6). Around the same time period, a different research agenda was exploring the sociocultural and sociopolitical aspects of teaching (for a recent account, see Gray and Morton 2018).

> This research revealed among other things that many aspects of identity – including, though not restricted to, matters of race, gender, and sexual orientation – were of the utmost importance in the language classroom. By the same token, the teacher too was not a neutral player in the classroom, but on the contrary, her positionality in relation to her students, and to the broader context in which the teacher was situated, was vital. (Varghese et al. 2005: 22)

These two conceptual and empirical lines of enquiry have coincided to create a growth in the area of language teacher identity research. The analysis later in this chapter will contribute to that growth by offering some perspectives on the contexts under examination.

In this chapter we begin with a theoretical discussion, based on the conceptual and empirical literature in the area of language teacher identity, which will lead us to the position we take in the present research. Just like identity itself is present in everything we are and everything we do, the language of identity is ubiquitous in everything we say. Therefore all of the language already analysed in Chapter 5, related to topic and the various categories of contextual metalanguage, are direct indicators of identity formation, affiliation and display. In addition and arguably even more closely associated is the language of reflection investigated in Chapter 7. In fact, we had long discussions about which linguistic items to present in this chapter and which to present in the next chapter. In the end, our choices were merely pragmatic rather than based on any perceived difference in their affiliation to one topic or the other, which we see as inextricably linked, and the analysis presented below should be considered in the context of all of the empirical analysis in this book. However, for research purposes, some compartmentalisation is required, and certain lexico-grammatical choices can provide a more direct lens on the articulation of identity in TEC. For the purposes of this chapter, and based on previous research (Farr 2005a), the realm of pronominal use is explored. It is considered in the corpus at large and then more specifically in relation to the probable influencing variables as presented in Chapter 4: novice and experienced student teachers, face-to-face and on-line discourse modes, and degrees of expert scaffolding present in the different contexts.

6.2 WHAT IS LANGUAGE TEACHER IDENTITY?

As a starting point, and in order to contextualise the analysis, we will address the incredibly complex question: what is language teacher identity? There are multiple perspectives on language teacher identity depending on one's theoretical and practical affiliations. However, there are now some shared conceptual understandings about the nature of teacher identity. Firstly, identity is inextricably linked to its social, cultural and political contexts, and is highly dependent on variables such as setting (institutional, informal and so on), other participants (peers, colleagues, bosses, employees and so on), and expectations and purpose of the interactions (Duff and Uchida 1997). In terms of the influence of others, Nunan views identity 'as the construct of a sense of self(selves) through interaction, so it is based in no small part on my own interpretation of how others see me – which is not the same as how they actually see me' (2017: 164). Inherent in the construct of identity is the difference between what Buzzelli and Johnston (2002) call 'assigned identity', which is imposed by others, and 'claimed identity', which is claimed by oneself for oneself. Assigned and claimed identities may or may not align, for example, the case of an adolescent claiming the identity of an adult but their parent assigning the identity of a petulant teenager. Sometimes, encountering new contexts or people can cause identity stress or crisis when one's claimed identity is not aligned with that assigned by the new contexts or people. This assigned/claimed distinction is an important one in the LTE context and one which will be drawn on during the analysis later in this chapter. Secondly, identity is not a static concept but is, rather, highly dynamic (Pennington and Richards 2016: 6; Varghese et al. 2005: 22–3). One's identity can change in different contexts and most people have multiple identities (professional, social and so on). It can also evolve and develop over time, for example, when someone starts a new job, moves to a new town or takes a new university programme of study. This can also mean that one's many identities can be in conflict with each other, for example, being a parent and being a teacher to your own child. And while identity has very close connections with the concept of 'role', it has been argued that they are distinguished by the fact that 'identities are more complex and, in some ways, more insidious. We can, and do, switch roles' (Nunan 2017: 166). Thirdly, language and discourse are key to the construction, negotiation and maintenance of identity (Gee 1996). As the present study is essentially a discourse analysis, we affiliate ourselves strongly with this position. However, we also acknowledge that identity in its entirety cannot be uncovered through language, particularly the language in the TEC data, which was not produced

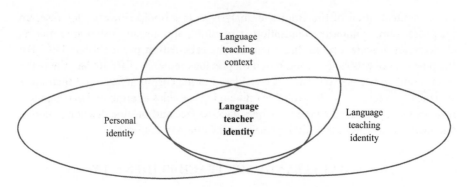

Figure 6.1   Language teacher identity

specifically for the purposes of displaying one's identity. It would probably be more discernible in other types of discourse, for example, narratives or interviews specifically around topics of identity.

Taking these three understandings as a given, we next try to unpack the various components of language teacher identity, illustrated by the (possibly, overly) simple framework proposed in Figure 6.1. The basic premise is that personal (or autobiographical, see Pennington and Richards 2016: 10) identity combines with language teaching identity and language teaching context in many ways, and the juncture at which they overlap is where language teacher identity evolves. Firstly, personal identity is influenced by a range of individual background considerations, including one's race, ethnicity, autobiography, physical characteristics, abilities, skills, social status, lifestyle choices, values, traits and personality characteristics, among other variables. As Farrell puts it 'who I am is how I teach; the person (teacher) cannot be separated from the craft (teaching)' (2017: 183). Also at play here are one's affiliations with different professional, political or social groups, what Gee has labelled 'affinities' (2001). From this perspective, identity 'can be viewed first in terms of the unique set of characteristics associated with a particular individual relative to the perceptions and characteristics of others' (Pennington 2015: 16). Secondly, the language teaching context, which can be incredibly varied and variable, is strongly determined by the prevalent sociocultural influences at play, for example, preferred teaching methodologies (if any), educational and cultural ethos, and national/local policies and regulations.

Thirdly, Freeman (2016: 35) defines language teaching identity as the overlap between 'professional socialisation' and 'language socialisation'. He bases the idea of professional socialisation on Lortie's (1975) 'apprenticeship of observation', which refers to the process of acculturation that takes place during the time we all spend as students in a classroom. In other words, it is our experience of teaching from a student perspective which gives us one perspective on it. It allows a student to see what a teacher does and how s/he does it (the behaviour) but not necessarily the reasoning behind it. To illustrate this, Fiona very recently had a discussion with her thirteen year-old daughter, who was dissatisfied with her science teacher's practice of asking students to say their test result scores aloud in front of the whole group. She couldn't understand why the teacher would want to 'embarrass them like this' – and apparently they were embarrassed whether they received 10 per cent or 100 per cent. Fiona tried to explain that the teacher was probably doing it so that all students would make an effort to study as they wouldn't want to be known to do badly. Of course, she didn't concede that this was a good reason (and Fiona is inclined to agree with her), but at least she could appreciate that it was more well-intended than the reason she had assigned to this teaching practice. In agreement with Freeman (2016), and Pennington and Richards (2016: 5), we contend that formal and informal teacher education programmes of study and related professional activities must also inevitably influence the professional socialisation process, although their impact is largely unknown and has been questioned by some. 'Second language teacher education, like any other form of activity, has its particular social facts that express recognizable shared meanings and understandings. Using these facts creates mutually accepted, shared identities' (Freeman 2016: 36). The second component of language teaching identity, according to Freeman, is language socialisation or 'the experience of language in the world', which could be experience of one's first or any other languages. The intersection between professional socialisation and language socialisation becomes language teaching identity, and based on our illustration in Figure 6.1, the overlap between language teaching identity and individual identity is where language teacher identity develops.

The conceptualisation of identity in this way perhaps hides some of its complexities but it is useful for illustrative purposes. For new teachers first encountering the language teaching classroom, they very often take on what Zimmerman (1998: 90) calls a 'situated identity', which is a traditional or formal role in the classroom as leader of the pedagogic context, most often based on their apprenticeship of observation. 'Such an institutionally defined and supported default teacher identity is natural for inexperienced teachers to assume, since it provides a degree of structure and hierarchy for making a class run well' (Pennington and Richards 2016: 8). The converse of this is what Zimmerman (1998: 91) calls a 'transportable identity', which is more relationship and student-centred, and as such, more informal and personal. While this can be favoured by students as a relaxed and laid-back approach, it can be less efficient for the teacher who may not yet be fully versed in appropriate pedagogic skills and competencies. In certain contexts, this can lead to difficulties achieving pedagogic outcomes and can also create or augment discipline problems.

Defining language teacher identity is not easy, and in many cases is not desirable. However, if one is to conduct research in this field, it is necessary. We finish this section with a recent quotation from Barkhuizen (2017: 4), derived from a content analysis of all forty-one chapters in his edited volume on language teacher identity. Interestingly, the various components of language teacher identities that he lists align with what we see in the analysis in this chapter and in Chapter 7.

Language teacher identities (LTIs) are cognitive, social, emotional, ideological, and historical – they are both inside the teacher and outside in the social, material and technological world. LTIs are being and doing, feeling and imagining and storying. They are struggle and harmony: they are contested and resisted, by self and others. They are core and peripheral, personal and professional, they are dynamic, multiple, and hybrid, and they are foregrounded and backgrounded. And LTIs change, short-term and over time – discursively in social interaction with teacher educators, learners, teachers, administrators, and the wider community, and in material interaction with spaces, places and objects in classrooms, institutions and on-line.

6.3 COMPETENCES OF LANGUAGE TEACHER IDENTITY

Another, more practice-based lens through which identity can be viewed is through a competences framework. In 2012, Richards identified the 'dimensions of teacher knowledge and skill that seem to be at the core of expert teaching competence and performance in language teaching' (2012: 46), and in 2016, with Pennington, he elaborated these as foundational and advanced competences of language teacher identity as per the following framework.

A. Foundational competences of language teacher identity:
   1. Language related identity, based on one's language background and language proficiency. Central to this discussion is whether one is a first or other language speaker of the language being taught (Aneja 2016; Ellis 2016; Wolff and De Costa 2017). First language speakers may have a confident and strong affiliated linguistic and cultural identity, but may lack confidence in their ability and identity as a purveyor of the grammatical and other rules of the language. Second or other language teachers may have the reverse in terms of identity, although this simplistic and binary illustration does not always hold true (Pennington and Richards 2016: 11–13).
   2. Disciplinary identity, or how one associates with the field of language teaching. This is shaped by one's formal education in the area of applied linguistics or TESOL, as well as by one's professional experiences both inside and outside the formal classroom context. This idea aligns well with the notion of content and pedagogic knowledge as presented in Chapter 2 of this book (see also Richards and Farrell 2011 for a discussion of disciplinary knowledge and pedagogical content knowledge) (Pennington and Richards 2016: 13–14).
   3. Context related identity, refers to the different conditions created by the context in which one is teaching. A binary distinction can be made between 'favouring conditions' with positive potentials for teaching (for example, good resources, supportive leadership), and 'disfavouring conditions' where negative influences constrain good teaching and learning (for example, poor pay and conditions, unqualified or incompetent staff). When disfavouring conditions are prevalent, teachers may be constrained in the application of good teaching practices and may become disheartened or demotivated, which in turn can have a negative effect on their practices. A teacher's classroom identity is also related strongly to a national, regional and school culture and is shaped by it, as discussed in the previous section (Pennington and Richards 2016: 14–15).

4. Self-knowledge and awareness of one's strengths and weaknesses and how to teach to the best of one's abilities based on this understanding. This is based on constructing a self-image and an awareness of one's teaching that incorporates personal qualities, values and ideals into good teaching performance. This construction is often developed and articulated through teacher narratives, which are integral to many teacher education and development programmes (Pennington and Richards 2016: 15–16).

5. Student-related identity (student knowledge and awareness), or a focus on the learner as a characteristic of skilled teacher behaviour. A teacher's identity develops through their interactive relationship with their students and is partially defined by it. There is a strong concern about their own role in relation to their students, for example, as a facilitator, a mentor and so on (Pennington and Richards 2016: 16–17).

B. Advanced competences of language teacher identity:

6. Practised and responsive teaching skills (knowledge into practice), or moving from theoretical knowledge, through a process of reasoning, into practices and skills needed in teaching contexts. During a teacher education course, new teachers are supported in doing this through the practicum, which allows them to apply the knowledge they have gained from coursework to the classroom. Their sense of identity as a teacher and confidence in their ability to do this grows with both formal education and practice, but even more substantially through prolonged teaching experience (Pennington and Richards 2016: 17–19).

7. Theorising from practice (practice into knowledge), happens when teachers evolve in terms of their understanding of teaching, based on their practice. They develop a personal understanding of teaching that integrates beliefs, theories and principles (Borg 2006). 'This takes language teacher identity beyond training (Richards 1998) to a higher level of reflection that seeks to relate individual classroom actions and decision-making to each other and to higher principles' (Pennington and Richards 2016: 19). Teacher research (Burns 2010) and development through such activities as seminars, peer coaching, cooperative development and so on (Johnson 2006) have been cited as ways in which such theoretical knowledge generation and identities can develop among the profession of teachers.

8. Membership in communities of practice and profession, helps to grow and influence a teacher's identity, as discussed in more detail in Chapter 3 of this book.

6.4 RESEARCHING LANGUAGE TEACHER IDENTITY

Empirical investigation of the complex notion of language teacher identity poses many challenges, primarily because it is only apparent through perceptible, overt demonstrations on the part of the teacher, which means that much of what constitutes identity remains hidden to the observer. In addition, even if they are observable, Farrell (2017: 187) comments that 'from a research perspective, these professional roles are not easily isolated or even measured'. As we interpret it, the following factors should be taken into account before any attempt at researching language teacher identity in any way, other than at a theoretical or conceptual level. Language teacher identity may be:

1. visible or invisible, for example, one's appearance is visible whereas one's opinions are not;
2. on-display or off-display, for example, one may choose to dress in a way that reflects a particular ethnic or religious affiliation, or one may not;
3. shared or individual, for example, within a community of my immediate colleagues, we might share a belief about the importance of continuous assessment but I might be alone in my belief that group-based continuous assessment is most effective;
4. claimed or assigned, for example, when Fiona was appointed as Dean of Teaching and Learning in her university recently, the broader academic community assigned her that identity in very obvious ways long before she was ready to claim it for herself. In fact, she experienced a little imposter syndrome in the initial weeks and months. So, at first there was a conflict between her assigned and claimed identities, but these soon came to align with each other more easily.

Having accepted that these factors play an influencing role in any attempt at research, one also needs to decide on the appropriate theoretical framework(s) to help interpret evidence and articulate the interpretations. This is no easy task. Exploring the theoretical and empirical accounts is when 'things become a bit murky' and choices are hard to make (Barkhuizen 2017: 2). Making sense of language teacher identity can be approached from a number of theoretical perspectives associated with the fields of general education, psychology and linguistics, among others. Varghese et al. (2005: 21) advocate for the use of multiple frameworks in order to offer range and complexity in interpretation: 'while in isolation each theory has its limitations, an openness to multiple theoretical approaches allows a richer and more useful understanding of the processes and contexts of teacher identity'. They illustrate this through the use of three different frameworks across three individual studies: Tajfel's (1978) social identity theory, Lave and Wenger's (1991) theory of situated learning and Simon's (1995) concept of the image-text. Through the interpretation of the various data sets collected across the studies, they identify the strengths and weaknesses of the adopted approach to make the case that multiple perspectives may help to eliminate weaknesses inherent in each. If you decide to embark on a deeper exploration of language teacher identity and want to better understand a range of perspectives, we suggest you read Brakhuizen's 2017 edited collection, which includes coverage from a number of interpretations and in many contexts: teacher autonomy and agency; sociolinguistics; social justice; multilingualism; distance learning; teacher research; teacher education; social practice; race; and feminism, among others.

In this chapter, we rely more heavily on social identity theory and the theory of situated learning and their associated concepts to help articulate our interpretation of identity in the TEC data. We acknowledge that these theories do not adequately account for the influence of power relations and hierarchies present in some of the contexts from which the data come (see Chapter 4), but fully recognise that the concept of 'role' within identity makes assumptions about power and control (Richards 2017: 141), and so will explicitly make comment on these in our analysis. We also acknowledge that the data comes from a range of teacher education contexts and related tasks and it was not constructed or influenced in any way to attempt to elicit more overt signals of identity. In other words, the participants were not explicitly asked to talk about their identity unless this was naturally part of the task for the purposes of the teacher education programme and not for the purposes of our research on teacher identity. This inevitably means that overt markers of identity in the discourse are more difficult to find, or that we sometimes have to rely on implicit interpretations based on our own understandings and participation in the context under scrutiny. An advantage of this, we would argue, is that the participants' expressions of identity may be more authentic. We will return to this discussion below. For now, we align ourselves with Farrell's clear articulation, that 'researching professional role identity really means reflecting on how we "see" ourselves as language teachers and how others "see" us as language teachers' (2017: 187). In the context of the typical requirements of ELTE programmes, the ways in which teachers see themselves is inevitably challenged and necessarily evolves as they assume many new roles and related identities. A key challenge imposed by this unique context is for teachers to 'reposition themselves from their identity as a student-teacher to that of a classroom teacher' (Richards 2017: 139), and we will illustrate below how this creates an identity challenge, and sometimes crisis, particularly in the focused arena of teaching practice feedback and its ensuing discourse.

6.5 PRONOUN USAGE IN TEC

As identity is a construct of how I see myself and of how I think others see me, an obvious, and recognised, starting point for linguistic analysis is pronominal usage. 'Pronouns are the main linguistic resources through which actors manage [the] shift in their own standing relative to the framework of reference' (Hanks 1990: 137). This short section details how personal and possessive pronouns, as well as possessive adjectives, present themselves in TEC in terms of frequency. Table 6.1 shows the relative order of frequency and the raw frequency totals.

Even a cursory glance at the results in Table 6.1 indicates that this is very much an *I, you, they* and *we* kind of language, in that order. Typical of a narrative genre, particularly in spoken discourse, we see *I* and *you* featuring at the top of the list. These pronouns are often indicative of sharing personal experiences, and thoughts and opinions relative to the context, all of which are highly associated with the expression of one's sense of identity as a language teacher. We can hypothesise that many of the instances of *I* are the teachers talking about their personal stories, and that the occurrences of *you* may represent the interlocutor asking questions, advising, evaluating or co-constructing the narrative. *They, them* and *their*, in relatively high frequencies, positions the expression of identity in relation to others present or perhaps outside the teaching context. They could, for example, be referring to their EFL learners, tutors or lecturers on the programme of study, published materials' writers or

Table 6.1   Personal and possessive pronouns, and possessive adjectives in TEC

	Personal pronouns (subject)	Freq.	Personal pronouns (object)	Freq.	Possessive pronouns	Freq.	Possessive adjectives	Freq.
1	I*	18,428	Them	1,465	His	137	My	3,078
2	You*[1]	10,766	Me	2,511	Mine	33	Your	1,874
3	They*	4,270	Her	312	Ours	6	Their	1,157
4	We*	2,251	Us	250	Theirs	6	Our	390
5	She*	671	Him	127	Yours	5	Her	312
6	He*	531			Hers	2		

* indicates that all contractions are included also, for example, *I'm*.
[1] Identical/repeated form frequencies are included in total in the first instance on this table. They are not differentiated by grammatical or syntactic category at this stage of the analysis. The items affected are *you, your,* and *his*.

researchers, or other non-present peers (Riordan 2018; Vaughan 2010). And finally worth mentioning is the relatively high number of *we, our* and to a lesser extent *us* in the data. These may point to a joint enterprise, endeavour or community of practice (Lave and Wenger 1991; and see Chapter 7). In any case, it is highly likely that they indicate a sense of belonging to a group and some level of shared identity.

Frequency lists do two things. They allow us to get an overview of the genre that is under scrutiny and the nature of the language contained within, and they allow us to make informed hypotheses in relation to high and low frequency items. The brief commentary on Table 6.1 in this section was in effect the formation of a number of hypotheses which will now be investigated more thoroughly in the various micro-contexts, as well as through a more detailed view of pronoun usage through the concordancer tool.

6.6 PRONOUN USAGE AMONG NOVICE AND EXPERIENCED STUDENT TEACHERS

It might be expected that novice and experienced student teachers would find themselves at different points of the continuum of identity formation and expression, or at least in terms of their confidence in that language teacher identity. This section will explore whether this manifests itself through their use of pronouns in the relevant corpora. Firstly, we will examine personal pronouns (subject) in the novice and experienced student teacher corpora. Given that the data from novice student teachers is almost three times the size of the data set from experienced student teachers the results are all normalised to words per million (WPM) and Chart 6.1 presents the relative frequencies.

We can see from Chart 6.1 that novice student teachers use more personal pronouns (87,873) overall than their experienced counterparts (70,581). While the gap isn't very big (just over 17,000), it may suggest that the novice student teachers are more preoccupied with their own personal experiences and sharing them with others, as most of

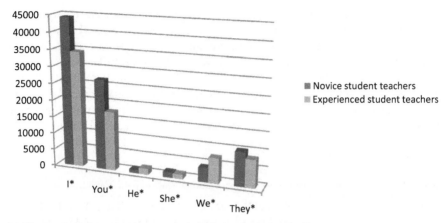

* indicates that all contractions are included also, for example, *I'm*.

*Chart 6.1   Personal pronouns (subject): novice and experienced student
teachers (WPM)*

the difference can be accounted for in the discrepancies between *I* and *you*. It is likely
that the requirements of the programme to review, in detail, their own local experiences in reflective practice contexts accounts for this pattern. This will be discussed
further below and in Chapter 7. On the other hand, while the experienced teachers
also have relatively high occurrences of these two pronouns, they may be less preoccupied with their own personal experiences and rather focused on engaging in a more
objective and professional type of discussion, either in written or spoken modes. Their
personal teaching experiences may also seem somewhat distant to them as they do not
teach while engaging in this part of their PhD studies. The slightly higher frequency
of *they* for the novice student teachers is likely to signal references to the EFL learners
they teach as part of their teaching practice. These learners inevitably take primacy of
place in any discussion of their practice teaching sessions. The pronoun which is of
most interest at this point is the novice teachers' lower use of *we*. Given the importance
of social models of education and the building of professional communities, it will be
interesting to investigate whether this is accounted for by their more peripheral sense
of belonging to the professional community at this stage of their education. In other
words, they may not yet have formed, or feel they legitimately belong to, a teaching
community and therefore talk about *I* and *you* rather than *we*. We will investigate these
hypotheses further below. As this section is looking at the novice and experienced
student teacher data in a relative way, the focus is on the three pronouns which show
the highest levels of divergence: *I, you* and *we*.

6.6.1 *I*

A focus on the self is a core component in the formation and articulation of identity.
For this reason, we will now explore how the novice and experienced teachers use

the pronoun *I* in their professional expression. With so many occurrences of this pronoun in the data, only significant reoccurrences and clusters will be examined here. A search for *I* in two- and three-word clusters, and related clusters (top 30) produced the results presented in Table 6.2. Various forms of the lemmas *know, feel* and *think* feature highly on the two- and three-word cluster list associated with the pronoun *I*. These are clearly important in the expression of cognition and emotion, both central to a teacher's identity. They are analysed in detail in Chapter 7 under the theme of reflective practice and therefore will not be addressed further here and are lowlighted in Table 6.2 for this reason.

Table 6.2   Two and three-word *I* clusters: novice student teacher data (top 30)

1	I WAS	1,314	I WAS PLEASED (57), I WAS LIKE (55), I WAS HAPPY (49), I WAS TRYING (42), I WAS A (41), I WAS JUST (39), I WAS TEACHING (38), I WAS ALSO (38), I WAS GOING (35), I WAS VERY (33), I WAS ABLE (31), I WAS DISPLEASED (24), I WAS THINKING (24), I WAS NOT (23), I WAS LOOKING (22), I WAS DOING (21), I WAS QUITE (21)
2	I THINK	1,303	I THINK THAT (199), I THINK I (125), I THINK IT (110), I THINK YOU (92), I THINK THE (87), I THINK IT'S (67), I THINK THEY (43), I THINK THAT'S (27), I THINK SO (25), I THINK IF (24), I I THINK (23), I THINK THIS (23)
3	I HAD	614	I HAD TO (74), I HAD A (51), I HAD PLANNED (30), I HAD THE (26)
4	I DON'T	519	I DON'T KNOW (231), I DON'T THINK (125), I DON'T HAVE (23), I I DON'T (20)
5	I WOULD	519	I WOULD HAVE (70), I WOULD SAY (66), I WOULD LIKE (55), I WOULD BE (32), I WOULDN'T HAVE (20)
6	I HAVE	504	I HAVE A (44), I HAVE TO (43), I HAVE BEEN (31), I HAVE LEARNED (20)
7	I MEAN	495	I MEAN I (78), I MEAN YOU (53), I MEAN IT (29), I MEAN THEY (23)
8	I DID	445	I DIDN'T (62), I DID NOT (45), I DIDN'T KNOW (39), I DIDN'T WANT (25), I DID FEEL (23), I DIDN'T HAVE (22), I DIDN'T THINK (21)
9	I FELT	383	I FELT THAT (132), I FELT THE (31), I FELT I (29), I FELT WAS (26), I FELT IT (21)
10	I FEEL	369	I FEEL THAT (139), I FEEL I (53), I FEEL THE (26), I FEEL LIKE (22)
11	I DIDN'T	307	I DIDN'T KNOW (39), I DIDN'T WANT (25), I DIDN'T HAVE (22), I DIDN'T THINK (21)
12	I I	294	I I I (27), I I THINK (23), I I DON'T (20)
13	I AM	292	I AM NOT (33)
14	I KNOW	286	I KNOW THAT (42), I KNOW I (35), I KNOW WHAT (20)
15	I JUST	281	

(Continued)

Table 6.2   Continued

16 THINK THAT	252	I THINK THAT (199), THINK THAT I (46), THINK THAT THE (28), I THINK THAT'S (27), THINK THAT WAS (26), DO THINK THAT (21)
17 DON'T KNOW	246	I DON'T KNOW (231), DON'T KNOW I (27), DON'T KNOW IF (21), DON'T KNOW WHAT (20), DON'T KNOW HOW (20)
18 I THOUGHT	244	I THOUGHT THAT (47), I THOUGHT IT (29), I THOUGHT I (29)
19 I DON'T KNOW	231	I DON'T (519), DON'T KNOW (246), I DO (192)
20 I COULD	**219**	**I COULD HAVE (68)**
21 THAT I	**216**	**FEEL THAT I (61), THINK THAT I (46)**
22 I THINK THAT	199	I THINK (1,303), THINK THAT (252)
23 I DO	**192**	**I DON'T KNOW (231), I DON'T THINK (125), I DON'T (39), I DO THINK (32), I DON'T HAVE (23), I DON'T (20)**
24 FEEL THAT	178	I FEEL THAT (139), FEEL THAT I (61), FEEL THAT THE (22)
25 I SAID	**170**	**I SAID I (22), I SAID IT (21)**
26 I SHOULD	**166**	**I SHOULD HAVE (84)**
27 THINK I	163	I THINK I (125), I THINK IT (110), I THINK IT'S (67), THINK IT WAS (37), DON'T THINK I (26), I THINK IF (24)
28 IT WAS	**152**	**THINK IT WAS (37)**
29 I WILL	**150**	
30 FELT THAT	150	I FELT THAT (132), FELT THAT THE (33)

Table 6.2 gives a sense of the novice student teacher discourse around the pronoun *I*. Much of the clustering happens with dynamic verbs. With some inevitable overlap between the categories, these verbs relate thematically to (1) teaching and learning (*I was teaching, I had planned, I have learned*), (2) effort expended more generally, but presumably on the job of teaching (*I was trying, going, looking, doing*), (3) cognition and emotion (*I was thinking, I didn't know, I feel that I*), and (4) critical review/explanation and evaluation (*I mean, I could have, I should have*). Where the sense is more stative, it is perhaps indicative of more profound markers of identity, for example, *I was happy, I was displeased*. Taking a similar approach with the more experienced teachers' data (minimum fifty occurrences because of the smaller data set) produced the clusters shown in Table 6.3.

The presence of clustering is lower in the experienced teacher data, but statistically this is probably due to the relatively smaller data set (about two and a half times fewer words in this corpus). Looking at individual clusters, there are some notable differences. Firstly, the experienced student teacher data illustrates a relatively lower occurrence of *I was*. When normalised to words per million, it occurs 4,043 times in the novice student teacher data and 1,898 times in the experienced student teacher data. This could be attributed to the nature of the tasks. In other words, the novice teachers are reflecting on their own recent teaching practices, while the experienced teachers are reflecting in a more general way (also evident in the analysis in Chapter 7). However, it could also signal that experienced teachers have moved from what Freeman (2016) calls 'articulation' to 'explanation' and have access to more related and precise language from the language teaching professional community and in this stage they may not feel the need or relevance of detailing every event, action or feeling related to a specific teaching context. This, however, is an expectation of the novice student teacher among their community of peers and also a requirement imposed by the academic leaders of the programme (lecturers, mentors, tutors and so on).

Secondly, two items in particular are notable by their absence in the experienced student teacher data, they are *I mean* and *I feel*. First at number 7 in the novice student teacher data, the relatively high frequency of *I mean* suggests that these teachers are being much more explicit in their discourse, as well as explaining and rearticulating much more. There is a potential sense of needing to be seen to be accountable, and this is very much part of their novice identity. It first occurs, in any of its forms, on the experienced teacher cluster list at number 32, which is a significant twenty-five places lower. At number 24 in the novice data, *feel* first appears, while it is not present in the experienced teacher data listed in Table 6.3. In fact, it is only to be found in cluster number 49, meaning twenty-five places in the difference between the data sets. Again the discourse is telling as a marker of identity here. The higher presence of *I feel* in the novice data suggests that they are expressing themselves with more of a lack of confidence and a higher degree of uncertainty. This may simply be a pragmatic strategy by the novice student teachers, but even if this is the case, its higher use is indicative of their less established place in the context of professional teaching and their emerging identity within this community (see also Chapter 7; Copland 2012).

A final comparative observation is in relation to the presence of *I should (have)* at number 26 in the novice student teacher data and not at all in the top 30 clusters in the experienced teacher data. In fact, it isn't to be found even in the top 100 clusters. The novice student teacher identity as someone in need of change and development through an evaluation and modification of their teaching practices is apparent here. The emerging picture of language teacher identity suggests that the novice teachers are comparatively more hesitant and less confident, see themselves as needing to be more explicit and accountable for their teaching, and also in need of change and development. To get a more nuanced and detailed sense of identity through the pronoun *I*, we now focus on *I am*.

6.6.2 *I AM*

We ran searches for *I am* in the data, and from the many occurrences we focused on the lines and extracts which gave a stronger explicit articulation of teacher identity. By categorising the results, a number of themes emerged. These are discussed in the following sections and lines from the concordances are used to illustrate.

A. Expressions of personal identity and its relevant or potential impact on teacher identity

Table 6.3   Two and three-word *I* clusters: experienced student teacher data (top 30)

1	I THINK	359	
2	**I HAVE**	318	
3	**I WAS**	225	
4	**I DON'T**	134	I DON'T KNOW (52)
5	**I AM**	123	
6	**I WOULD**	117	
7	**I I**	92	
8	I KNOW	91	
9	**I CAN**	90	
10	**I HAD**	84	
11	**I WILL**	74	
12	I DID	71	
13	**I NEED**	68	I NEED TO (56)
14	I JUST	67	
15	**NEED TO**	66	I NEED TO (56)
16	**I DO**	60	I DON'T KNOW (52)
17	**I NEED TO**	56	I NEED (68), NEED TO (66)
18	**I BELIEVE**	55	
19	THINK THAT	52	
20	**THAT I**	52	
21	I DON'T KNOW	52	I DON'T (134), I DO (60), DON'T KNOW (52)
22	DON'T KNOW	52	I DON'T KNOW (52)
23	**I DIDN'T**	50	
24	**WANT TO**	49	I WANT TO (26)
25	**BELIEVE THAT**	48	I BELIEVE THAT (34)
26	**I COULD**	45	
27	I FOUND	43	
28	THINK IT'S	41	I THINK IT'S (39)
29	I THINK THAT	40	I THINK (359),THINK THAT (52)
30	**I WANT**	39	I WANT TO (26)

Earlier, in Figure 6.1, we identified personal identity as one of three key and overlapping components of language teacher identity and here we see this being manifested in the discourse of both the novice and experienced teachers in Figure 6.2. Personal traits such as being a good planner (line 1), a people person (line 2) and not being a perfectionist (line 3) expressed because they are deemed to be relevant to the novice's positioning of themselves as teachers. This carries through to the experienced teachers in terms of achieving goals (line 2), being patient (line 4) and funny (line 5). Age, geographical origin, marital status and having children (lines 4 and 5 for novices, and 1 and 2 for experienced teachers) are also expressed through their narratives as part of their identity, and probably as a conscious or subconscious strategy to form a community (see Chapter 7). As such there is little difference between both groups.

B. Expressions of language-related identity

As discussed earlier, Pennington and Richards (2016: 11–13) theorise what they call language related identity, as one of their foundational teacher identity

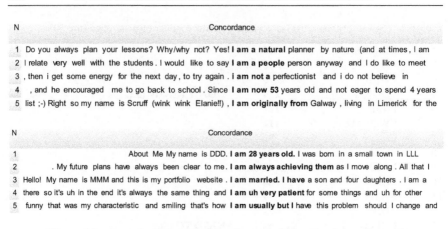

Figure 6.2   I am *for the expression of personal identity: (a) novice and*
(b) experienced student teachers

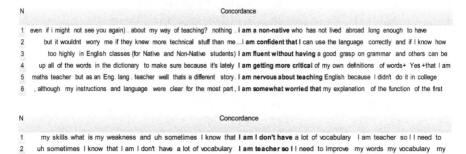

Figure 6.3   I am *for the expression of linguistic identity: (a) novice and*
(b) experienced student teachers

competences. The key concepts here are language background and language proficiency. In relation to status as a non-native teacher, we see explicit mention of this as a weakness by one of the novice student teachers in Figure 6.3 (line 1). Although the vast majority of the experienced student teachers are non-native speakers, they don't refer explicitly to this at all but rather to their need and desire to improve their vocabulary. We can assume though that the implicit meaning is that this needs to happen because they are non-native speakers and as such don't have intuitive access to the lexis of the language. In terms of the language proficiency of the native-speaking novice student teachers, two perspectives are present in the data. Line 2 expresses confidence in their language use as a native speaker, and line 3 expresses an acknowledgement of fluency as such, but also admits that this does not necessarily entail a good understanding of grammar. This later sentiment is echoed in lines 4–6 in more general terms as anxiety about the ability to understand and explain the English language without possessing explicit or formal knowledge of it. Clearly then, in this language teaching context, linguistic identity is significant, and is part of what Freeman calls 'language teaching identity' (see above). While this is present in both sets of data, we were somewhat surprised not to see any/more expressions of non-nativeness in the experienced teacher data, given that most of them are second language English speakers, and for many this is their first extended period of time in an English-speaking country. Perhaps it is precisely their status as experienced teachers and PhD students that is preventing them from discussing this as they may worry that it would be perceived as a professional weakness by others if they were to do so.

C. Expressions of disciplinary identity as a teacher

In this section, we are including expressions of affiliation to both the discipline (English language or TESOL) and to the teaching profession. There are numerous examples to be found in both the novice and experienced student teacher data, and so the figures in this section represent just a sample of these. Figure 6.4 includes some of the data from the novice student teacher corpora.

The concordance lines in Figure 6.4 illustrate the full gamut of identity representation. In many cases the expression is quite explicit and mentions words like teacher or identity. Here we can see that some of the teachers feel quite sure and confident about their identity, or some aspects of it, in expressions like: *I am a creative teacher* (line 1), *found who I am as a teacher* (line 8), *in the classroom I am entirely more myself than ever* (line 19), *I have truly exploited this TP module fully and I am happy with the results* (line 25), *I am showing my identity more strongly* (line 41), *I am viewing myself as professional teacher* (line 50). Others are conscious of the transition from a previous teacher identity in a different disciplinary and educational context (contextual identity, see Figure 6.1 above) and therefore the adjustment to English language teaching is still a novelty and sometimes a challenge: *I am a qualified Science teacher* (line 3), *I am used to being more of an authoritative figure* (line 47), *I am used to being more in control as a secondary school teacher* (line 48), *I am used to teaching maths and science students* (line 49). In some cases, the teachers feel that their identity is evolving and that they have come part of the way on the journey but still have a way to go: *who I am as a teacher is less explicit* (line 9), *I am becoming more and more aware of my ability as a teacher* (line 10), *I am in a half learned stage* (line 27), *I am still solidly in the developmental stage* (line 43), *I am trying to change my natural style* (line 46). And at the other end of the spectrum we find those who identify themselves as being at the start of their teaching journey with quite a way to go before feeling confident in their identity in the form of competences: *how can I say that I am a good teacher* (line 2), *I am exposed to them in the classroom* (line 20), *I am kind of shaking when they ask me a question* (line 29), *I think I am not a good teacher* (line 33), *I am still struggling* (line 44).

Where the expression of identity is more implicit, it tends to focus on feelings and actions, often transitory, based on a particular event or a series of happenings. This illustrates very well the non-stable nature of identity and identity formation and how it is linked to the various roles we play as teachers. Again, these range from the more positive emotions, for example, *excited* (lines 4 and 13), *comfortable* (line 15), *glad* (line 24), *intrigued* (line 28) and *interested* (line 39), to those more in the negative realm, for example, *annoyed* (line 7), *nervous* (line 13), *difficult* (line 22), *not enjoying* (line 34) and not *positive* (line 36).

N	Concordance
1	. However , through this experience , I've realized that while **I am a creative teacher** and (hopefully) an engaging one , that
2	and they were not giving her equal rights . now , how can i say that **i am a good teacher** if after these three months this is the result? as
3	Galway , living in Limerick for the past five years more or less and **I am a qualified Science** teacher (with ZERO jobs) so I am now
4	feel capable of understanding how to use/manipulate resources . **I am actually quite excited** about the last few weeks as we get to do
5	a chance to teach academic writing as I really do love writing . **I am also interested in** academic spoken discourse though so I'd like
6	exercise I did with the class. I felt that they responded well to it. **I am also looking forward** to feedback with Laura as it will be
7	so you know there's the adjectives that take the -ing and the -ed so **I am annoyed I feel** annoyed but something is annoying so you
8	in the classroom . This semester I think I have finally found who **I am as a teacher.** I am much more aware of my teacher presence ,
9	better teacher was stronger than the need for an A. However , who **I am as teacher is** a little less explicit . I know that I like it (although
10	standard and that that was not it. So what all of this tells me is that **I am becoming more and** more aware of my ability as a teacher and
11	in it). But I have since grown to relate more to my students and **I am beginning to realise** the difficulties they encounter (both in the
12	a secondary school teacher would make this course easier but **I am beginning to wonder.** The people that have no experience are
13	weeks , I get to prepare my own lesson using authentic materials . **I am both excited and** nervous about this as the class has to be
14	it comes to designing / using our own material next week for TP **I am certainly inspired to** look at literature in this way and perhaps
15	would also like to work on my teacher presence . I do feel that once **I am comfortable with the** new class that this won't be an issue but
16	university outside of TP which has really boosted my confidence as **I am constantly learning new** things or being asked new questions
17	them . I was trying to include more fun activities in my lesson and **I am continually seeing the** benefits of doing so. Two of the students
18	like others might have . Although challenging , it was so useful and **I am delighted that I** am taking it up again . This semester I am
19	elicited really well . I feel very comfortable in the classroom and **I am entirely more myself** than ever now , which was one of the
20	language point more as to be able to overcome them when **I am exposed to them** in the classroom . This is also true of any
21	beneficial . My struggle with a more detailed lesson plan continues . **I am fighting against it** because I often find the best lessons happen
22	used to being more in control as a secondary school teacher . Also **I am finding difficult judging** their previous (prior) knowledge as I
23	everything's going so far. My evaluation is more or less positive; **I am getting really encouraging** feedback so all in all I'm quite
24	on what my 'summary of teaching' contained last semester, and **I am glad to say** that throughout this semester I have built on what I
25	. In doing this I feel I have truly exploited this TP module fully and **I am happy with the** results, though I recognise I have a long way to
26	with? (Why?) I was pleased with my overall lesson plan. I feel **I am improving and the** more I practise writing my lesson plans, the
27	the complexity of this level of grammar but don't like the confusion , **i am in a** half-learned stage and it is annoying , and the book is not
28	I think a lesser teacher would not have made it seem as desirable . **I am intrigued by Suggestopedia**, and its claims that learners can
29	I think whatever group I had last week I got rattled again and now **I am kind of shaking** when they ask me a question I'm going no
30	in the classroom , and send them the disc itself later? Therefore **I am more at ease** in the classroom . And the supervisors can go look
31	me less nervous or in need of planning for every second. Overall **I am much happier as** a teacher than I was last semester. I'm more
32	level and it is something I am excited to work on. I feel that **I am much more aware** of TTT and STT in my classes and take all of
33	job much better than i do mine .) I came over to uI because i think **i am not a good** teacher and I need /ed to improve . teachers here
34	and your classes? My golden rule is keep it simple and have fun . If **I am not enjoying what** I am doing and how I am doing it, how am I
35	bring in more authentic material to the classroom . Upon reflection **I am not entirely sure** if the material was actually that authentic . It
36	, down . :I How I feel about my own teaching ... At the moment **I am not feeling very** positive . Though it is early days, I feel my
37	this phase of learning (rewarding good behaviour) . personally **i am not fond of** behaviourism . when i consider the drills , i think
38	maths. Well thats how I feel about teaching! Gotta go Second Post **I am now offically a** blogger . Woohoo!! Look at me blogging . All the
39	Englishes; these will form the first part of my TP considerations . **I am particularly interested in** sociolinguistic competencies and I
40	o What often one student will enjoy another student won't . **I am really learning that** there are many learner types and not
41	the self to the classroom is quite a positive thing , however now that **I am showing my identity** more strongly in the classroom , there must
42	classes but the biggest change is the degree of preparation . **I am still preparing** a lot . I prepare the vocabulary , grammar etc. to
43	. And I do expect to be somewhat fluid as a teacher , especially as **I am still solidly in** the developmental stage of my career . But, it
44	aspect(s) of your teaching would you like to develop in the future? **I am still struggling to** find a way to get some of the Japanese
45	I understand the importance of more precise planning especially if **I am trying something new!** Perhaps I am trying to change my
46	precise planning especially if I am trying something new! Perhaps **I am trying to change** my natural style because I am being observed
47	acquire a second language . Regarding to how they relate to me, **I am used to being** more of an authorative figure in the classroom
48	to be some what more easy going and this is difficult for me as **I am used to being** more in control as a secondary school teacher .
49	because it has been awhile since I learned a language and **I am used to teaching** maths and science students. Also I have very
50	and more experienced classmates. All this for me, highlights that **I am viewing myself as** professional teacher in, at least, some

Figure 6.4   I am *for the expression of disciplinary identity: novice student teachers*

The data also clearly portrays the identity of a novice teacher as someone engaging fully in their own professional development, often through their involvement in teaching practice, which is a fully accredited module and is more or less obligatory for all students on the MA programme depending on their prior experiences (see Chapter 4). It is highly unusual for a student to be exempted from Semester 1 and Semester 2 TP modules as they don't have substantial experience when they begin the programme. Even if this is the case, they often opt to do it as a way to further their professional development. Positive engagement in the TP module is explicit in lines 6, 18, 23 and 25, while a more general developmental focus is apparent in lines 32, 38, 40, 45 and 48. In both cases, an awareness of an evolving and dynamic teacher identity is very much present. It is also interesting and reassuring to see that some of the novice teachers may see this development as directly linked with exploration and research, for example, line 5 mentions an interest in academic spoken discourse, and a fuller extract in 6.1 gives more context.

Extract 6.1 (Mode 5: On-Line Blogs)

NST: This week has been for the most part overrun with thoughts of our theses. Next week is the big thesis presentation and so this is occupying most of our minds. I really like my topic and it's something that is so useful to me with regard to CPD as it's making so much more aware of academic writing and related fields and also so much more interested in EAP. This is helping me a lot in my position in the regional writing centre and is something I would have liked to bring into the classroom in TP. EAP is a goldmine for language teachers and I do think it's a pity that we haven't had a chance to use that at all. The MA qualifies us to teach it right? But I'd love to have a chance to teach academic writing as I really do love writing. I am also interested in academic spoken discourse though so I'd like to teach both. I think that this is again leading me back to genre and I'm glad that we talked about radio broadcasts and language of persuasion in the TP class as the genre element seems to be a nice base from which to grow a language lesson, next week I'm doing Irish sport so I'm trying to think of a good, useful and relevant way to introduce the idea.

Moving to the experienced teacher data, in some ways professional identity expression is similar but there are also some significant differences. Figure 6.5 provides some illustrative examples.

Similar to the novice student teachers we see the experienced teachers expressing confidence in their identity and ability as a teacher (lines 1–4, 32), but without the strong negative evaluations and uncertainties of the former group (see also LIWC analyses in Chapter 7). We see them expressing their identity in positive ways, for example, line 17 (enthusiasm), lines 24–5 (happiness), without the level of negativity found in the novice data. There is a similar focus on development, but this time in more independent ways in their teaching (lines 16, 40–3), rather than in the TP context. There are also strong suggestions of development through attendance at CPD events such as conferences (line 35), and with a specific

N	Concordance
1	collage science 2008. Teaching Philosophy As a teacher I believe **I am a facilitator to** my students . I love teaching when the learning
2	so could you say don't be so bossy 1 it, the status is for example , **I am a more experienced** teacher I know what's good I know
3	situation these days in that I teach students individually , so **I am able to assign** homework on a case by case basis, which I
4	be happier with my assessment and examination process, for **I am able to tailor** assessments and examinations for each
5	we like (for example , songs, films , or texts) of our preference . **I am also trying to** overcome this either by offering different
6	profession . This portfolio portrays where I have been , who **I am and where I** intend to go with regard to my profession . It has
7	of my education background and my reflection on it, where **I am and where I** want to go as a teacher , and strategies to reach
8	ok ok you're not given anybody any no or I just reflect on how **I am as a teacher** maybe not a specific class do you think that's
9	with my students. In fact, I don't even let them know when **I am assessing them, for** it is for my benefit not theirs. The
10	study program and one year in the doctoral degree , I can say that **I am at the midle** level of my career . As a teacher , I want to reach
11	focusing on the students if they do not respond or engage well . **I am aware that there** is a problem somewhere . I ask myself who
12	learning about the word "how" . This is one of the main reasons **I am carrying on with** my research studies . 1. Using technology in
13	the college roles will be changed . I am asking this because now **I am conscious regarding our** changing teaching methods and
14	as a native or first language (Ireland) . For my formal education , **I am consistent to focus** on the field of English education . I did my
15	that I am good at teaching English. Also, I am happy with what **I am doing. Therefore, I** am sticking to it. However , teaching was
16	experience and improve their language skills. To this day, **I am educating myself on** what is new in the teaching field to
17	, is not a profession alone , but rather a calling and a passion that **I am enthusiastically associated with** as a teacher . Atkins & Brown
18	like evaluated by others yeah mhmm because will be like here **I am forced someone is** observing me evaluating me mhmm but
19	philosophy also it encourages me to uh reflect who I who **I am from the past** until until now . I go through some points for
20	what I have what I did so far and it's helped me to know where **I am going+ Ah hah** +and um how I could help um a GBLL and
21	figure out ways to overcome and prevent it. I definitely know that **I am going through "teacher** burnout" at the moment because I do
22	that it took me about 4 years to discover what I'm good at and **I am good at teaching** so I stuck to it and because to become good
23	what you are good at, and then you need to stick to it. I know that **I am good at teaching** English . Also, I am happy with what I am
24	with reflective practice activities as a professional? for me **I am happy especially with** the technology and the internet in my
25	to stick to it. I know that I am good at teaching English. Also, **I am happy with what I** am doing . Therefore , I am sticking to it.
26	and control will definitely make them stressed or depress and **I am highly against this.** Make the homework short, brief and to
27	beckground , I do believe that I have strong foundation and **I am in the right** tract to achieve my goal to be a better teacher .
28	awareness and keep their will to become better professionals . **I am looking forward to** attend this conference in Corpus
29	and hard . There are just too many tasks and demands ," then **I am not, for sure,** giving myself any reason not to burn out. I try;
30	I had achieved . However , now when I look back at that stage, **I am not sufficiently satisfied.** This is because I have since learned
31	education pathways and trainings have shaped me as what **I am now as a** teacher . With the clear idea in my mind of what
32	of my career as a teacher. The key point I keep in mind is that **I am now doing a** professional job, and I need to make effective
33	build an enjoyable and supportive atmosphere in my classroom . **I am open to my** students and I try to get to know my students
34	does the result of the test or exam perfect how good teacher **I am or not?** mhmm so this area still vague So in terms of
35	attended or that you have planned to attend and this is one I **I am planning to attend** in Newcastle+ Uh huh +the IBACS
36	helped me in developing teaching process . One of the things that **I am planning to do** is to engage myself with more research in
37	it happens to me a lot, I really need to examine the messages **I am sending myself about** the job as a teacher . If every day I am
38	English. Also, I am happy with what I am doing . Therefore , **I am sticking to it.** However , teaching was not the easiest career
39	, using different teaching strategies and methods , I believe that **I am still a learner.** The more I learn , the more I discover how
40	of teaching more than 2,000 students in various institutions , and **I am still learning about** the word "how" . This is one of the main
41	and inventions . As far as my teaching experience is concerned , **I am still learning and** making discoveries about myself and about
42	hope so mhmm from the day one I said teaching until now **I am still learning mhmm** mhmm reading is a big part of the
43	a pronunciation instructor . Now, as I write my PhD dissertation , **I am still striving to** improvement my pronunciation instructional
44	feel anxious , since I was at my first stage of teaching prefession . **I am sure that I** have learnt a lot from our PhD program and from
45	evaluated by other students and also you in the classroom and **I am sure the problem** will be solved as he will start thinking
46	it in class for 10-15 mins and let them enjoy the rest, themselves . **I am sure they will** solve the rest themselves or come back to you
47	for Academic Purposes (EAP) instructor in China . Currently , **I am teaching Chinese students** of various ages and levels via an
48	board . That night , I could not sleep thinking of different solutions . **I am the type of** lecturer who needs interactivity . My lectures are
49	ok because sometimes you're like you don't like to look like **I am weak in this** ok sometimes aren't you emotional like do
50	is exactly this because the experience does count so the reason **I am working with more** experienced teachers is exactly this I

Figure 6.5   I am *for the expression of disciplinary identity: experienced student* teachers

focus on their students (line 47). This focus on students is what Pennington and Richards (2016: 16) called student-related identity (see earlier discussion). Overall, we see the same types of expression but this time they are more confident, more positive and signal more independent teacher thought and action than in the novice student teacher data. In these ways the data suggests that the experienced teachers are the same plus different. In another way, we can see a very clear difference, which is obviously associated with the career stage (mid-career in most cases) of the more experienced teachers. Lines 6 and 7 contain examples of teachers expressing where they are and where they want to go as professionals, line 10 talking about mid-career explicitly, and line 15 giving a considered account that this teacher is happy with their career choice and is going to stick with it (also in line 38). These are all indicators of serious consideration about teaching as a career and as a profession in relation to their own identity and choices. On the other hand, one of the teachers raises the problematic and prevalent issue of teacher burnout (line 21), and acknowledges that they are experiencing this. Extract 6.2 extends the context of this discussion.

Extract 6.2 (Mode 5: On-Line Blogs)

EST: This time of year, I usually go through what most refer to as 'teacher burnout'. I find myself less excited and passionate about planning my lessons and I begin to rely on textbooks more than my own creative abilities. Many things contribute to this, mainly stress and mental fatigue. I believe that burnout is a normal part of any career, especially teaching, but it is important to recognize it is happening and figure out ways to overcome and prevent it. I definitely know that I am going through 'teacher burnout' at the moment because I do not look forward to planning my lessons at the moment, and I find myself using convenient, pre-made materials. There is nothing wrong with using convenient materials. As teachers, it's important to find materials and shortcuts to make our lives more manageable in and out of the classroom, but when we take our own unique skills as a teacher and our students' needs and interests out of the equation, the result is a classroom with an unmotivated and most-likely bored teacher and students which lowers the likelihood of learning outcomes. So it's time to make a change! In order to reverse my 'teacher burnout,' I plan to do the following: * yoga/meditation * exercise * create something for myself in order to reignite my creativity in all areas of my life * give my students more control of their lessons * get plenty of sleep.

How do you recognize the signs of 'teacher burnout,' and what do you do to correct it?

In this case, the teacher acknowledges the issue and the main cause, illustrates some of the symptoms in the classroom, and then turns to find ways to solve it in a positive way. This perceptiveness, resilience and future-oriented identity is much more typical of teachers with more experience and more resources available to them to respond in a professional way.

D. Expressions of identity as a student

In this context of a formal education programme, which has the strong potential to impact on a teacher's identity, the role of the individual as both a teacher of English, plus an MA/PhD student has been shown to create a sort of identity tension (Farr and Riordan 2015). Elsewhere, and more specifically in the TP feedback context, Farr (2011) has written of this tension in terms of the necessity to present oneself as an *expert novice*. While the tension itself may not explicitly be present in the discourse, a further examination of the *I am* concordance reveals that this identity is certainly very present among the two groups under scrutiny. Figure 6.6 presents those lines from the data which we feel show a strong student identity rather than a teacher identity, though, of course, these are inextricably linked.

Figure 6.6   I am *for the expression of student identity: (a) novice and (b) experienced student teachers*

Although both groups explicitly express their identity as students, there is a difference. The lines from the novice student teacher data are almost all representations of themselves as student teachers rather than research students, despite the fact that one third of the credit for their MA programme is for the research component. They are immersed in the world of classroom practice and teaching preparation, teaching methodologies (behaviourism and suggestopedia), linguistics and pragmatics. So, as students of TESOL, they present themselves as relative novices, and despite the fact they are postgraduate students at MA level, this is rarely mentioned in the data. The experienced teachers, on the other hand, consistently present themselves as PhD and research students, presumably because they are already qualified teachers and so are now assuming a new identity at this higher educational level. They seem to be loud and proud in their mentions of 'research' and 'PhD'. We do also see their identity as language learners coming through, as discussed earlier in relation to their identity as non-native speakers (see lines 3, 12 and 13).

In summary then, the *I am* concordance data presents four types of identity (personal, linguistic, disciplinary and student). In the case of personal identity, the groups show very similar expression, including information on background, age, heritage, geographical affiliation, marital status and parentage. When it comes to linguistic and student identities, the groups are broadly similar except for some issues about native and non-native speaker status, and student teacher versus PhD student/researcher. In both of these categories, the novice and experienced teacher groups display similar trends with some nuanced differences. However, when it comes to professional or disciplinary identity the disparities become more obvious. Here the novices express themselves more hesitantly and less confidently, in much need of further change and development, and all the while they provide more explanation of their thoughts and actions and seem to be conscious of their responsibility to account for themselves. Clearly then, their identity as teachers is generally still at a relative embryonic stage and they are in the peripheries in terms of their membership of the professional teaching community, but very much comfortable in their identity as student teachers.

6.6.3 We

Chart 6.1 showed quite a comparative quantitative discrepancy between novice and experienced teachers' use of *we* (4,222 versus 7,418 occurrences per million words). Given the importance of social and scaffolded learning in teacher education contexts, as well as the pivotal place of a community of practice, this pronoun can be quite telling in terms of in- and out-group membership. This section therefore builds on earlier work by Farr (2005b), which explored *we* specifically in the TP feedback context. In order to establish the nature of the quantitative difference in use of *we* between the two teacher groups, cluster analysis is our first point of departure. The top 30 three-word clusters in both sets of data were extracted. Chart 6.2 illustrates the shared clusters from the top 30 and the quantitative differences between them.

Looking at the data in Chart 6.2 gives us an idea of the clusters which account for the major difference between the use of *we* in both data sets. The short answer is that

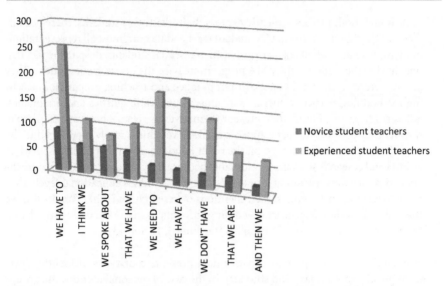

Chart 6.2   Quantitative differences between shared we *three-word clusters in novice and experienced student teacher data (WPM)*

all of them do. Three items show fifty or fewer in the difference (*we spoke about, that we are, and then we*), two between fifty and 100 (*I think we, that we have*) and the remaining four (*we have to, we need to, we have a, we don't have*) more than 100 in the margin. It is interesting to note that two modal items expressing obligation (*we have to, we need to*), in this case self-imposed obligation, feature in the most highly used items, comparatively speaking. Although these items set the novice teachers and the experienced teachers apart quantitatively, this is only part of the story. Table 6.4 shows the top 10 from the remaining clusters (of the original top 30 list), which are exclusive to one set or the other.

Looking at the lists in Table 6.4 gives us an indication of some of the possible qualitative differences in the use of *we* between the groups. In the novice data we see

Table 6.4   *We* clusters exclusive to experienced and novice student teachers (top 10)

Novice student teacher only	Experienced student teacher only
YOU KNOW WE	WE WE CAN'T
WE HAD TO	THE WAY WE
WE HAD A	AND HOW WE
WHEN WE WERE	WE ARE GOING
THIS WEEK WE	WE ARE DOING
THAT WE WERE	WHAT WE HAVE
WERE TALKING ABOUT	WE ARE NOT
WE HAD THE	WE DO HAVE
WE WERE TOLD	WE THINK WE
WE WERE TALKING	A TEACHER WE

the discourse marker, or hedge, *you know*, possibly complementing the high occurrences we saw of *I mean* earlier to signal more hesitation and a lack of confidence in their group identity (Sert and Asik 2019). Also present is evidence of some sort of authority over the group, evident in *we had to* and *we were told*. These are again strong indicators of the power dynamic between these novice teachers and the programme lecturers, tutors and mentors, who may have a limiting influence on how these teachers express their individual identity. *When we were* and *this week we* suggest tight temporal and accountability obligations on the group, most probably around their teaching practice module. And the two clusters containing *talking* are likely to emanate from the novice teachers recounting what happened in their TP classes with their English language learners, as well as reflecting on the events of other content-based modules in the recent past. Both of these requirements were task specific. Turning to the experienced teachers, the data begins to tell a slightly different story. *The way we, and how we, a teacher we* and *we are doing* suggest a relatively deep level of professional reflection and analysis. *We we can't* and *we are not* suggest a confident identity in taking a stance, and making critical decisions and choices. This confidence is again apparent in the emphatic *we do have*, which features highly for this group of experienced teachers.

The comparisons and contrasts around *we* thus far are interesting in accounting for the quantitative differences between the two groups of teachers; however, none of the analysis up to now gives us much insight into who exactly the *we* is referencing in the discourse. In order to establish this, it is necessary to look more qualitatively at the corpus data to determine if any of our earlier hypotheses can be upheld. To do this, we begin with a concordance analysis of *we are*.

6.6.4 *We are*

The data reveals that there are different referents of the pronoun in *we are* concordance lines in the novice data. Essentially, *we* is used when the novices want to refer to themselves as students, as student teachers, as teachers, or simply a group of people in a more general sense (see also Riordan 2018; Vaughan 2010). There are sixty-five examples of *we are* in the data and Figure 6.7 presents some examples to illustrate each of these four uses.

Identity as a student on an MA programme is articulated a number of times in the data in relation to course content and course requirements (for example, lines 1, 8, 15, 16, 17, 24, 25), which is related to, but slightly different from, their identity as student teachers. As student teachers the novices talk about the teaching practice component of the programme very specifically (for example, lines 2, 4, 7, 13, 15, 18, 20, 21, 22, 23, 27, 28, 32, 33), which places them as peripheral participants in the community of practice of fully fledged teachers. On a few occasions, we get the sense of a more independent teacher identity being presented, which is not directly associated with the practice context, although it is founded on it (for example, lines 5, 6, 26, 29, 34). This gives a glimpse of the novices beginning to feel like full members of a community of professional teachers. Finally, we get some more general uses, as are found in most discourses recounting human experience (for example, lines 3, 19, 30, 31).

N	Concordance
1	... but possible . well , i am glad that time has arrived and that **we are about to do** the exams althought i am not doing a lot in
2	your lesson but that we can supplements and that's where **we are adding to the** lesson yeah even bringing in the
3	Intelligences theory is really interesting! Its great to think that **we are all intelligent in** some way and that we as teachers
4	but I'll see if I can change anything in the next few lessons as **we are allowed to create** our own materials . Watch this space!
5	level of student the following week . I think , as teachers , **we are always inevitably pressed** for time . It's been the case in
6	in the communicative language teaching classroom **we are always trying to** maximize participation and
7	with Laura was also very positive . I think it's a great thing that **we are being supervised by** a person who doesn't know us; it's
8	all made it through the ups and downs of semester one and **we are coming up to** the final hurdles of semster 2, and of
9	Irishosaru's comment , I agree , it's a different level of grammar **we are dealing with in** class, compared to what you will
10	well to Anna and I as a team and they seem to enjoy the tasks **we are developing. As do** we . They responded well to different
11	, making overt links between exercises highlighting why **we are doing certain tasks.** Encouraging students to repeat and
12	to look at that page hold your book up and say this is what **we are doing have a** look at this I want you to look and answer
13	couple of weeks left teaching right it is lucky actually that **we are doing the feedback** today because I have so many
14	forgot to ask you should I be looking at instead of just thinking **we are doing the first** half of this unit ah of which that is going
15	good I know . I hope . And one last rant in relation to this topic . **We are expected to do** a certain amount of observations and
16	I'm half way through the semester . The sheer volume of tasks **we are getting in each** class for each module is tricky to keep
17	Hard to believe that we have 6 weeks done already , and **we are half way through** the semester . I thought that early on
18	the same time . Yeah what I had yeah . Yeah. Because we are **we are here to be** trained+ Mmhm . +you know we're not we're
19	. I had a bad class today . Fine , every teacher has them , **we are human, humans make** mistakes and all that . I don't like
20	agree with Mckenna too Feedback is great at this stage when **we are learning. The only** way to improve is to know your
21	of your teaching would you like to develop in the future? As **we are moving on to** creating our own lessons this week , I
22	classes. I must preface this by saying I fully understand why **we are observed and overall** I feel that it is a necessity and the
23	sure I understand :) Roadrunner , i think yes. It's important that **we are prepared for whatever** they may throw at us. In saying
24	a teacher training course+ Mmhm. +and if you remember that **we are still learning until** the very day we finish and for years
25	me something . so far i have only seen videos of the methods **we are studying in various** teaching sections lead by "famous"
26	do a lesson plan ... :(LATERS! I agree with Witch's comment . **We are teaching grammar. I** feel like in the earlier stages we
27	hi tis me and 2o2 here!! What would we be teaching? If **we are teaching non-native** speakers , then I'd say no. Sorry ,
28	the next four weeks . I was apprehensive about starting again . **We are teaching the Upper** Intermediate group , only a few
29	shy away from authority but we as we when perhaps when **we are teaching we feel** it's not okay to say I'd like you to put
30	them though as they were a stepping stone to get us to where **we are today. So do** others agree with Scruff in that some
31	about the Irish language dying here in Ireland . Here , **we are trying to fight** for the language to survive and in other
32	that there are some slight mistakes in some of the textbooks **we are using. Has anyone** else noticed mistakes or errors?
33	ideas at the same time . Yeah what I had yeah . Yeah. Because **we are we are here** to be trained+ Mmhm . +you know we're
34	to some activities and not so well to others . The more in touch **we are with the culture** of our learners , the easier it is for us as

Figure 6.7   We are *in novice student teacher data*

The experienced data is similar in all ways except one. These teachers do not identify with the peripheral membership of being a student teacher. Even though they often present themselves as students, they are confident in their self-portrayal as professional teachers, discussing and reflecting on their practice in general. So, qualitatively, there is just this one distinguishing factor, but a quantitative glance at the data can present another perspective. Chart 6.3 presents a comparison of the relative number of occurrences of *I am* versus *we are* in both sets of data, normalised to words per million as the novice student teacher corpus is much larger than the experienced student teacher data.

These results show that relatively speaking, both groups of teachers use *I am* more frequently than *we are*, but the relative difference is much more pronounced in the novice student teacher data. And while *I am* indicates roughly similar relative frequencies among both groups, suggesting that they both have strong individual identities, when it comes to collective identity, the difference of 365 occurrences clearly

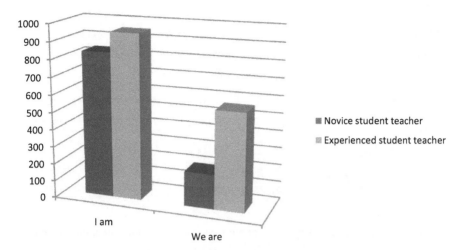

Chart 6.3   I am *and* we are *in novice and experienced student teacher data (WPM)*

demonstrates that the experienced group is displaying an identifiable stronger collective identity through the use of *we are*. This is the strongest indicator so far that experienced teachers identify themselves as part of an identifiable and more professional community or peers, perhaps formed during the programme, perhaps before or most probably both. They feel more confident expressing themselves as part of a group, and perhaps feel more entitled to speak on behalf of others. The novice student teachers on the other hand are still firmly in an individual identity mode of expression in this respect. To investigate this further, we ran searches for all of the first person singular and first person plural pronouns and possessive adjectives for both groups. Chart 6.4 presents the results.

The data on Chart 6.4 further strengthen the hypothesis that the experienced teachers express themselves as a collective much more frequently than the novice student teachers. The converse is also true, that the novices show a relatively stronger individual identity compared with their experienced counterparts. Given that this and previous sections have shown that most of the pronoun use is accounted for in the first person singular and plural, and given their function in the expression of individual and collective identity, these will be the sole focus of the comparative analysis across face-to-face and on-line modes, and also in the individual and scaffolded discourse modes.

6.7 PRONOUN USAGE IN FACE-TO-FACE AND ON-LINE MODES: *I* AND *WE*

This section briefly explores the question of whether the teachers are more likely to articulate their identity through expressions containing personal pronouns when speaking face-to-face or when communicating in the various on-line modes detailed in Chapter 4. Table 6.5 presents the results numerically for *I* and its inclusive *I am*,

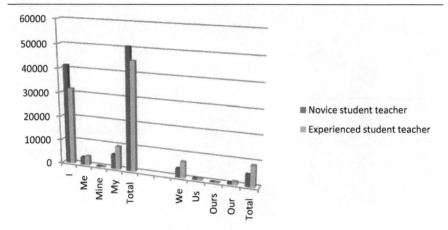

*Chart 6.4   First person singular pronouns and possessive adjectives: novice and
experienced student teachers (WPM)*

Table 6.5   *I* and *we* in face-to-face and on-line modes (WPM)

	Face to face	On-line
I	39,668	37,703
I am	404	1,439
We	5,222	3,508
We are	319	272

and *we* and *we are*. Chart 6.5 presents the same data visually in a bar chart. The data
are normalised to words per million although these comparative corpora are relatively similar in size, with the face-to-face data accounting for 244,729 words, and the
on-line 198,707 words.

These results suggest that there are no major differences between the on-line and
face-to-face modes in terms of the usage of *I* and *we*, at least quantitatively. Analogous
with the overall frequencies in TEC, *I* enjoys much more prominence in the data,
marginally more so in the face-to-face discourse, although *I am* tends to prefer
on-line contexts. Perhaps the on-line modes allow for slightly freer expression of
one's identity in more stative ways, although the difference really isn't significant. *We*
is a little more interesting in that it shows a higher frequency in face-to-face modes.
This may be to do with the expression of group responsibility and accountability
when speaking directly to other interlocutors. In other words, it is more face-saving
to display knowledge, narrate and perhaps assume responsibility for things that may
have gone wrong as a group rather than as an individual when being held accountable
in a face-to-face scenario. We hypothesise that this may also have to do with the fact
that in many of the face-to-face contexts there is an expert present, and also assessment is a factor that may have an influence, for example, in TP feedback. We explore
this further in the scaffolded and individual contexts in the next section.

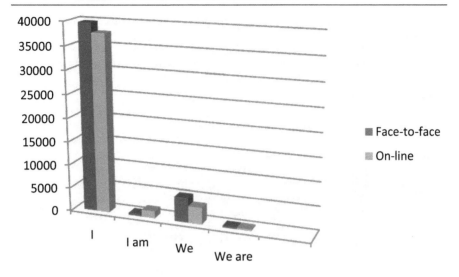

Chart 6.5   I and we in face-to-face and on-line modes (WPM)

6.8 PRONOUN USAGE IN INDIVIDUAL AND SCAFFOLDED MODES:
I AND *WE*

Another way to slice and explore the data in order to gain further insights is to examine contexts where the teachers are communicating alone versus contexts where the teachers are present but a mentor, supervisor or lecturer is also part of the interaction. Comparing the data in this way should allow us to see if there are any notable influences from a more expert and more authoritative person's presence. The role of institutional and disciplinary power in identity projection is the main consideration in this section. Again, Table 6.6 presents the results numerically for *I* and its inclusive *I am*, and *we* and *we are*, while Chart 6.6 presents the same data visually in a bar chart. The data are normalised to words per million as the individual data is 116,777 words, and the scaffolded is 269,624 words.

Here again we see the familiar pattern of the significantly higher presence of *I* in both sets of data, when compared with *we*. The disparity between *I* in the individual and scaffolded contexts is striking, with an approximately 20,000 occurrences difference. This suggests that the participants are more comfortable portraying an

Table 6.6   *I* and *we* in individual and scaffolded contexts (WPM)

	Individual	Scaffolded
I	58,102	38,627
I am	2,166	8,033
We	4,222	15,659
We are	231	857

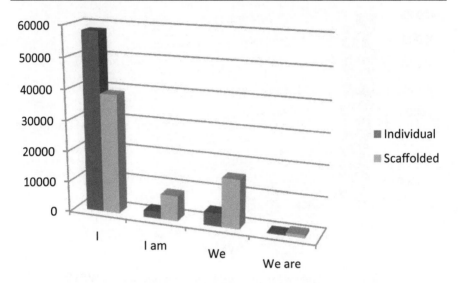

Chart 6.6   I and we *in individual and scaffolded contexts (WPM)*

individual identity when communicating alone and a collaborative identity when experts are present, and corroborates what we found in the last section. The higher occurrence of *we* in the scaffolded contexts may also point to the experts expressing their identity as part of the community of practice of qualified and experienced English language teachers, possibly trying to include the novices in that *we*. A closer look at the TP feedback context, which has a much higher proportion of teacher educator talk relative to the student teacher or novice, provides some insights into this hypothesis. In this context there are 167 occurrences of *we* in the data, only forty-five of which are student teacher talk with the remaining 122 being contained in the supervisor's talk. Already we begin to understand the relatively higher frequency of *we* in scaffolded contexts. To examine this more closely we isolated the 122 supervisor spoken occurrences of *we* and investigated how they are being used in TP feedback (see also Farr 2005b for a more detailed account). A number of uses and referents emerge, most of which include the student teacher as well as the speaker/supervisor.

A. *We* as humans in general (inclusive)

This use of *we* includes the supervisor and the student teacher, and is a general reference to people as part of the human race. This represents collective common identity and is articulated by the supervisor, who in this context has the power to make such assertions, regardless of whether they are factually accurate. Extract 6.3 presents one typical example from supervisor talk, and in fact, she contradicts herself towards the end of the same turn, but still chooses to express a collective identity at the beginning.

Extract 6.3 (Mode 1: Face-to-Face Teaching Practice Feedback Interactions)

TPS: Yeah because it might be because I was brought up on this type
of food and **we all** like we fo= **we all** like to stay with the
foods **we're** brought up with and no= because it's you could it
would be to elicit vocabulary because it's very tasty because
I don't I no lon= I'm a vegetarian I no longer eat beef so this
I have to choose fish so these these are the sorts of reasons

B. *We* as Irish people (inclusive)

Extract 6.4 illustrates how the supervisor invokes a shared sense of cultural and linguistic identity by talking about a particular trait of Irish English pronunciation, the pronunciation of 'th' in the same way as 't' or 'd'.

Extract 6.4 (Mode 1: Face-to-Face Teaching Practice Feedback Interactions)

NST: Try and correct it but I know I don= I know I don't pronounce
my T Hs.
TPS: The the T H you because **we** do dental most Irish speaker= I mean
all of us would do dental Ts where it should be
NST: Mm
TPS: And **we** don't
NST: Right mmhm
TPS: But if you're teaching on a at an international level if you're
teaching it is a sound that you need to actually have
NST: Mmhm

This is an interesting extract in terms of identity because the supervisor is criticising a very personal part of the novice's identity which has direct relevance for being a teacher, that is, their pronunciation. She is also setting herself apart as an expert who knows the correct pronunciation of these sounds, and their appropriate technical descriptions, which has the potential to further threaten the face of the teacher. In the event of this double face threat, she attempts to invoke a shared Irish cultural identity through the use of *we* twice, and *all of us*. Here she includes herself, although clearly this is not something that she herself actually does.

C. *We* as the teaching profession (inclusive)

Extract 6.5 presents a good example of when the supervisor is trying to include both themselves and the student teacher on the same plane of being a teacher, in this case prone to making incorrect assumptions. By including herself the supervisor diminishes the risk of face threat and potential insult.

Extract 6.5 (Mode 1: Face-to-Face Teaching Practice Feedback Interactions)

TPS: Yeah and sometimes those sort of lessons that challenge **us** to
do that turn out to be the better lessons at the end of the

```
          day whereas if we think we got a lesson with loads of differ-
          ent activities we can just sit back and say oh that will carry
          itself it doesn't carry itself it never carries itself
NST: Mm
```

D. *We* as the experts in applied linguistics or teacher education (exclusive)

The final use of *we* in the data is very different from the three just discussed in the sense that the supervisor portrays her identity as being different from the novice teacher. She presents herself as the expert purveyor of linguistic knowledge who is in a position to educate the teacher, on the assumption that they need to be educated. This is clearly a *we* which excludes the teacher as a novice but includes all other professionals who have acquired the same level of linguistic prowess as the speaker assumes for herself. This is despite the fact that the student teacher may actually possess this knowledge already, which is hinted at by their rather impatient *yeah, yeah*, in the final turn of extract 6.6.

Extract 6.6 (Mode 1: Face-to-Face Teaching Practice Feedback Interactions)

```
TPS: These are what we call lexical sets Mathew okay they they come
     looking looking at that one you're looking at vocab more often
     this is a set a set of words which relate to each other in some
     way
NST: Yeah
TPS: Now their definitions are only meaningful relative to each
     other
NST: Yeah, yeah
```

6.9 SUMMARY

This chapter explored the very complex concept of language teacher identity, which has been theorised and investigated from a range of perspectives in the literature. As a concept, teacher identity became important with the advent of the teacher as a cognitive being. With active thought and purposeful decision-making, the notion of a teacher's identity became relevant. A teacher's identity is determined by a number of profes-sional (role-related) and personal factors, including their personal and professional (teaching and language) backgrounds, as well as teaching context related influences. All of these factors integrate and influence in implicit ways to determine a teacher's identity at any given moment, an identity which is fluid and dynamic in the short and long term. The biggest difficulty in investigating teacher identity empirically is the fact that it is non-tangible and can only be assumed from observation, or from narrated accounts from teachers, and even these may not be entirely accurate as individuals are not always conscious of, or have the ability to articulate, their identity accurately.

The TEC corpus provided the data to explore language teacher identity in this chapter. As a proxy for explicit discussions of their identity, the teachers' discourse was investigated for signals of identity. An obvious, and well-documented, linguistic system through which to explore identity in discourse is the participants' use of pronouns to speak about themselves as individuals and as part of a professional or personal community. Therefore the chapter began with a general examination of how pronouns are used in TEC, and this was followed by a more detailed look at how the novice and experienced teachers use *I* and *we* to talk about their professional role identity. There are some commonalities across groups but they differentiate themselves in two main ways. Firstly, the novices are much less assured and confident in the ways in which they express and portray themselves as teachers, and still portray a strong learner and student identity. And secondly, the experienced teachers (and the teacher educators) very explicitly identify with their professional community of practice in ways that we don't see among their less experienced counterparts, with a much better established collective identity. Clearly, the novices are on a journey and in transition towards a more fully fledged and confident teacher identity. For some, this may mature during the course of their academic programme and for many it will most likely happen when they begin their professional careers as teachers.

6.10 TASKS

1. Read either the special issue of *TESOL Quarterly* (Vol 50, Issue 3, 2016) or *The Modern Language Journal* (Vol 101, Issue 1, 2017) on language teacher identity. Consider and discuss which article(s) you find most interesting, useful or controversial.
2. T. S. C. Farrell (2015) presents a useful self-reflective tool called the Tree of Life, which is divided into three parts:
   - *roots* are the early influences, usually at home, which provide the foundations shaping a teacher's early years (family values, heritage, religion, socio-economic status and so on);
   - the *trunk* represents early school experiences right up to the end of second level education (reminiscent of the 'apprenticeship of observation' discussed earlier in this chapter);
   - *limbs* signify any beyond school experiences which happen in adulthood.
       a. Consider, and record in writing, your own personal roots, trunks and limbs in terms of how they have influenced your personal teacher identity (considering that some experiences may cause you to decide not replicate them, for example an exclusively teacher-led classroom).
       b. When/if you feel comfortable, share your tree with another and discuss how each part of it has influenced your current language teacher identity.

7

DEVELOPING AND REFLECTING TEACHERS

7.1 INTRODUCTION

While there are various tools/activities that can be used to facilitate RP, Farrell (2016b: 237), when conducting research on articles published between 2009 and 2014, found that the most frequent tool used to facilitate the process was discussion (including teacher discussion groups and post-observation meetings), which was followed by journal writing, classroom observations, video analysis, action research, narrative and lesson study. He also found that out of the 116 articles surveyed 'no fewer than 50 of the studies reviewed [made] use of some kind of combination of on-line formats for reflection such as blogs, podcasts, chats, and forum discussions', which is what we examine in this chapter. Firstly, we outline some previous work on face-to-face and on-line RP.

In face-to-face third level contexts, Urzúa and Vásquez (2008) explored 'reflection for action' and identity for novice ESL teachers. Their data consisted of post-observation discourse and mentoring meetings. By examining the modals *will* and *going to* for future-oriented reflection and identity, they found that *will* and *be going to* occurred twice as much in the mentoring meetings compared to the supervision feedback. This, they argued, was possibly due to the nature of the meetings, whereby post-observation meetings often rely on past reflection, and the mentoring sessions lend themselves more to future-oriented talk, therefore multiple modes of expression can assist in the development of RP in differing ways. Moreover, Farr and Riordan (2015) used various modes of communication (face-to-face, discussion fora, blogs and chat sessions) with novice TESOL teachers in order to promote RP, and when examining evidence of reflective discourse across their data sets, they found more descriptive reflections occurring overall, possibly because the teachers were novices. Other levels of reflection were reached, namely critical and comparative (as per Jay and Johnson's (2002) framework as discussed in Chapter 3); and while blogs appeared to offer a lot in terms of expressing comparative reflections, it was the face-to-face modes that facilitated the deeper, critical reflections, possibly because in this context the joint effort by the student teachers and the peer tutor resulted in the co-construction of RP. Thus, modes of interaction and patterns of interaction affect RP.

RP in on-line modes has gained more interest recently (although Farrell 2016a suggests that this is an area in TESOL that warrants further exploration), and it has been found that using technology to write reflections allows languaging, which mediates learning (Faez et al. 2017: 11). It is often the asynchronous on-line modes (for example, discussion fora and blogs) that can facilitate RP (Biesenbach-Lucas 2004; Han and Hill 2006; Hubbard 2009; Kamhi-Stein 2000; Looi 2005; McPherson and Nunes 2004; Preece and Maloney-Krichmar 2003; Putnam and Borko 2000; Tu 2002). For example, Szabo and Schwartz (2011) used discussion fora with pre-service teachers for the enhancement of critical thinking skills. Through surveys and an analysis of postings, they noted evidence of increased critical thinking ability in the discussion threads, and the student teachers' reflections moved from surface level reporting of content to critical thinking regarding that content. Others discuss the use of diaries for RP, for example, for awareness-raising (Bailey 1990), providing feedback, promoting autonomous learning, confidence building, creating interaction outside the classroom, making the approach of learning a more process oriented one, and facilitating connections between course content and teaching (Porter et al. 1990). The last point in particular has echoes of Freeman's (2016) Design Theory seen in Chapter 2, in terms of giving student teachers tools to use and the opportunities to use them. Blogs can be used as on-line reflective diaries and to this end, Yang (2009) set up a collaborative blog for RP with EFL student teachers. When analysing the blog contents, he sorted the postings into the following five categories: theories of teaching; instructional approaches and methods; teaching evaluation methods and criteria; self-awareness; and questions about teaching and requests for advice. Yang's findings suggest that the student teachers were often more descriptive in their reflections than critical. However, he asserts that the instructors played a role during the process in that they posted questions in order to encourage more critical deliberations.

Regardless of the tools used, Farrell's (2016b: 240) extensive review mentioned earlier indicated that 'most TESOL teachers who engage in reflection become more aware of their practice'. He goes on to note that 'this greater level of awareness may lead to "improved" or "better" teaching, especially if the reflections lead to some definite conclusions that have direct implications for a teacher's classroom practices'. However, as noted above, student teachers need to be scaffolded in their RP journeys, and Borg (2018), as well as Farrell (2018), hold that teachers should be given training in what RP entails before expecting them to reflect on their practice, so they can, in Freeman's (2016) words, move from articulation of their practice to explanation of it. Cirocki and Farrell (2017: 6) sum up what it means to be a reflective practitioner nicely when they note,

No matter whether they are engaged in individual or collective deliberations, reflective practitioners (1) guide their teaching with different types of knowledge, including theoretical, empirical and practical; (2) examine their own teaching through different lenses and (3) incorporate the novel or alternative into their pedagogical practice to (4) optimise learning in the classroom as well as (5) develop their own teaching.

This is what we wanted to empower our novice and experienced teachers to do as part of their programmes of study from which TEC emanated.

While RP is very difficult to explore directly, we examine the use of language to show evidence of RP. Some research has already been conducted in this area, (for example, Farr and Riordan 2012, 2017; Murphy 2015; Riordan 2012, 2018), where linguistic indicators (verbs, nouns, adjectives and adverbs) are explored as a means to indicate reflective thought (see also Ullmann 2017 for an automated approach to finding keywords that are specific to an RP writing model). We build on this research in the context of TEC, as will be seen in the following sections. This is considered important as 'determining how students use language to construct their narratives can facilitate gaining a clearer understanding of the scope and facets of their reflections and their representational or communication approaches' (Lin et al. 2016).

7.2 THE LANGUAGE OF REFLECTION

To offer a general overview of the language of reflection found in TEC as a whole, the top 20 most frequent nouns, verbs, adjectives and adverbs were extracted from the overall TEC frequency list, as presented in Table 7.1.

As seen, the nouns all contain metalinguistic tokens related to teaching and learning (which can be used for either the articulation or explanation of their practice, see Freeman's Design Theory in Chapter 2), for example, *students, lesson, teachers, plan, English* and *classroom*. This is the focus of the teachers' discussions, and as discussed in depth in Chapter 5, these metalinguistic items have distinct functions. Some patterns, coinciding with research mentioned earlier, can be seen across the other word classes, for example, a lot of items in the verbs category show verbs of cognition, namely *think, know, learn, feel* and *want*. These verbs help the teachers to express their thoughts and desires, and to explain their beliefs and values, which is, as outlined in Chapter 3, all part of RP. We recognise that some of these verbs may be used as spoken discourse markers also (for example, in the construction *you know*), but for now these functions have not been disregarded from the data. As well as this, the verbs category and the adverbs category exemplify the language of narration, for example, verbs facilitating narration, *be, have, do, say, was, is, were, are, been* and *being*, and also adverbs marking time and boundaries between events, namely *then, now, here, always* and *sometimes*. In order for teachers to reflect, they need to think back on experiences and tell their stories, and the language of narration is key in doing this. The adjectives category and the adverb category show evidence of stance, and evaluation, for example, through adjectives such as *good, better, interesting, happy* and *pleased*, and adverbs such as *just, really, actually* and *quite*. Again, as part of RP, teachers are encouraged to offer opinions, reactions and thoughts while making evaluations, with the aim of revising their thinking and, in turn, future actions. Lastly, the adverbs category shows evidence of rationalisation, for example, *so* and *as* where the teachers are rationalising their thoughts and actions, again, a requirement of RP. This linguistic analysis is in line with previous research stating the importance of cognition (Borg 2003) in teacher RP: the importance of discussions that include 'sharing, discussing, questioning and reasoning about their teaching experiences' (Ashraf and Rarieya 2008: 270), and the importance of spaces to share emotions and relieve stress (Murray-Harvey et al. 1999; Zembylas 2003). Thus, the functions of cognition,

Table 7.1 Top 20 nouns, verbs, adjectives and adverbs in TEC

Nouns	Freq.	Verbs	Freq.	Adjectives	Freq.	Adverbs	Freq.
1 STUDENT(S)	3,724	WAS/IS/ WERE ARE/BEEN/ BEING	14,734	GOOD BETTER	1,480	SO	3,286
2 LESSON	2,021	DO/DID/ DON'T/ DIDN'T/ DOING	6,590	DIFFERENT	756	AS	3,137
3 CLASS	1,914	HAVE/HAD/ HAS	5,777	KIND	564	JUST	1,948
4 TEACHER(S)	1,377	THINK/ THOUGHT	2,915	RIGHT	487	THERE	1,751
5 TIME	1,298	KNOW	2,591	LITTLE	419	WELL	1,662
6 THING(S)	1,184	TEACH(ING)	2,512	INTERESTING	384	VERY	1,334
7 LANGUAGE	909	LIKE	2,495	IMPORTANT	383	THEN	1,242
8 WAY	852	SAY/SAID	1,503	NEW	354	REALLY	1,042
9 PLAN	677	GO(ING)	1,471	SURE	353	ALSO	957
10 PRACTICE	669	LEARN(ING)	1,381	DIFFICULT	304	NOW	770
11 WEEK	665	FEEL/FELT	1,344	ABLE	261	ACTUALLY	647
12 WORK	571	GET/GOT	1,331	PERSONAL	242	EVEN	537
13 EXPERIENCE	529	USE	710	HAPPY	216	QUITE	523
14 ENGLISH	527	MEAN	614	GREAT	192	MAYBE	497
15 LEVEL	509	NEED	614	HARD	181	HERE	391
16 CLASSROOM	452	SEE	591	LONG	176	ALWAYS	380
17 WORDS	444	LAUGHING	565	USEFUL	176	SOMETIMES	336
18 FEEDBACK	443	WANT	525	AWARE	165	AGAIN	333
19 QUESTIONS	414	MAKE	503	PLEASED	163	STILL	323
20 PEOPLE	411	GIVE	417	REFLECTIVE	156	OVERALL	258

narration, stance and evaluation, and reasoning appear to be core linguistic devices in the realisation of RP (these are somewhat similar to the categories outlined by Ullmann 2017, namely reflection, description of an experience, feelings, personal beliefs, recognising difficulties, perspective, and outcome and intentions).

With this in mind, going back to the frequency lists, we combined the occurrences of words (in the top 300 items) which can fall into the functions of (1) cognition, (2) narration, (3) stance and evaluation, and (4) questioning and reasoning. Most of the items categorised in Table 7.1 formed part of this analysis but other items outside the word classes were also included, for example *but*, *how* and *why* for questioning and reasoning. The distribution of these functions across the top 300 items in the TEC frequency list can be seen in Chart 7.1.

There are 31,783 occurrences of narration in the top 300 items of the frequency list, which is followed by questioning and reasoning (21,097), stance and evaluation (16,836), and, finally, cognition (14,924). This high use of narration (verb forms and

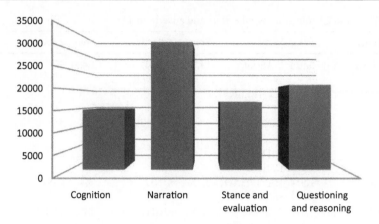

Chart 7.1   Indicators of reflection in TEC (WPM)

time references) is necessary in order for the teachers to situate their discussions, whether they are individually narrating for the reader, or co-constructing narration in groups. Questioning and reasoning follows in second place because the teachers are questioning themselves, their and others' practices, and making connections with theory in order to better understand themselves and the practice of teaching and learning. Therefore, within the TEC data, the student teachers typically reveal stance, make evaluations, express feelings and emotions and demonstrate cognition, awareness, and understanding of issues, concepts and events, within which they show awareness of the tools of the trade and the professional language use of the community (see Chapter 2). They do this because, as part of RP, they are evaluating thoughts and actions, using pre-existing knowledge and other lenses (students, peers and so on) to inform those thoughts and actions, and they are showing an awareness of their feelings, emotions and understanding of their practices. We suggest that narration allows a descriptive level of RP, whereas deeper levels of reflection might be attained through cognition, evaluation and stance, and questioning and reasoning. Three items from Table 7.1 (*overall, personal* and *reflective*) have been chosen to close this section. These are examined as we hypothesise that they represent reflective language in terms of a focus on the individual (*personal*) and a summarised reflection on practices (*overall* and *reflective*).

7.2.1 OVERALL

The word *overall* occurs 258 times in the corpus, and our initial assumptions are that this summative linking adjunct (Carter and McCarthy 2006) is being used to review or summarise reflections made by the teachers. Therefore, we examined the top 10 collocates one to the left and right of *overall* to give us an idea of what the teachers are talking about.

The teachers are being very specific in terms of discussing the *overall* issues of timing in a lesson, the plan and the theme of a lesson. Aspects of teaching practice

Table 7.2 Collocates of *overall* in TEC

Collocate 1L	Freq.	Collocate 1R	Freq.
The	31	I	57
But	10	Impression	37
Timing	10	Progression	28
And	7	The	23
Lesson	5	It	10
My	5	Lesson	7
So	5	Theme	7
An	4	Review	6
Plan	4	Though	5
That	4	They	4

being a high priority for the content of reflection was also found by Riordan (2018). The teachers are also using *overall* on a more macro-level by talking about their *overall impression* of something, their *overall progression* and their *overall review* of teaching, which was what the novice teachers were required to blog about on the MA programme. A closer examination of the most frequently occurring cluster, *overall I*, is warranted. This is an interesting one as the cluster *overall I* appears to be the end result of considering something and it appears to represent a positive tone. To be more precise, the cluster indicates the teachers' overall experiences of lessons which are taught on a weekly basis (75 per cent of all occurrences); their experiences of their programme in general (1.2 per cent of all occurrences); their general experiences (6.8 per cent of all occurrences); and of most relevance here, their development and growth as a teacher (17 per cent of all occurrences), the latter of which the concordances in Figure 7.1 show.

These ten examples of *overall I* representing teacher development and growth come only from the MA blogs. This is interesting in itself as it highlights the affordance of this mode for RP (see, for example, Killeavy and Moloney 2010; McLoughlin et al. 2007; Ray and Coulter 2008; Stiler and Philleo 2003; Yang 2009). This is explored further in Section 7.4 where face-to-face and on-line reflections are examined. The majority of examples in Figure 7.1 are all present and past reflections, while line 7 is a lovely example of future-oriented reflection, where hopes and desires are offered. The other examples are centred around the novice student teachers' confidence,

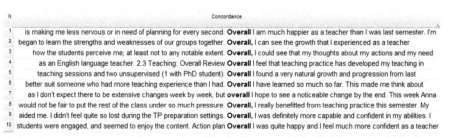

N   Concordance

1   is making me less nervous or in need of planning for every second. **Overall** I am much happier as a teacher than I was last semester. I'm
2   began to learn the strengths and weaknesses of our groups together. **Overall,** I can see the growth that I experienced as a teacher
3   how the students perceive me; at least not to any notable extent. **Overall,** I could see that my thoughts about my actions and my need
4   as an English language teacher. 2.3 Teaching: Overall Review **Overall** I feel that teaching practice has developed my teaching in
5   teaching sessions and two unsupervised (1 with PhD student). **Overall** I found a very natural growth and progression from last
6   better suit someone who had more teaching experience than I had. **Overall** I have learned so much so far. This made me think about
7   as I don't expect there to be extensive changes week by week, but **overall** I hope to see a noticeable change by the end. This week Anna
8   would not be fair to put the rest of the class under so much pressure. **Overall,** I really benefitted from teaching practice this semester. My
9   aided me. I didn't feel quite so lost during the TP preparation settings. **Overall,** I was definitely more capable and confident in my abilities. I
10 students were engaged, and seemed to enjoy the content. Action plan **Overall** I was quite happy and I feel much more confident as a teacher

Figure 7.1 Overall I *concordance: novice student teachers (Mode 5: On-Line Blogs)*

development, enhancement of their skills and changes in their perceptions of themselves. An example (an expansion of concordance line 6) can be seen in extract 7.1.

Extract 7.1 (Mode 5: On-Line Blogs)

NST: **Overall I** have learned so much so far. This made me **think about** 'what ifs'. **What if** I had had experience when I came here, **what would** TP do for me and upon a little investigation and by asking people who have experience, their approach makes sense to me. They **seem to be** focusing on developing themselves as teachers as opposed to being more prescriptive, what **I mean** is that they have a strong identity of themselves as teachers and TP for them is a way to fine tune this identity to be the best teacher they can by whilst being who they want to be.

This made me **think about** me as a teacher, **who am I? What kind of teacher do I want to be? Is TP having a washback effect on me?** For the most part I think not. **I do think** that I work hard and **I want to** do well, but **I also recognise** that the expertise available here **is extremely beneficial** and has helped progress quite quickly. **So, although,** marks are important, I **do think** that overall my drive to learn to be a better teacher was stronger than the need for an A. **However,** who I am as teacher is a little less explicit. **I know that I like it** (although **the pressure** of TP and being observed did make me wonder sometimes) and **I know that** I could be **really good** at it but at the moment I think I am somewhat like a neat jigsaw of things I learned in class and observations. **This is good,** it shows I can take what I see and hear about and put it into action and so far this **I know I can do.** This then leads me to my final section of the blog.

So for this semester I have **two main aims for TP**: to continue to progress methodologically and to apply the theory we cover to the classroom (this was the primary aim of TP last semester for me) and to introspectively develop my identity as a teacher, or moreover, document the development of my identity as a teacher. **I will do this** by trying out different things in my classes; different approaches etc. to see what is most natural for me.

TP starts next week, so I'm looking forward to seeing how it goes.

Here we see a novice student teacher asking multiple questions of himself, answering some of them but also including some specific actions for his own future development, which is precisely what we hope to see in reflective discourse. His reflections are honest while also being both confident and showing some vulnerability. This is a good reflective piece where all elements of reflective discourse are present, namely cognition, narration, stance, and questioning and reasoning. The teacher gives his opinions, thoughts and future intentions in order to develop and grow.

7.2.2 PERSONAL

Personal occurs 242 times in the corpus, and is considered worthy of analysis because it focuses on the individual. When examining the collocates of *personal*, *your* is the most frequent pronoun occurring to the left (fifty-six times), especially when queries from a lecturer or a peer tutor aimed to scaffold reflections (for example, *what is your personal opinion*). The tasks the teachers are set, whether structured or semi-structured, individual or scaffolded, have a clear impact on the teachers' reflective language. Interestingly, the next most frequent collocate is *my personal* (twenty-two occurrences). This occurs only in the data from the individual blogs by the MA students and the collaborative blogs by the PhD students, examples of which can be seen in Figure 7.2.

The novice student teachers are talking about their personal objectives and the aims of the lessons they are planning or teaching (lines 3–14 and 19–22), while the PhD students (experienced teachers) move up a level to talk about their personal teaching philosophies, enquires, interests and teaching styles (lines 1, 2, 15 and 18), as these were the broad discussion topics of the tasks that were set for them. Extracts 7.2 and 7.3 show two differing approaches to reflection by the novice and more experienced student teachers.

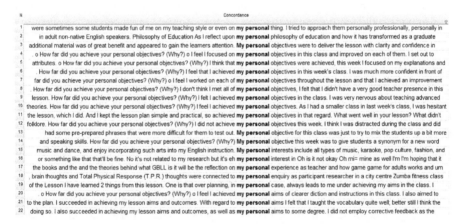

Figure 7.2   My personal *concordance: novice and experienced student teachers (Mode 5: On-Line Blogs)*

Extract 7.2 (Mode 5: On-Line Blogs)

As I reflect upon **my personal** philosophy of education and how it has transformed as a graduate student with the University of XXX Master of Arts in Teaching program and now as a PhD TESOL candidate at the University of Limerick, I realize that my core educational beliefs have remained since first becoming a teacher in 2002: Take an active role in your students' lives; always take students' multiple intelligences into account when planning lessons; and maintain a structured learning environment. Since becoming a teacher of speakers of other languages in 2008 and enrolling in the aforementioned graduate program, I have additional philosophical beliefs, in regards to education of non-native English speakers. For example, I now feel that foreign language instruction should be as communicative as possible. I have also embraced the importance of pronunciation instruction, and I hope to continue studying and improving upon my ability to teach English pronunciation.

Extract 7.3 (Mode 5: On-Line Blogs)

I don't think I met all of **my personal** objectives, I felt that I didn't have a very good teacher presence in this week's lesson. I became nervous and let that effect me. I could of had more authority during the class.

In extract 7.2, the experienced teacher is reflecting on her teaching philosophy (which, from anecdotal and personal experiences, many teachers find a difficult task), and she is using high-level jargon (demonstrating her knowledge of the professional community), while also naming theories such as multiple intelligences, demonstrating her alignment of theory and practice, an important element in reflection (and also Freeman's Design Theory as discussed in Chapter 2). She also expresses how her philosophy has developed over time, and her future hopes and desires. In the second extract, the novice student teacher is discussing more specific details of a lesson. The reflections appear to be less sure (*I don't think, I feel that I didn't*) and are more teacher- than student-centred compared to the previous extract, which is typical of novices at the early stages of their careers (see Farr and Riordan 2015; Riordan 2018). It could also be argued that the novice student teachers are, in the words of Freeman (2016), articulating their practice while the experienced student teachers are explaining their practice, thus having full membership in the community. While both of these examples of discourse are of absolute value for RP, this distinction demonstrates that further examination of the differences in novice and experienced reflections is warranted (and is explored in Section 7.3).

7.2.3 REFLECTIVE

Reflective occurs 156 times in the corpus, and collocates show that the most frequent word one to the right of *reflective* is *practice* (101 occurrences), which is followed by *teaching* (twelve occurrences). *Reflective practice* emerges as salient in particular due to the module on RP that the PhD students followed, discussions from which form part of TEC (see Chapter 4). Of these 101 occurrences of *reflective practice*, 56 per cent come from the lecturers where they are questioning the students about what they think RP is, their experiences of RP, and their opinions of its value, as seen in extracts 7.4–7.6.

Extract 7.4 (Mode 2: Face-to-Face Lecturer-Guided Group Discussions)

```
L:  So what you're saying is reflective practice is a process
    that leads you to professional development. Is that your
    understanding?
```

Extract 7.5 (Mode 2: Face-to-Face Lecturer-Guided Group Discussions)

```
L:  What about you guys what sort of reflective practice activities
    do you engage in?
```

Extract 7.6 (Mode 2: Face-to-Face Lecturer-Guided Group Discussions)

```
L:  Ok and the last question, what is your professional opinion
    of the value of reflective practice for language teachers? So
    you're experienced teachers now, what what do you think the
    value of reflective practice is if any?
```

This particularly highlights the importance of a lecturer/peer tutor (as well as the task) scaffolding student teacher reflections (Borg 2018; Coulson and Harvey 2013; Farrell 2018), leading reflective dialogue and making the process of RP an open classroom discussion (see Chapter 2 for more on scaffolding). The remaining occurrences (44 per cent) of *reflective practice* come from the experienced student teachers when they are answering the lecturers' questions/comments. They are therefore understanding RP in more depth by speaking about it, for example, Vygotsky (1983: 219) noted that 'thought is not merely expressed in words: it comes into existence through them' (see Chapter 2). This can be seen in the examples in extracts 7.7–7.10.

Extract 7.7 (Mode 2: Face-to-Face Lecturer-Guided Group Discussions)

```
EST: if you were to worried about improving you may go on the wrong
     way but that's a specific I think that's a specific type of
     problem that in general reflective practice should push you
     forward to more improve rather than had a negative effect
```

Extract 7.8 (Mode 2: Face-to-Face Lecturer-Guided Group Discussions)

```
EST: I think the value of reflective practice we have a very bad
     need of it and to learn from our areas because as the proverb
```

proverb says no one is perfect no human being is perfect so we
need to learn from our own mistakes and amend the errors

Extract 7.9 (Mode 2: Face-to-Face Lecturer-Guided Group Discussions)

EST: Yeah and I think I will also continue to do reflection as what
I have already done actually at the end of every semester and
at the beginning of every semester I actually think about what
I have already done what I want to do in the future but I don't
really put it in the one file which is or **reflective practice**
or reflective portfolio I just do it naturally without really
knowing what I was doing at that time. So now I know that it is
a kind of reflection and I know how to put it in one document

Extract 7.10 (Mode 2: Face-to-Face Lecturer-Guided Group Discussions)

EST: I would like to **do reflective practice** but some of the environment is not really supporting the practice

In these extracts, the experienced teachers are becoming more aware of RP through
discussing what it is (extracts 7.7, 7.8 and, in particular, 7.9), while also being cog-
nisant of the challenges when wishing to engage in RP (extract 7.10). These examples
highlight the importance of talking about something in order to more fully understand and make sense of it, which was our aim in all of the activities with the novice
and experienced teachers where social interaction is key for understanding processes
and practices in language teaching.

Moving on to the second most frequent collocate, *reflective teaching*, and as seen in
the concordances in Figure 7.3, this predominantly occurs in the experienced teachers'
individual portfolios (nine out of twelve), where they talk about their teaching philosophies, approaches to teaching, and reflective teaching as a means of development.

The example in extract 7.11 comes from an experienced teacher's portfolio, and
here he is making, what he sees as, the distinction between reflective teaching and professional development, again verbalising his thoughts into a deeper understanding.

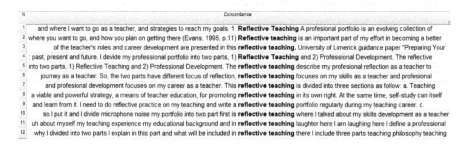

Figure 7.3   Reflective teaching *concordance (Mode 4: On-Line Portfolios)*

Extract 7.11 (Mode 4: On-Line Portfolios)

EST: The **reflective teaching** describe my profesional reflection as
     a teacher to improve my teaching skills, and the professional
     development describe my profesional reflection of my career
     journey as a teacher. So, the two parts have different focus
     of reflection, reflective teaching focuses on my skills as a
     teacher and profesional development focuses on my career as a
     teacher.

Therefore, so far, we have seen that there are specific linguistic items that can be found in reflective discourse, and these have functions including cognition, narration, evaluation, stance and reasoning. We also found that there are multiple means of reflecting on one's practice, and that the level of those reflecting (novice versus experienced), the mode of reflection (face-to-face versus on-line), the interaction patterns within reflective discussions (individual versus scaffolded) and the tasks the teachers are set may all have an impact on how teachers reflect. These are therefore explored in the following sections.

7.3 THE LANGUAGE OF REFLECTION AMONG NOVICE AND EXPERIENCED STUDENT TEACHERS

In order to explore any potential differences between the reflective practices of novice and experienced student teachers, we followed the same steps taken for Chart 7.1 by taking the words, under the functions cognition, narration, stance and evaluation, and questioning and reasoning, in the top 300 items in the frequency list and calculating their frequencies in the novice student teacher data compared to the experienced student teacher data. The results of this can be seen in Chart 7.2.

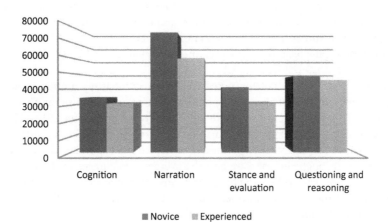

Chart 7.2   Indicators of reflection: novice and experienced student teachers (WPM)

The same pattern emerges as in Chart 7.1 with narration being the most frequent function, followed by questioning and reasoning, and then by stance and evaluation, and, finally, cognition. Furthermore, surprisingly, there are more examples of all of these functions in the novice student teacher data compared to the experienced teacher data. We imagined that the experienced teachers would have had produced more examples of cognition and questioning and reasoning as they might represent higher levels of reflection. However, those two functions have the least amount of difference between novice and experienced, and most difference lies between the functions of narration, and stance and evaluation. When looking at individual frequency list items that make up the chart, a notable difference between novice and experienced teacher data is the cognitive verb *know*, which occurs almost 7,000 times in the novice data compared to 3,500 times in the experienced data. A quick concordance search shows that *know* is used in the construction *you know* (not showing cognition, but rather having a discourse marker function – see Biber et al. 1999; Carter and McCarthy 2006) 55 per cent of the time in the novice data and only 27 per cent of the time in the experienced data. However, even taking these out of the frequency lists, cognition is still slightly higher in the novice data.

To examine this further, the LIWC 2015 program was used. It examines how words are used across texts by determining 'the degree any text uses positive or negative emotions, self-references, causal words, and … other language dimensions' (Pennebaker et al. 2007). It works using a tagging system based on its internal dictionary to define words within the target files. Output is generated in terms of:

- four summary variables, namely analytical thinking, clout, authenticity and emotional tone [this was added in the 2015 version];
- general descriptor categories (total word counts, words per sentence, percentage of words);
- linguistic dimensions (percentage of words that are pronouns, articles, auxiliary verbs);
- psychological construct categories (affect, cognition, and biological processes);
- personal concern categories (work, home, and leisure activities);
- paralinguistic dimensions (fillers, and non-fluencies);
- punctuation categories (commas) (Pennebaker et al. 2007: 4).

The LIWC programme has been noted to accurately identify emotion in language use (Tausczik and Pennebaker 2010), but like all text analysis programmes, it does not flawlessly capture the meanings of all words (Servi and Elson 2012). However, combined with a CADS approach, it can be used to support emerging patterns. For our analysis, all the sub-corpora pertaining to novice and experienced student teachers were run through the software and the average percentages of the output were compared against each other. The first area of analysis includes the dimensions affect, cognition, and focus on past, present and future time, as we take them to broadly relate to affect, cognition and narration in Chart 7.3.

Similar to Chart 7.2, there is more cognition overall, and more affect, cognition and tense usage in the novice data, therefore upholding the corpus-based findings.

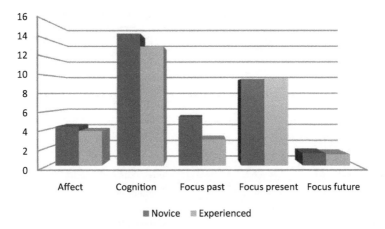

Chart 7.3   LIWC (2015) variables: novice and experienced student teachers

Higher levels of cognition compared to affect were also found in medical students' reflective writing by Lin et al. (2016). In both data sets, there is a lack of focus on the future, which is disappointing because forward thinking and future actions are key to RP and teacher development. While the percentile differences in each dimension are minimal, the only striking trend is that the novices focus on the past nearly twice as much as the experienced teachers. This could be because the novices' reflections are focused on what happened retrospectively in classrooms, rather than the broader topics the experienced teachers reflected on, for example as seen in the previous section, their teaching philosophies, interests and teaching styles (see also Farr and Riordan 2017). In order to confirm this, frequency lists for novice and experienced teacher data were compared against TEC as a whole, and the keywords in Table 7.3 were found (only content words from the keyword lists are included in the table).

While there are many similarities here, we can see that teaching/learning strategies, the English language and processes in teaching, and learning and development are key to the novice data sets, while portfolios, teaching philosophies and the topics of students' PhDs are core to the experienced teachers (Technology, Zumba, and Saudi students as participants). Therefore, there is a broad range of reflection topics in the PhD data sets as they have more knowledge and experience, and professional language use (see Chapter 2) to draw on, and the tasks they were set also reflected this. This highlights once again the impact the task has on reflective practices.

Other output from the LIWC programme are the four summary variables; analytical thinking, clout, authenticity and emotional tone. According to the LIWC website:

- analytical thinking 'captures the degree to which people use words that suggest formal, logical, and hierarchical thinking patterns';
- clout 'refers to the relative social status, confidence, or leadership that people display through their writing or talking';

Table 7.3   Novice and experienced student teacher keywords relative to TEC

Novice student teacher keywords	Experienced student teacher keywords
Example	Reflective
Program	University
Strategies	Portfolio
English	Technology
Experience	Career
PhD	Professional
Process	Education
Evaluation	Reflect
Reflect	PhD
Learning	Evaluation
Development	Saudi
Education	Philosophy
Professional	Website
Career	Program
University	Zumba

- authenticity refers to the fact that 'when people reveal themselves in an authentic or honest way, they are more personal, humble, and vulnerable';
- emotional tone combines positive and negative emotional dimensions into a single variable and 'the higher the number, the more positive the tone. Numbers below 50 suggest a more negative emotional tone.'

The findings from these four dimensions are presented in Chart 7.4.

While Charts 7.2 and 7.3 showed that cognition was lower in the experienced student teacher data compared to the novice student teacher data, we see here that

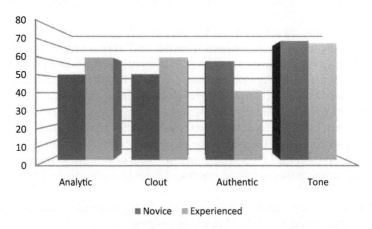

Chart 7.4   *LIWC (2015) summary variables: novice and experienced student teachers*

Table 7.4 Most frequent cognitive constructions with *I*

	Novice student teachers	WPM	Experienced student teachers	WPM
I* know	304	936	50	422
I* think	252	776	64	540
I* feel	106	326	5	42

analytical thinking (which is needed for deeper levels of RP) is higher amongst the experienced teachers, as is clout (meaning the more experienced teachers are showing more confidence). This demonstrates that the experienced teachers have the tools, past experiences and career maturity to reflect in analytical and confident terms. They have also completed a module on reflective practice, which points to the importance of teaching teachers how to reflect (Coulson and Harvey 2013; Farr and Farrell 2017; Farr and Riordan 2017). Something also worth noting is that the authentic dimension is higher in the novice data. This could be because the novices are more vulnerable in their speech and writing (as was found by Riordan 2018), while the experienced teachers feel the need to show more confidence, less vulnerability and therefore protect their face (Brown and Levinson 1987), or indeed just draw on their experience for more confident reflections. Tone in both data sets is similar (70 per cent in novice data and 69 per cent in experienced data) and the fact that is it over 50 per cent means there is an overwhelming positive tone in TEC.

To examine cognition further, using corpus linguistic techniques, the top three most frequent cognitive verbs (*know, think* and *feel*) in the TEC were searched for in the construction *I* think/feel/know*, the results of which can be seen in Table 7.4. These verbs were also among the top 20 most frequent cognitive verbs in the Longman Spoken and Written English (LSWE) corpus, a 40 million word corpus of spoken and written texts of various registers (Biber et al. 1999).

The novice teachers use these verbs of cognition much more than the experienced teachers in this construction. The most striking difference in Table 7.4 is that the construction *I* feel* is almost eight times more frequent in the novice data compared to the experienced data, which supports the suggestion that the novices are being more open and vulnerable in sharing their feelings compared to the experienced teachers, which is of importance in terms of humanistic approaches, as discussed in Chapter 2. The constructions *I* think* and *I* feel* are examined more qualitatively in later sections, and *I* know* is examined here in relation to analytical thinking.

7.3.1 *KNOW*

Concordance analysis of *I* know* reveals that it occurs in the constructions illustrated in Table 7.5. We see that the novice and experienced teachers use the structure in the negative construction the majority of the time (87 per cent and 83 per cent), and the positive construction is used more by the experienced teachers than the novices (17 per cent and 6.6 per cent). Extracts 7.12–7.14 present examples of how this is used across both data sets.

Table 7.5   *I* know*: novice and experienced student teachers

Constructions	Novice	Experienced
I didn't/don't know/never (negative)	263/304 = 87%	53/64 = 83%
I know/now know (positive construction)	20/304 = 6.6%	11/64 = 17%
I you know (hesitation)	18/304 = 5.9%	0
I + modal know (might, wouldn't)	3/304 = 1%	0

Extract 7.12 (Mode 1: Face-to-Face Teaching Practice Feedback Interactions)

NST: Em another thing as well was they were asking me the dictionary I kind of bent down I didn't know what to do there because
they were showing me the dictionary and **I didn't know** whether
to stay standing or to I was I was crouched down

TPS: What were they showing you in it Petra?

NST: They were asking me to they were like kind of turning their
books towards me and then going 'It's not in the dict the
dictionary doesn't give a good e explanation' and then they
were showing me the dictionary see I didn't want to take the
dictionary off them

TPS: No

NST: +and I didn't want to impose on them either so I **didn't know**
what to do

TPS: Well why not ask them to to tell them instead of showing you
say 'okay I've looked up the dictionary too so tell me what
are you saying to me?'

NST: Mmhm

TPS: Cos there's no point in them showing you their writing

NST: Yeah

In extract 7.12, we see the novice student teacher reflecting on her lesson with a TP supervisor, and asking for help as she did not know what to do in a certain situation, therefore not having sufficient experience to make in-action reflections, and showing genuine vulnerability. This novice needed the assistance of the supervisor to validate her classroom actions. A more mature reflection emerges in the following extract from a novice student teacher blog.

Extract 7.13 (Mode 5: On-Line Blogs)

NST: With regard to my teaching identity, this week was actually
quite enlightening. I had a lot of fun and there was a very
clear learning outcome. The students also really enjoyed the
lesson and I felt very comfortable with them whilst still
maintaining the teacher's role. So all in all I felt I was more

myself than ever. I also was brought a little back to earth this week as more and more I've been feeling quite confident as a teacher but today I was reminded that each situation will bring me something new to learn. That is that I had quite a dominant student in the class and **I didn't know** how to deal with it at the time. She is very capable and really lovely and she did try to encourage other people to speak so it was more so that the other students became quite shy in her presence. I think that the other students present (as there weren't many present) were the quite ones anyway so it was perhaps a strange mix and I noticed that when a student presented an opinion which she would question, the students would very quickly cave and allow her to continue. I **did not know** what to do. I couldn't move her without being obvious and I didn't want to discourage her, I tried to ask the other students questions in order to include them but that created a student-teacher dialogic as opposed to a student-student dialogic which would have been the aim.

So overall, it was a good week and I learned a lot about myself as a teacher and gaps in my approach that I can work on - with just two more weeks to work on them !

This is a very interesting post with lots of cognition, namely feelings, descriptions of events and attempts at understanding the events. All of this shows the novice is coming to a better understanding of himself as a teacher, although it lacks a critical or forward-looking element. Both these extracts come from novice teachers, and the second one shows how blog writing facilitates a much deeper explanation of events compared to face-to-face TP feedback. However, the assistance of the supervisor in TP feedback is also invaluable, hence highlighting the necessity of a range of modes and interaction patterns for RP in order to help teachers mature in their levels of community membership. It could also be that the second teacher is simply better at reflecting than the first.

Extract 7.14, also seen in Chapter 6, shows a more confident tone.

Extract 7.14 (Mode 5: On-Line Blogs)

EST: This time of year, I usually go through what most refer to as 'teacher burnout'. I find myself less excited and passionate about planning my lessons and I begin to rely on textbooks more than my own creative abilities. Many things contribute to this, mainly stress and mental fatigue. I believe that burnout is a normal part of any career, especially teaching, but it is important to recognize it is happening and figure out ways to overcome and prevent it. I definitely know that I am going through 'teacher burnout' at the moment because I do not look forward to planning my lessons at the moment, and I find myself using convenient, pre-made materials. There is nothing wrong with using convenient materials. As teachers, it's important to find materials and shortcuts to make our lives more manageable in and out of the classroom, but when we take our own unique skills as a teacher and our students' needs and interests out of the equation, the result is a classroom with an unmotivated and most-likely bored teacher and students which lowers the likelihood of learning outcomes. So it's time to make a change! In order to reverse my 'teacher burnout,' I plan to do the following: * yoga/meditation * exercise * create something for myself in order to reignite my creativity in all areas of my life * give my students more control of their lessons * get plenty of sleep.

How do you recognize the signs of 'teacher burnout,' and what do you do to correct it?

This comes from the collaborative PhD blogs, where one teacher writes a post for others to engage with. This teacher is drawing on her experience in order to discuss teacher burnout, giving examples, and therefore showing self-awareness and issues in her teaching. She offers some action plans to deal with this and tries to engage the others also. This is a much more mature, confident and experienced post, once again showing that experience offers teachers more to draw on, resulting often in deeper reflections. We can therefore say that while novices can and do reflect at various levels and in differing ways, the more experienced teachers have more knowledge of teaching to exploit, which can enhance their reflections. The experienced teachers' more intense formation in RP is also crucial in the realisation of these more confident levels of reflection. The following section examines the impact of the mode on RP.

7.4 THE LANGUAGE OF REFLECTION IN FACE-TO-FACE AND ON-LINE REFLECTIONS

Once again, using the words from the top 300 items in the frequency list in Chart 7.1, the frequencies of the functional categories of reflection in the face-to-face data compared to the on-line data were calculated, and the results can be seen in Chart 7.5. This chart is similar to Chart 7.1 for the face-to-face corpus, showing that narration is the most frequent function, followed by questioning and reasoning, stance and evaluation, and, finally cognition. However, the on-line data shows more evidence of cognition than stance and evaluation. This could partly be because some of the items included in the category of stance such as *like*, *just* and *kind* are much more frequent in spoken data compared to written (Biber et al. 1999). This is not to say that there is no evidence of stance and evaluation in the on-line data, but the most frequent features in the data are those which are more dominant in face-to-face communication. In fact, on-line modes are known for being conducive to the expression of feelings (Deng and Yuen 2011; Derks et al. 2008; Killeavy and

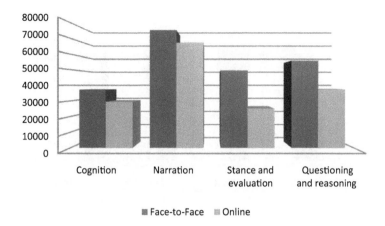

Chart 7.5   Indicators of reflection: face-to-face and on-line (WPM)

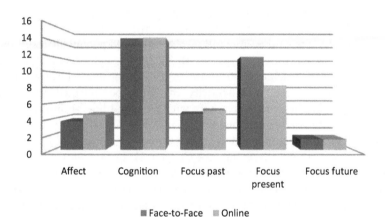

Chart 7.6   LIWC (2015) variables: face-to-face and on-line

Moloney 2010). In addition, it was initially surprising that cognition is higher in the face-to-face data, but on closer inspection this is because the discourse markers *you know* and *I think* are pushing the frequencies of these items up in the face-to-face mode.

Chart 7.6 shows the LIWC variables of affect, cognition and tenses across the face-to-face and on-line data. We can see once again that cognition is higher than affect in on-line and face-to-face modes. The only marked difference is that a focus on the present is higher in face-to-face discourse, possibly because speech is in real time, while on-line modes promote narration and a focus on the past (Deng and Yuen 2011; Lucas and Fleming 2011; Murray and Hourigan 2008; Stiler and Philleo 2003; Yang 2009). If we examine the four summary variables across the face-to-face and on-line data, we see the patterns in Chart 7.7.

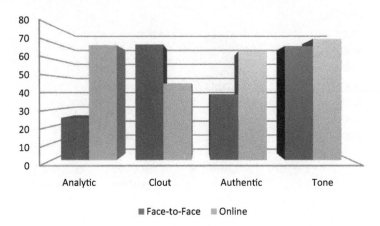

Chart 7.7   LIWC (2015) summary variables: face-to-face and on-line

There is more evidence of analytical thinking in the on-line mode compared to the face-to-face. This is because when writing in on-line environments, people have time to think about what they are writing, and this could potentially result in more advanced and logical thinking (Kunz et al. 2003; McLoughlin and Mynard 2009; Preece and Maloney-Krichmar 2003; Riordan 2011; Szabo and Schwartz 2011). Also higher in the on-line mode is authenticity. This might be explained by the fact that the participants find it easier to be more vulnerable and honest on-line compared to face-to-face for face-saving reasons, as was found by Killeavy and Moloney (2010), and Riordan (2018), and is important when considering the benefits of humanistic approaches to learning (see Chapter 2). In line with this assumption is the fact that clout is higher in face-to-face contexts than on-line, therefore the teachers are showing a more confident tone when in face-to-face conversation than in their writing, again highlighting the impact of face on collaborative discussions. Showing confidence during face-to-face conversations is of importance because the teachers are sharing their knowledge and learning from each other through mutual engagement in their CoP (Lave and Wenger 1991; Wenger 1998), whether they are at the articulation or explanation stage of membership (Freeman 2016). Tone is similar across both data sets and is positive. As noted earlier, the construction *I* feel* is investigated, as this structure was not only one of the top three most frequent cognitive verbs but also much more frequent on-line compared to face-to-face.

7.4.1 FEEL

Concordance analysis of *I* feel* reveals that it occurs in the following constructions as shown in Table 7.6. The face-to-face mode shows equal amounts of positive and negative feelings, while the on-line mode has more, albeit minimal, negative feelings. Also, and in line with earlier findings which showed more cognition than affect in the data sets, 61 per cent of the usage of *feel* in speech was cognition, while

Table 7.6   *I* feel* in face-to-face and on-line data

Constructions	Face-to-face	On-line
Positive feeling, for example, feel happy, feel comfortable, didn't feel terrible, didn't feel stupid, didn't feel out of my depth	7/36 = 19.5%	2/75 = 3%
Negative feeling, for example, feel guilty, don't feel comfortable, feel nervous	7/36 = 19.5%	5/75 = 7%
Cognition, for example, feel sth. was better, more effective, feel I've learned, feel I should have done sth	22/36 = 61% Positive remarks: 4/22 = 18% Negative remarks: 6/22 = 27% Neutral: 12/22= 55%	68/75 = 90% Positive remarks: 32/68 = 47% Negative remarks: 23/68 = 34% Neutral: 13/68 = 19%

90 per cent of its on-line usage was cognition. When looking through the concordance examples *of I* feel* for cognition in the face-to-face modes, the comments were predominantly neutral (55 per cent), followed by negative and positive comments. The on-line data sets are different in that the comments were predominantly positive and negative, with the least amount of neutral comments (19 per cent). This could indeed indicate that the teachers are not 'sitting on the fence' in the on-line environments, and are being more honest and open with their feelings and opinions, which is reflected in the lower levels of neutrality in the on-line modes. Similar findings were also reported by Riordan (2018).

Extracts 7.15–7.17 furnish some examples of the various feelings and reflections expressed in the on-line modes. The first extract comes from a self-reflection in a novice teacher's blog.

Extract 7.15 (Mode 5: On-Line Blogs)

NST: This was my favourite lesson in the semester so far, and **I really feel** that as the teacher there was great STT [Student Talking Time] along with great S-T [student-teacher] rapport. The <u>affective filter</u> of the students was quite low, and I could see that there was active learning going on. We were all working together, and if needed they could ask for help. There were a few laughs - content related- and I felt that on a whole this lesson was quite positive.

Here, the novice student teacher is reflecting on a lesson in a positive light. Something we find encouraging is that she is using other lenses (Brookfield 1995) to support her reflection, therefore pushing her into deeper levels of reflection, rather than simply retelling events. For example, she uses Krashen's (1983) Affective Filter Theory to support her point, and she uses terminology such as *active learning* to show her knowledge and understanding of the field of teaching and learning, or in other words, showing her understanding of the tools required for teaching (see Freeman's Design Theory in Chapter 2). Of course, the on-line modes lend themselves to these deeper levels of thought, as the teachers have time to think about events from various angles and lenses. Extract 7.16 comes also from a novice student teacher blog, in a teacher's overall final review of teaching at the end of the semester.

Extract 7.16 (Mode 5: On-Line Blogs)

NST: In the beginning **I did feel** that being observed affected my teaching as it made me extremely nervous, the idea of someone watching you and grading you. I am now very glad that this was the case. In my future career I will never have a problem with someone sitting in and observing a class that I am teaching.

This teacher is offering a very honest reflection about being observed while teaching, which many teachers feel anxious about (Farr 2015). In a short post, we see that she values being observed for her own professional development, and we also see evidence of forward reflecting in the final sentence (however idealised this may be). Again, the task is having an impact here in that the overall review encourages teachers to reflect on a macro-scale on the semester as a whole, but the on-line environment is allowing time to nourish these reflections. The final extract exemplifies what a blog can offer to a novice teacher in terms of reflecting on her own RP.

Extract 7.17 (Mode 5: On-Line Blogs)

NST: Now that we're reflecting on every class, it feels like a burden. Not because it's required coursework, but because you can't 'un-see' something, just as you can't un-learn something (which I suppose is different than forgetting it). So, now that I've 4 years of experience teaching, I find it very difficult to reflect on only one aspect of a class afterward. Because, inevitably, all the aspects are linked. If, for example, if I try to reflect on my seating arrangements, it naturally leads me to think about monitoring and then monitoring leads onto CCQ-ing [concept checking questioning] and CCQ-ing leads onto feedback and feedback into motivation and so on and so forth. I suppose the sign of a good teacher is one who's able to simultaneously monitor all of these things as they're occurring in 'real time' (aka the classroom) and fine-tune his/her teaching at the moment, but I'm not quite to that stage yet. I do have moments of 'meta-monitoring' during class sometimes, where I'm aware in that instant that something is or isn't working and

```
I can pinpoint the reason why, as opposed to just having a
vague feeling that it's not working as I did in my first years
teaching.
     But, back to my point. While I understand that reflection
is necessary to develop into a more fully aware teacher, it
can also be mentally/emotionally exhausting, especially for
someone who has more introverted tendencies and might take
a class that goes poorly to heart. Perhaps this is just a
personal problem. I often feel that my self-reflections are
incomplete if I choose to limit them by only focusing on one
aspect of a class, as I feel it gives an incomplete picture.
But, I'm not sure what else to do within the time constraints.
I suppose that's the purpose of the blog - to provide an
additional forum in which to provide feedback, but I feel it
saps my creativity that I could be using to plan lessons. I
still don't feel that I'm explaining my point particularly
well and I don't want it to feel that I'm giving out about
the course requirements, as I feel they are, in general, good
ones. It's just that I imagine some people take blogging and
reflecting lightly, as more of something to do to fill a
requirement, but I don't because I find it genuinely helpful.
But, if you're giving it your all, it can be severely deplet-
ing. That's all.
```

The teacher here is offering a very honest post about the demands put on them by
the reflective process, which she refers to as a *burden*, and something which is both
mentally and emotionally exhausting. She rationalises this point for the reader, and
offers a lovely example of how various classroom aspects are in fact linked, and therefore thinking about one aspect leads on to another. She, without naming it, addresses
the act of in-action reflection (Schön 1991) where she notes that 'good teachers' can
monitor their actions in class ('meta-monitoring'); however, she admits that she has
not yet reached that level of proficiency. This is because reflection-on-action (Schön,
1991) is often easier for the more novice teachers. She finishes her post showing deep
awareness of the values of RP, but an honest overview of the time required to do it
well. If we compare the last three reflections to extract 7.18, we see how face-to-face
reflections can differ.

Extract 7.18 (Mode 3: Face-to-Face Peer Tutor-Guided Group Discussions)

```
NST1: And I still find that after this I'm still today is the last
      day we're ever gonna be together lecturing and I still feel
      that my my knowledge of grammar hasn't improved sufficiently
NST2: Yeah
NST3: Especially like XX I might learn stuff but still you might
      just you know know the names of the tenses
```

NST1 is reflecting on the fact that she has not developed her knowledge of grammar to an acceptable level, and while there is mutual support from the other members in the group, we see no evidence of rationalisation, no attempts at surmising why this might be, and no level of responsibility on the part of the teachers. This is not to say that face-to-face reflections are not worthwhile, but development of thought needs time and space, or the voice of an experienced other who can ask relevant questions to scaffold the reflections, an example of which can be seen in the TP context in extract 7.19.

Extract 7.19 (Mode 1: Face-to-Face Teaching Practice Feedback Interactions)

```
NST: I think that would I need to picture of myself different from
     them em
TPS: Do you feel that you kind of relate to them more as your peers
     rather than your students?
NST: Yeah definitely like I I feel strange if I'm trying to approach
     that from a teacher perspective I still I don't feel comfort-
     able with that yet
TPS: Ok have you read that chapter that was a up on Sulis?[1]
NST: In the classroom
TPS: Yeah and cause a lot of those thoughts and issues were dealt
     with
```

This student appears to have difficulty with the fact that she is doing her weekly teaching practice with learners her own age. She is therefore struggling with her own identity as a teacher (Riordan and Farr 2015) and, while in this example there is clear evidence of her trying to understand the issue at hand (compared to the previous extract), the TP tutor is playing a key role in scaffolding her thoughts. Accordingly, it could be that on-line reflections can be deeper because of the mode, but face-to-face reflections can deepen with the help of more experienced others.

We can therefore say that on-line modes offer more with regard to analytical thinking as teachers have time to deliberate their thoughts, and therefore use more knowledge, experience, reasoning and analysis to develop and deepen their reflections. This is not to say that reflection cannot happen in face-to-face modes, as deeper levels of reflection may emerge from collaborative dialogue with more experienced others when scaffolding occurs. With this in mind, the following section examines the impact of the speaker paradigms on RP.

7.5 THE LANGUAGE OF REFLECTION IN INDIVIDUAL AND SCAFFOLDED MODES

Once again, the words used in the top 300 items in the frequency list for Chart 7.1 were examined in the individual compared to the scaffolded data, the results of which can be seen in Chart 7.8.

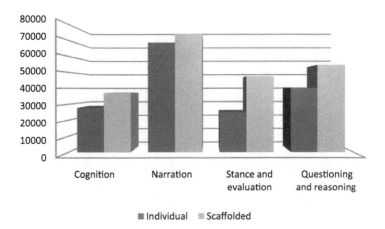

Chart 7.8   Indicators of reflection: individual and scaffolded (WPM)

As with novice versus experienced, and face-to-face versus on-line data, these trends bear resemblance to those seen in Chart 7.1, showing that narration is the function with the highest frequency, followed by questioning and reasoning, stance and evaluation, and, finally, cognition for the scaffolded data sets, while there is more cognition than stance in the individual data sets. It is worth reminding ourselves that the individual data sets consist of blogs and portfolios, and are therefore in written language, hence contain more evidence of cognition. Also, similar to results for Chart 7.5, the features of stance such as *like*, *just* and *kind* are much more frequent in face-to-face compared to written language, therefore resulting in higher levels of stance features in scaffolded contexts. When going through the frequency lists for any deviations, it was found that the cognitive items *know* and *think* were much higher in the scaffolded data compared to the individual data, and this is because these items are being used in their discourse marker functions in the forms, *you know* and *I think*. Interestingly, another difference in the data sets is that the cognitive verb *feel/felt* occurs much more in the individual data compared to the scaffolded data (*feel* is twice as frequent, and *felt* is almost four times as frequent), which could be indicative that individual spaces are needed for students to openly share their feelings and emotions (see also Riordan 2018). In general, the scaffolded data sets contain more evidence of all functions compared to the individual data sets, thus reinforcing the significance of having collaborative discussions for RP (Mann and Walsh 2013), and of social learning in general, as discussed in Chapter 2.

Chart 7.9 shows the variables of affect, cognition and tense references across the individual and scaffolded data.

The recurring trend of cognition being higher than affect is present. Interestingly, there are no major differences in terms of affect or cognitive processes whether reflections are individual or scaffolded. The only marked difference is that there is more of a focus on the present in the scaffolded data and more focus on the past in the individual data. This could be a result of the tasks, as those that were individual

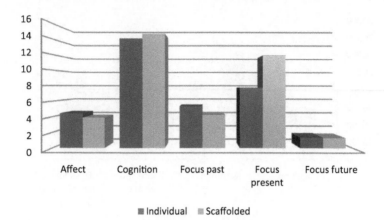

Chart 7.9   LIWC (2015) variables for individual and scaffolded data

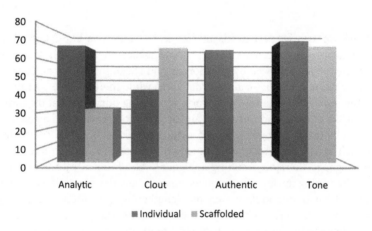

Chart 7.10   LIWC (2015) summary variables for individual and scaffolded data

were retrospective in nature (blogs and portfolios), therefore a narrative tense would derive from this. The four summary variables across the individual and scaffolded data can be seen in Chart 7.10.

Here we can see that analytical thinking is higher in individual reflections than the scaffolded ones. This was initially somewhat surprising as we assumed that the scaffolded reflections would be higher in terms of analysis because the lecturer was assisting in the RP process. However, the task type is obviously important here, as the individual reflections were on-line, through blogs and portfolios, which are both very well known for the promotion of analytical thinking skills (Farias and Ramírez 2009; Parkes and Kajder 2010; Pryor and Bitter 2008; Yang 2009). Also higher in the individual data is authenticity, therefore being honest and vulnerable may be easier when writing and, indeed reflecting, in a private space, which the results on *feel* and *felt* being higher in the individual data discussed earlier support. This also reinforces what was found in the

Table 7.7   *I* think* in the individual and scaffolded contexts

Constructions	Individual	Scaffolded
Cognition – mental state, opinions and so on	66/66 = 100%	221/236 = 94%
Hedge	0	12/236 = 5%
Unsure	0	3/236 = 1%

previous section where on-line modes facilitate more honest and open reflections, as the individual data sets are from on-line environments. Clout is higher in the scaffolded discussions, again reinforcing what was found in the previous section, that teachers might feel the need to show more confidence in group settings than individual ones, which is important for shared learning. Once again, the tone is similar and positive in both data sets. In order to examine the issue of analytical thinking a little more, *think* (one of the top three most frequent cognitive verbs) is analysed below.

7.5.1 THINK

The construction *I* think* occurs 380 times (WPM) in the individual data and 875 times in the scaffolded data. It must be borne in mind that the scaffolded data sets are predominantly face-to-face, which account for the very high frequency of this item, as Biber et al. (1999) note that *think* is especially frequent in conversation. Table 7.7 shows its uses across the data sets. In all cases, *I* think* is being used in a cognitive/mental manner in the individual data sets and the majority of time in the scaffolded data sets. The teachers are expressing their thoughts, opinions and beliefs about various issues, which is key to reflection. Extracts 7.20–7.21 exemplify how this is realised in the data sets.

Extract 7.20 (Mode 5: On-Line Blogs)

```
NST: I really did feel the presence of the observer this week and
     I also think the students noticed it. I think they were much
     more reserved than they usually would be.
```

Extract 7.20 comes from a novice blog, where the teacher is reflecting on the presence of the observer, and uses evidence of the students' behaviour to make her point, therefore showing awareness of events. Unfortunately, this teacher does not expand on her opinions, nor does she offer suggestions for how this could be dealt with in future lessons, which would in fact strengthen her reflections. A more developed reflection can be seen in extract 7.21.

Extract 7.21 (Mode 5: On-Line Blogs)

```
NST: One thing I didn't think went so well was the listening.
     I really liked the idea of splitting up the comprehension
```

questions and having each of them only answer one. They can be so overwhelming to do in a chunk at the end of a lesson, and I was purposefully trying to avoid having to read out the answers myself, since I thought doing so last time led to way too much TTT [Teacher Talking Time]. So I decided to try something new. But, the listening itself was hard to comprehend. I'm not sure any of them actually got the answer to their individual question, except the girl who had the first one. And I'm not sure how well that activity tested their comprehension of the listening. If none of them got the answer to their own question right, then they were sharing the wrong information with each other. I should've maybe tested the answers first before sharing them, but I couldn't think of a way to do that without rendering the sharing point obsolete.

This post is a lovely example of reflection in terms of Jay and Johnson's (2002) levels of descriptive, comparative and critical reflection, outlined in Chapter 3. The novice teacher begins her description of the event by explaining that she believed the listening task in a given lesson did not work well (descriptive). She then goes on to discuss why she thought this, namely there was too much TTT. This is an example of comparative reflections where she is integrating her knowledge of good practice in language teaching in order to rationalise her reflections. She moves on to discuss the perceived issues she had with the new listening task, and after using evidence from the lesson (comparative reflection), she makes reference to what she should have done, thereby showing a better understanding, moving into the critical level of reflection. The differences in the levels of analytical thought and reflection in these blog posts (extracts 7.20 and 7.21) demonstrate either differing abilities, effort or interest on the part of the novice teachers with regard to RP. In support of this point, Coulson and Harvey (2013: 402) highlight that 'not all teachers are disposed to reflect'. Extract 7.22 is a good example of how collaborative reflections can happen.

Extract 7.22 (Mode 3: Face-to-Face Peer Tutor-Guided Group Discussions)

NST1: I think that the purpose of learning a language is to
    communicate
PT: Mmh
NST1: And so yeah I I don't think I mean we all can communicate but
    we all don't have perfect grammar
NST2: True
NST1: And I think that that really needs to be emphasised and I
    think that many students have never either been told that or
    don't personally feel like that's possible
PT: Mmhm

The teacher is voicing her opinions, and the peer tutor and one other student are facilitating her thought process simply by using response tokens (*mmhm*, *true*) to show listenership (Bublitz 1988; Duncan and Fiske 1977; Farr 2003; Gardener 2001; McCarthy 2002, 2003; Schiffrin 1987), involved communication, and to will the teacher to continue. Some might argue that this is not scaffolding; however, we argue that they are keeping the line of communication open so the teacher can rationalise and explain her thoughts.

Interestingly, while there are 236 (raw) examples of *I* think* in the scaffolded data, there are 191 examples of *do you think* coming from the lecturer, the peer tutor or the peers, which shows evidence of the more experienced other feeding cognitive thought. Examples can be seen in extracts 7.23–7.24.

Extract 7.23 (Mode 2: Face-to-Face Lecturer-Guided Group Discussions)

```
L:   Reflective practice what is it what does it mean to me what are
     your opinions on it what do you think reflection reflective
     practice is what does it mean to you?
EST: I think it's like feedback I can give to myself
L:   Mhmm
EST: How I can see how weak and strong points in my work
L:   Feedback from who?
EST: It's em self feedback
L:   Ok
EST: Yes its … or auto feedback
L:   Mhmm mhmhm
EST: Well I don't know I think does this also mean like student com-
     prehension affect this feedback or not I'm just asking myself
L:   Mhmm
EST: Does the result of the test or exam perfect how good teacher
     I am or not?
L:   Mhmm
```

The lecturer opens by asking the questions about what RP is and what it means to the teachers. One teacher replies by saying it is feedback, and in order to get more from the teacher, the lecturer asks who the feedback is from. This second question by the lecturer then prompts the teacher to delve more deeply into what feedback could be useful for RP, and the use of response tokens by the lecturer, along with prompts, leads the teacher to realise that self-reflections, student feedback and exam results could all be potential lenses for the teacher to view his teaching and development. This collaborative discussion therefore gave this teacher a more developed and nuanced understanding. In fact, guiding students to understand their values, beliefs, classroom events and so on is important and often lies with the lecturer/mentor (Coulson and Harvey 2013). The lecturer can also try to engage teachers in more future-oriented talk as in extract 7.24.

Extract 7.24 (Mode 2: Face-to-Face Lecturer-Guided Group Discussions)

```
L:   Yeah do you think you feel you'd like to try something new now
     because you've got so many new?
NST: Yeah I'm going to try different methodologies of teaching and
     and moving away from the PPP although it does have its place
     but I want it to be more task based
L:   Yeah what about you? What are your plans?
```

The lecturer is encouraging the teachers to try to think about their future plans. The response is very welcome as the teacher is considering trying different methodologies, which shows advancement in her development and also her knowledge and understanding of the field. Peers can also encourage reflective and analytical thought as seen in extract 7.25.

Extract 7.25 (Mode 5: On-Line Blogs)

```
EST: Another question is regarding technology based environments
     such as www.futurelearn.com which is kindly introduced by
     Dr XXX. What do you think will be the future of learning and
     teaching based on this phenomena? Do you think it will come
     fast and we will stop going to teach in colleges within a few
     years? Or do you think the college roles will be changed. I am
     asking this because now I am conscious regarding our chang-
     ing teaching methods and habits in future based on our use of
     technology in the past-time. How we can facilitate it?
```

Here we see how a collaborative blog used by the experienced teachers can encourage self-reflection on a topic, in this case, technology in education, while also encouraging their peers to reflect on the issue.

In general, there does not appear to be significant differences with regard to individual or scaffolded reflections; the individual reflections are on-line and therefore allow the teachers more time to think and process their ideas, and they possibly allow for more open and honest reflections as they are private spaces. The scaffolded discussions can push reflections deeper and can prompt understandings of issues that might not come if reflecting alone.

7.6 SUMMARY

This chapter has explored the language of reflection, where we found functions of narration, cognition, stance and evaluation, and questioning and reasoning being core to this. The trend in general seems to be that in TEC as a whole, there is more evidence of narration, followed by questioning and reasoning, then stance and evaluation, and finally cognition. We believe that narration is required for the teachers to situate their discussions, and questioning and reasoning follows because the teachers are questioning themselves, their and others' practices, and making connections with theory in order to better understand themselves, teaching tools, and the overall practice of teaching and learning. Within these reflections, stance, evaluations, feelings, emotions and cognition are expressed. Doing this is part of RP; therefore, through language, teachers can make better understandings of issues in teaching and learning, and situate themselves within the explanation/full membership stage of community membership (Freeman 2016, see Chapter 2).

We also examined potential differences between novice and more experienced student teachers' reflections and found that novice teachers demonstrate less analytical thinking, possibly because they have less experience to draw on than the experienced teachers do. The more experienced teachers are more confident while the novices are more vulnerable in their articulations. We also believe that the mode impacts on this as do interaction patterns. The fact that the experienced teachers had more intense RP training (an entire module) could also be a factor in the higher levels of analytical thought and confidence in their reflections, therefore supporting the point made that teachers need to be taught how to reflect (Borg 2018; Farrell 2018).

Another distinction we made was between reflections in on-line and face-to-face modes, and to this end, we found that there were more expressions of emotion and feelings on-line as well as analytical thinking, for which on-line spaces are celebrated. The face-to-face mode appears to encourage teachers to be confident in their discussions with one another, which is of utmost importance for social and shared learning within a CoP. The final distinction we made was between participant paradigms, namely individual and scaffolded reflections, and we found more evidence of openly sharing feelings and analytical thought in the individual data sets, although this was more than likely a result of the mode (on-line). Similar to the differences between face-to-face and on-line modes, the scaffolded discussions allow teachers to show confidence thus enhancing shared and collaborative learning. Furthermore, we saw evidence that scaffolded reflections might become deeper with the help of the more experienced other/teacher educator, or that new avenues for reflection might be prompted.

RP is therefore evidenced as a complex process, with many variables affecting one another, for example, the level of teacher experience, the mode, participant paradigms, the context and the task types. To help teachers to become reflective practitioners, we believe that they need to be educated and supported in appropriate RP processes, and be offered a combined approach of various modes of communication, various speaker paradigms, and various tasks and contexts within a social constructivist environment. In line with Coulson and Harvey (2013: 408), our research shows that 'exploring the diversity of reflective tools and media offers more inclusive practice and encourages cognitive and creative approaches to reflection that may lead to aesthetic and emotional knowing'. We will therefore continue to create 'an effective climate and context for reflection' (Coulson and Harvey 2013: 403) at our institution in order to prepare our teachers to be reflective practitioners.

7.7 TASKS

1. Reflect on your teaching philosophy in your own time and take some notes. Then, in groups of three to four, reflect on your teaching philosophy by discussing your notes with one another. For you, what were the advantages of both individual and collaborative reflections?
2. Examine one or two extracts from your own reflections on teaching in terms of the language you use (for example, nouns, verbs, adjectives and adverbs, as seen in Section 7.2). Are they similar to the findings in this chapter? Share your findings with a peer and discuss what information such as this can tell you about your own reflective writing.

NOTE

1. Sulis (Sakai) is the Virtual Learning Environment used at the university from which the data emanates.

8

CONCLUSIONS

8.1 INTRODUCTION

In this book we have endeavoured to show how a CADS approach was successfully used to investigate the social interactions of student teachers with peers, lecturers, tutors and TP supervisors across a variety of communication modes. This has made it possible to expand data-led research within the CoP and RP research paradigms and thereby bring a more bottom-up perspective to the existing academic literature in these fields. From this, a wealth of insights has been gained as to the complex processes involved in student teacher socialisation into the ELTE CoP, professional identity formation and the journey towards becoming reflective practitioners. Moreover, we have achieved a more finely nuanced understanding of the mechanisms by which student teachers learn and grow professionally, and how best this can be fostered and guided in the scaffolded environment of pre-service (MA) and CPD type (PhD) TESOL programmes. In this final chapter, we review the key trends uncovered in the data analyses, from which we offer some suggestions in terms of their implications for research in the CoP and RP fields, and for future directions in ELTE.

8.2 KEY FINDINGS

In line with the data-led approach argued for in this book, the analysis began with initial, exploratory CL investigations. The first layer of analysis was concerned with establishing student teacher participation levels across the various modes (see Chapter 4) and exploring the role of participant paradigm in promoting student teacher engagement, and therefore community building. As the highest levels of teacher participation recorded were for those face-to-face and on-line modes featuring peer tutor-guided discussions, this provided strong evidence of the valuable contribution that peer tutors can make in encouraging collaborative dialogue and shared learning on ELTE programmes alongside lecturers and TP supervisors, thereby supporting earlier claims made by Farr and Riordan (2015) and Riordan (2018). The varying student teacher participant levels observed also offered early indications that the distinct modes, and the specific participant paradigms featured in each case, might contribute in different ways to community formation. From the second layer of CL analysis, also presented in Chapter 4, areas of lexical saliency in TEC were identified as an initial platform from which to explore lexical, interactional and discourse features associated with social and collaborative learning in an ELTE environment. This suggested that the student teachers' use of metalanguage, personal pronouns and cognitive/evaluative expression might be areas meriting further quantitative and qualitative analyses to gain insight into the fabric and workings of this CoP and the processes by which student teachers become socialised into its norms and practices. These initial CL findings thereby shaped the route that the following chapters would take, with Chapter 5 focusing on metalanguage, Chapter 6 on language teacher identity, and Chapter 7 on reflective practice, with some inevitable overlaps.

8.2.1 METALANGUAGE AND TOPIC

The student teachers' use of metalanguage was investigated with a view to gauging the extent to which they were becoming familiar with the professional terms associated with the profession of teaching English, how this newfound knowledge was being evoked and articulated, and what this might mean in terms of student teacher learning. It was also anticipated that the findings would add to our understanding of the knowledge base of the CoP and, therefore, its shared repertoire. The initial measurement of distributional trends for metalanguage use across the various face-to-face and on-line modes offered early indications of the role they might play in creating a useful and safe space for student teachers to articulate the discursive practices of the professional community they were entering, and therefore their contribution to professional identity formation and alignment. In this regard, the on-line modes were found to be more conducive to metalanguage use than others, especially the portfolios and the blogs where significantly more individual items were found than in chat and the discussion fora. Meanwhile, in the face-to-face data, the lecturer and peer tutor-guided group discussions revealed a higher level of use than in the TP feedback interactions. Further qualitative analyses of these trends in relation to key contextual variables revealed that participant paradigm and the novice/experienced status of the student teachers were the main determining factors for the outcomes observed. The varying levels of metalanguage use observed within modes across the specified subcategories also suggested different levels of engagement with the CoP by the student teachers in each grouping. This was seen to be indicative of either partial or full membership of the TESOL teaching community. It also provided insights as to the ways in which membership role and status were being evoked and manifested by student teachers at each stage of their professional development.

Crucially, the findings for metalanguage use also provided a platform from which to explore topics of interest and concern to the student teachers and the wider ELTE community, as further evidence of community building and shared repertoire. This revealed student teacher engagement with a wide and diverse range of topics and that important links were being made between educational/linguistic theory and practice. In their social interactions and reflective writing across the various modes, there was also strong evidence of awareness-raising and learning in relation to key areas of professional knowledge as well as the norms and practices of the CoP, at both local and international levels. What was also striking was that some of the face-to-face and on-line modes were found to play an important role in the affective realm of communication, often serving as an outlet for stress and frustration and a space for mutual emotional support by peers. This was especially evident in those modes featuring peer tutors, which again emphasised the valuable contribution they can make as part of a holistic approach to teacher education. Meanwhile, modes involving lecturers and TP supervisors were found to be instrumental for awareness-raising and targeted scaffolding around subject knowledge and practical aspects of English language pedagogy. The findings in this area thereby provided further empirical evidence of student teacher socialisation and learning, as well as adding to our understanding of the rich fabric and complex workings of this professional teaching community.

8.2.2 LANGUAGE TEACHER IDENTITY

In the analysis framed around language teacher identity, a further layer was added to the picture being built of student teacher socialisation and learning, with a focus in this case on professional identity formation. To gain insight into how professional identity was being evoked and articulated, and what this might reveal, personal pronoun use was explored from a comparative novice/experienced student teacher perspective using frequency lists and concordances. Pronoun references showed evidence of both *I* and *you* for individual and joint identity construction, with *we* indexing CoP alignment, both of which are required for community members. The analysis also demonstrated that, as might be expected, at the early stage of their professional development, the novices were more preoccupied with individual rather than the group identity. Moreover, they portrayed a more hesitant and less confident identity than their experienced student teacher counterparts, who were typically more confident and assured in terms of their place in the professional teaching community.

However, a more finely nuanced examination based on the cluster *I am* revealed a number of emerging identities for student teachers in both groupings, which were, on occasion, realised differently by each. For instance, in both cases, a personal identity emerged, with little difference shown between the groupings. A language-related identity was also evident with a focus on the status of non-native English speaker teachers. Interestingly, while this was referred to by the novices, it was not discussed by those in the more experienced grouping, which may have been due to the fact that many of those involved came from precisely this background. This suggests that they may have avoided this issue in order to uphold a confident and assured teacher identity. A disciplinary identity also emerged; however, in the case of the novices, there was instability in terms of the nature and levels of confidence being expressed. This suggested a state of flux in their identity construction, as well as various levels of maturity across the novice spectrum. Interestingly, the novice student teachers' professional development was viewed in terms of their MA programme. By contrast, the experienced student teachers were generally found to be more confident and positive about their professional identity. They were also seen to focus on professional development in more independent ways. This indexes both time and experience as core to the construction of a professional identity. The final aspect of identity revealed related to a student identity; in this regard, the novices referred to themselves as student teachers whereas those in the more experienced cohort described themselves as PhD students. What was further striking in the data was the saliency of *we* in the experienced student teacher data, which was used by those in this grouping to align themselves with the teaching CoP. By contrast, the novices were found to depict a peripheral identity in the sense that, at this stage of their professional development, they did not yet perceive themselves to be fully part of the professional teaching community, or at least did not articulate this.

From this, further investigations were undertaken to explore the ways in which teacher identity was being constructed across the various face-to-face and online modes, taking into account also individual and scaffolded paradigms. While few differences were generally observed in this regard between the face-to-face and online modes, *we* featured significantly higher in the former data. This was attributed to two possible reasons; firstly, that a group identity needed to be explicitly marked when in the presence of interlocutors, and secondly, that in the face-to-face modes, there was a more experienced other present, which could have had an impact on the perceived need to index group identity. Furthermore, the individual and scaffolded data comparison seemed to show that the student teachers were more at ease displaying an individual identity when in collaborative settings, and that the scaffolded other could play a key role in aiding their identity construction. The analysis of identity construction thereby confirmed that using data to examine the construction of identity for novice and experienced student teachers is a worthwhile endeavour, and that the amount of experience has implications for identity construction, with novice identities constantly being shaped and reshaped as they progress in their socialisation into the CoP. A further key finding from the analysis was that having access to various social spaces (online and face-to-face), as well as different patterns of interaction (individual and scaffolded), would seem to impact on the identities being portrayed at various times. It has also provided evidence that various levels of participation are acceptable and indeed essential within a CoP framework. From the findings for teacher identity formation, we turn next to those relating to the theme of reflective practice.

8.2.3 REFLECTIVE PRACTICE

It was intended that the examination of reflective language across the various TEC modes and data sets would add a final crucial layer to the account being provided of the role and nature of student teacher interactions in the scaffolded environment of postgraduate TESOL programmes. In this regard, the findings in this area support the previous conclusions reached in the areas of teacher socialisation and identity formation, as well as correlating with the existing research literature in the RP field. For example, there was strong evidence of cognitive thought (*think, know* and *learn*), of narration (*be* and *do*), of stance and evaluation (*good, better* and *interesting*) and of rationalisation (*so* and *as*). This aligns with the research discussed in Chapter 3 where RP is viewed as providing a valuable platform and space for teachers to express their thoughts and wishes, to explain their beliefs and values, and to reflect retrospectively and on future events, in order to understand them more fully, to offer opinions, reactions and thoughts while at the same making evaluations with the aim of revising thinking and actions, and to rationalise thoughts and actions.

The use of CL methods and tools made it possible to trace the frequency of the specified core linguistic devices in the realisation of RP, with items relating to narration found to be the most salient, followed by those associated with rationalisation, stance, evaluation and, lastly, cognition. The analysis also revealed that RP can be realised in many ways, and that the level of the reflections of novice/experienced student teachers, the mode of reflection (face-to-face/online) and the interaction patterns observed within reflective discussions (individual/scaffolded) all appeared to impact on how student teachers reflect. For example, when comparing the novice/experienced student teacher discourse, the former were found to focus more on the past while there was a general lack of future-oriented reflection by both cohorts. Interestingly, more qualitative follow-up analyses revealed that the novices tended to focus retrospectively on classroom events and experiences, while the more experienced student teachers reflected on a broader range of topics, which was attributed to their more substantive knowledge and experience. Moreover, there was greater evidence of analytical thinking on the part of the latter while greater vulnerability was displayed by the former. This suggested that the more experienced teachers had the necessary tools, past experiences and professional maturity to be able to engage in reflection of a more analytical kind, and to do so with greater maturity and confidence.

The comparative analysis of face-to-face/on-line modes showed that the former type facilitated a focus on the present, where the online modes were more conducive to analytical reflection of the retrospective kind. This was attributed to the greater amount of time and space offered in on-line modes for thinking and reflecting. Furthermore, during on-line reflections, it is likely that student teachers feel less vulnerable as face-saving or power issues are not at play in the same way as would be typical of face-to-face contexts. This may also explain why there was stronger evidence of open and frank reflection in online modes. Despite this, face-to-face reflections were also found to be fruitful, with many examples of highly beneficial scaffolded reflections across the various contexts.

The final variable explored in the analysis was the nature and effectiveness of individual/scaffolded reflections. In this regard, the scaffolded contexts revealed a stronger focus on the present while the individually produced discourse was more often linked with the past, with the nature of tasks featured across the various modes likely to have been a major influence. Interestingly, there was also evidence of more analytical thinking in the individual reflections. In this case, the fact that these were also on-line may help to explain this finding given that on-line modes are well suited to the promotion of analytical thought. A further trend observed was that there was more honesty and vulnerability in the individual data. Here, the importance of the more experienced other in scaffolding RP was emphasised and exemplified in the discourse. It was also noted that not all student teachers are willing to fully engage in RP, or are suited to this educational approach, which is an important factor that should be borne in mind by teacher educators. In general, the individual reflections allowed the teachers more time to think and process their ideas, and allowed for more open and honest reflections, while the scaffolded discussions seemed to foster deeper reflections with the aid of the more experienced other. In these ways, the analysis has provided a wealth of insights concerning the nature of the language of reflection. It has also underscored the merits of encouraging RP via multiple avenues, including a range of face-to-face and on-line modes, with varied participant paradigms, while at the same time emphasising the impact of individual preferences, abilities and learning styles on the nature and quality of the reflections engaged in by student teachers. The overriding conclusion reached from the analysis is that one of the key ways of socialising student teachers into a CoP is by encouraging them to reflect deeply, both collaboratively and individually, on their practices.

8.3 IMPLICATIONS

The findings presented have many important implications for ELTE. The analysis of metalanguage and topic, teacher identity and reflective discourse has brought to light the important benefits that can be gained for student teachers at different stages of their professional careers from social interaction across a range of face-to-face and on-line modes. In particular, it has uncovered the kind of mediation and guidance that lecturers, TP supervisors and peer tutors can provide, all of which is key to scaffolding learning and promoting inclusivity. This was seen to be of vital importance on pre-service teacher education programmes involving novices, and for all programmes where there are student teachers from international backgrounds as they are likely to need more targeted support around language use. The research reported on has also underscored the supportive, complementary role that peer tutor-guided discussions can play in the socialisation process, especially in the affective and reflective realms of communication.

The exploration of teacher identity has also revealed key differences in identity construction between novice and experienced student teachers, which can help to inform teacher education programmes. For instance, our findings and conclusions suggest that creating opportunities for dialogic interaction between student teachers at different stages of their professional careers might enhance the development of professional identities in each case. For novices in particular, engaging in collaborative dialogue with more experienced teachers is imperative to help them to feel part of the community and to enable a more confident, secure and self-assured identity to emerge. Meanwhile, the findings relating to RP have further suggested that while various modes and participant paradigms are beneficial, teacher educators must take into account the level of experience, the context and the task types featured, as these can impact on the quality of reflective discourse. A further implication is that teachers need explicit training to understand and engage in RP and that teacher educators must be aware that some student teachers may be less predisposed to RP than others, and may therefore need more encouragement and support.

As illustrated, the findings confirm the wide range of cognitive, social and affective benefits that can be accrued when student teachers engage in social interactions with peers and more expert others across varied modes of communication for the purpose of collaborative dialogue, shared learning and reflective practice. These findings are important as they provide empirical support for the growing theoretical arguments made for the development of holistic approaches to teacher education (Farr and Riordan 2015; Farrell 2016a; Mann and Walsh 2017; Riordan 2018). Beck and Kosnik (2006) believe that a constructivist approach in teacher education is not merely an interesting concept but may also assist with some of the practical problems facing teacher education today. Accordingly, reflection and discussion are the key concepts that can be taken from this theory and incorporated into teacher education programmes. This book has demonstrated the ways in which this can successfully be achieved, thereby offering obvious practical applications that can help to advance teacher education approaches in terms of the design of module content and tasks on future ELTE programmes and in relation to the modes of communication made available to students.

REFERENCES

Ädel, A. (2010), 'How to use corpus linguistics in the study of political discourse', in McCarthy, M. and O'Keeffe, A. (eds), *The Routledge Handbook of Corpus Linguistics*, London: Routledge, pp. 591–604.

Ädel, A. and Reppen, R. (2008), 'The challenges of different settings: An overview', in Ädel, A. and Reppen. R. (eds), *Corpora and Discourse. The Challenges of Different Settings*, Amsterdam: John Benjamins, pp. 1–6.

Ahmed, M. K. (1994), 'Speaking as cognitive regulation: A Vygotskian perspective on dialogic communication', in Lantolf, J. P. and Appel, G. (eds), *Vygotskian Approaches to Second Language Research*, Westport: Ablex, pp. 157–71.

Akbari, R. (2007), 'Reflections on reflection: A critical appraisal of reflective practices in L2 teacher education', *System*, 35: 2, 192–207.

Aljaafreh, A. L. and Lantolf, J. P. (1994), 'Negative feedback as regulation and second language learning in the zone of proximal development', *The Modern Language Journal*, 78: 4, 465–83.

Anderson, C. W. (1989), 'Implementing instructional programs to promote meaningful, self-regulated learning', in Brophy, J. (ed.), *Advances in Research on Teaching: Teaching for Meaningful Understanding and Self-regulated Learning, Vol. 1*, Greenwich, CT: JAI Press, pp. 311–34.

Andrews, S. (1999), 'Why do L2 teachers need to know about language? Teacher metalinguistic awareness and input for learning', *Language and Education*, 13: 3, 161–71.

Andrews, S. (2001), 'The language awareness of the L2 teacher: Its impact upon pedagogical practice', *Language Awareness*, 10: 2–3, 75–90.

Aneja, G. A. (2016), '(Non)native speakered: Rethinking (non)nativeness and teacher identity in TESOL teacher education', *TESOL Quarterly*, 50: 3, 572–96.

Antón, M. (1999), 'The discourse of a learner-centred classroom: Sociocultural perspectives on teacher-learner interaction in the second language classroom', *Modern Language Journal*, 83: 3, 303–18.

Ashraf, H. and Rarieya, J. F. A. (2008), 'Teacher development through reflective conversations – possibilities and tensions: APakistan case', *Reflective Practice*, 9: 3, 269–79.

Atkinson, D. (2002), 'Toward a sociocognitive approach to second language acquisition', *Modern Language Journal*, 86: 4, 525–45.

Bailey, K. M. (1990), 'The use of diary studies in teacher education programs', in Richards, J. C. and Nunan, D. (eds.), *Second Language Teacher Education*, Cambridge: Cambridge University Press, pp. 215–26.

Bakhtin, M. M. (1981), *The Dialogic Imagination. Four Essays by M. M. Bakhtin., C. Emerson and M. Holquist*, Austin: University of Texas Press.

Barkhuizen, G. (2017), 'Language teacher identity research: An introduction', in Barkhuizen, G. (ed.), *Reflections on Language Teacher Identity Research*, London and New York: Routledge, pp. 1–11.

Bax, S. (1997), 'Roles for a teacher educator in context-sensitive teacher education', *English Language Teaching Journal*, 51: 3, 232–41.

Beauvois, M. H. (1998), 'Conversations in slow motion: Computer-mediated communication in the foreign language classroom', *Canada Modern Language Review*, 54, 198–214.

Beck, C. and Kosnik, C. (2006), *Innovations in Teacher Education*, Albany: State University Press.

Berry, R. (2005), 'Making the most of metalanguage', *Language Awareness*, 14: 1, 3–20.

Biber, D. (2006), *University Language. A Corpus-Based Study of Spoken and Written Registers*, Amsterdam: John Benjamins.

Biber, D., Conrad, S. and Leech, G. (2002), *Longman Student Grammar of Spoken and Written English*, New York: Longman.

Biber, D., Johansson, S., Leech, G., Conrad, S. and Finegan, E. (1999), *Longman Grammar of Spoken and Written English*, London and New York: Longman.

Biesenbach-Lucas, S. (2004), 'Asynchronous web discussions in teacher training courses: Promoting collaborative learning-or not?', *AACE Journal*, 12: 2, 155–70.

Bizzell, P. (1982), 'College composition: Initiation into the academic discourse community', *Curriculum Inquiry*, 12: 2, 191–207.

Black, P. and Plowright, D. (2010), 'A multi-dimensional model of reflective learning for professional development', *Reflective Practice*, 11: 2, 245–58.

Borg, S. (1999), 'Studying teacher cognition in second language grammar teaching', *System*, 27: 1, 19–31.

Borg, S. (2003), 'Teacher cognition in language teaching: A review of research on what language teachers think, know, believe, and do', *Language Teaching*, 36: 2, 81–109.

Borg, S. (2006), *Teacher Cognition and Language Education: Research and Practice*, London and New York: Continuum.

Borg, S. (2009), 'English language teachers' conceptions of research', *Applied Linguistics*, 30: 3, 358–88.

Borg, S. (2018), *Teacher Evaluation: Global Perspectives and their Implications for English Language Teaching*, London: The British Council.

Brandt, C. (2006), 'Allowing for practice: A critical issue in TESOL teacher preparation', *ELT Journal*, 60: 4, 355–64.

Breen, M. P., Hird, B., Milton, M., Oliver, R. and Thwaite, A. (2001), 'Making sense of language teaching: Teachers' principles and classroom practices', *Applied Linguistics*, 22: 4, 470–501.

Breen, P. (2006), 'The education of language teachers in East Asia', *Asian EFL Journal*, 4: 4, 1–13.

Brookfield, S. (1995), *Becoming a Critically Reflective Teacher*, San Francisco: Jossey-Bass.

Brown, G. and Yule, G. (1983), *Discourse Analysis*, Cambridge: Cambridge University Press.

Brown, J. S., Collins, A. and Duguid, P. (1989), 'Situated cognition and the culture of learning', *Educational Researcher*, 18: 1, 32–42.

Brown, P. and Levinson, S. C. (1987) *Politeness: Some Universals in Language Use*, Cambridge: Cambridge University Press.

Browne, H. D. (2000), *Principles of Language Learning and Teaching*, New York: Longman.

Bruner, J. (1985), 'Vygotsky: A historical and conceptual perspective', in Wertsch, J. V. (ed.), *Culture, Communication and Cognition. Vygotskian Perspectives*, New York: Cambridge University Press, pp. 21–34.

Bublitz, W. (1988), *Supportive Fellow-Speakers and Co-operative Conversations*, Amsterdam and Philadelphia: John Benjamins.

Bullough, R. V., Young, J. R., Hall, K. M., Draper, R. J. and Smith, L. K. (2008), 'Cognitive complexity, the first year of teaching, and mentoring', *Teaching and teacher Education*, 24: 7, 1846–58.

Burgess, H. and Mayes, A. S. (2008), 'Using e-learning to support primary trainee teachers' development of mathematical subject knowledge: An analysis of learning and the impact on confidence', *Teacher Development*, 12: 1, 37–55.

Burnett, C. (2003), 'Learning to chat: Tutor participation in synchronous online chat', *Teaching in Higher Education*, 8: 2, 247–61.

Burns, A. (2010), *Doing Action Research in English Language Teaching. A Guide for Practitioners*, New York: Routledge.

Burns, A., Freeman, D. and Edwards, E. (2015), 'Theorizing and studying the language-teaching mind: Mapping research on language teacher cognition', *The Modern Language Journal*, 99: 3, 585–601.

Buzzelli, C. A. and Johnston, B. (2002), *The Moral Dimensions of Teaching: Language, Power and Culture in Classroom Interaction*, New York: Routledge Falmer.

Byram, M. (1997), *Teaching and Assessing Inter-cultural Communicative Competence*, Clevedon: Multilingual Matters.

Calderhead, J. and Gates, P. (1993), 'Introduction', in Calderhead, J. and Gates, P. (eds), *Conceptualizing Reflection in Teacher Development*, London: Falmer Press, pp. 1–10.

Carlson, H. L. (1999), 'From practice to theory: A social constructivist approach to teacher education', *Teachers and Teaching: Theory and Practice*, 5: 2, 203–18.

Carter, K. (1995), 'Teachers' knowledge and learning to teach', in Houston, W. R. (ed.), *Handbook of Research on Teacher Education*, New York: Macmillan, pp. 291–310.

Carter, R. and McCarthy, M. (2006), *Cambridge Grammar of English: A Comprehensive Guide to Spoken and Written Grammar and Usage*, Cambridge: Cambridge University Press.

Castro, M. C. A. (2006), 'Let's chat: An analysis of some discourse features of synchronous chat', *Journal of English Studies and Comparative Literature*, 9: 1, 77–94.

Chappell, P. (2017), 'Interrogating your wisdom of practice to improve classroom practices', *ELT Journal*, 71: 4, 433–44.

Chen, Y., Chen, N.-S. and Tsai, C.-C. (2009), 'The use of online synchronous discussion for web-based professional development for teachers', *Computers and Education*, 53: 4, 1155–66.

Cirocki, A. and Farrell, T. S. C. (2017), 'Reflective practice for the professional development of TESOL practitioners', *The European Journal of Applied Linguists and TEFL*, 6: 2, 5–24.

Coates, J. (1996), *Women Talking to Women*, Oxford: Blackwell.

Copland, F. (2010), 'Causes of tension in post-observation feedback in pre-service teacher training: An alternative view', *Teaching and Teacher Education*, 26: 3, 466–72.

Copland, F. (2012), 'Legitimate talk in feedback conferences', *Applied Linguistics*, 33: 1, 1–20.

Cornford, I. (2002), 'Reflective teaching: Empirical research findings and some implications for teacher education', *Journal of Vocational Education and Training*, 54: 2, 219–35.

Cotterill, J. (2000) *Representing Reality in Court: Power and Persuasion in Trial Discourse as Exemplified by The People V Orenthal James Simpson*, unpublished PhD thesis, University of Cardiff.

Coulson, D. and Harvey, M. (2013), 'Scaffolding student reflection for experience-based learning: A framework', *Teaching in Higher Education*, 18: 4, 401–13.

Coutinho, C. P. (2010), 'Challenges for teacher education in the learning society: Case studies of promising practice', in Yang, H. H. and Chi-Yin-Yuen, S. (eds.), *Handbook of Research on Practices and Outcomes in E-learning: Issues and Trends*, New York: IGI Global, pp. 385–401.

Crookes, G. (2003), *A Practicum in TESOL. Professional Development through Practice*, New York: Cambridge University Press.

Cunningham, F. M. (2001), *Reflective Teaching Practice in Adult ESL Settings*, Washington: ERIC.

Cutting, J. (1999), 'The grammar of the in-group code', *Applied Linguistics*, 20: 2, 179–202.

Cutting, J. (2000), *Analysing the Language of the Discourse Community*, Oxford: Elsevier.

Dakowska, M. (1993), 'Language, metalanguage, and language use: A cognitive, psycholinguistic view', *International Journal of Applied Linguistics*, 3: 1, 79–99.

Daniels, H. (2007), 'Pedagogy', in Daniels, H., Cole, M. and Wertsch, J. V. (eds.), *The Cambridge Companion to Vygotsky*, Cambridge: Cambridge University Press, pp. 307–31.

De-Guerrero, M. C. M. and Villamil, O. S. (2000), 'Activating the ZPD: Mutual scaffolding in L2 peer revision', *Modern Language Journal*, 84: 1, 51–68.

Deng, L. and Yuen, A. H. K. (2011), 'Towards a framework for educational affordances of blogs', *Computers and Education*, 56: 2, 441.

Derks, D., Fischer, A. H. and Bos, A. E. R. (2008), 'The role of emotion in computer-mediated communication: A review', *Computers in Human Behavior*, 24: 3, 766–85.

Dewey, J. (1933), *How We Think*, Chicago: Henry Regnery.

Diaz, R. M., Neal, C. J. and Amaya-Williams, M. (1990), 'The social origins of self-regulation', in Moll, L. C. (ed.), *Vygotsky and Education. Instructional Implications and Applications of Sociohistorical Psychology*, Cambridge: Cambridge University Press, pp. 127–54.

Dilthey, W. (1976), *Selected Writings, H. P. Rickman*, Cambridge: Cambridge University Press.

Dippold, D. (2009), 'Peer feedback through blogs: Student and teacher perceptions in an advanced German class', *ReCALL*, 21: 1, 18–36.

Donato, R. (1994), 'Collective scaffolding in second language learning', in Lantolf, J. P. and Appel, G. (eds.), *Vygotskian Approaches to Second Language Research*, Westport: Ablex, pp. 33–56.

Ducate, L. and Lomicka, L. (2008), 'Adventures in the blogosphere: From blog readers to blog writers', *Computer Assisted Language Learning*, 21: 1, 9–28.

Duff, P. A. and Uchida, Y. (1997), 'The negotiation of teachers' sociocultural identities and practices in post-secondary EFL classrooms', *TESOL Quarterly*, 31: 3, 451–86.

Duncan, S. and Fiske, D. (1977), *Face-to-Face Interaction: Research, Methods and Theory*, Somerset, NJ: John Wiley and Sons.

Dyment, J. E. and Connell, T. S. (2011), 'Assessing the quality of reflection in student journals: A review of the research', *Teaching in Higher Education*, 16: 1, 81–97.

Edge, J. (1992), 'Co-operative development', *English Language Teaching Journal*, 46: 1, 62–70.

Edge, J. (2002), *Continuing Cooperative Development. A Discourse Framework for Individuals as Colleagues*, Ann Arbor: University of Michigan Press.

Elliott, D. (2009), 'Internet technologies and language teacher education', in Thomas, M. (ed.), *Handbook of Research on Web 2.0 and Second Language Learning*, New York: IGI Global, 432–450.

Ellis, E. M. (2016), '"I may be a native speaker but I'm not monolingual": Reimagining all teachers' linguistic identities in TESOL', *TESOL Quarterly*, 50: 3, 597–630.

Evison, J. (2013), 'Turn openings in academic talk: Where goals and roles intersect', *Classroom Discourse*, 4: 1, 3–26.

Faez, F., Cooke, S., Karas, M. and Vidwans, M. (2017), 'Examining the effectiveness of online discussion forums for teacher development', in Farrell, T. S. C. (ed.), *TESOL Voices: Insider Accounts of Classroom Life*, Virginia: TESOL Press.

Fantilli, R. D. and McDougall, D. E. (2009), 'A study of novice teachers: Challenges and supports in the first years', *Teaching and Teacher Education*, 25: 6, 814–25.

Farias, G. M. and Ramírez, M. S. (2009), 'Reflective teacher assessment through evidence e-portfolio, an experience in contrast with reflective diaries', *American Educational Research*

Association On-line, <http://www.ruv.itesm.mx/convenio/catedra/recursos/material/ci_14.pdf> (last accessed 22 March 2019).

Farr, F. (2003), 'Engaged listenership in spoken academic discourse: The case of student-tutor meetings', *Journal of English for Academic Purposes*, 2: 1, 67–85.

Farr, F. (2005a), 'Reflecting on reflections: The spoken word as a professional development tool in language teacher education', in Hughes, R. (ed.), *Spoken English, Applied Linguistics and TESOL: Challenges for Theory and Practice*, Hampshire: Palgrave Macmillan, pp. 182–215.

Farr, F. (2005b), 'Relational strategies in the discourse of professional performance review in an Irish academic environment: The case of language teacher education', in Schneider, K. and Barron, A. (eds), *Variational Pragmatics: The Case of English in Ireland*, Berlin: Mouton de Gruyter, pp. 203–34.

Farr, F. (2010), 'How can corpora be used in teacher education?', in O'Keeffe, A. and McCarthy, M. (eds), *Routledge Handbook of Corpus Linguistics*, London and New York: Routledge, pp. 620–32.

Farr, F. (2011), *The Discourse of Teaching Practice Feedback. An Investigation of Spoken and Written Modes*, New York: Routledge.

Farr, F. (2015), *Practice in TESOL*, Edinburgh: Edinburgh University Press.

Farr, F. and Farrell, A. (2017), 'PENSER: A data-informed reflective practice framework for novice teachers', *The European Journal of Applied Linguistics and TEFL*, 6: 2, 85–103.

Farr, F., Murphy, B. and O'Keeffe, A. (2004), 'The Limerick Corpus of Irish English: Design, description and application', in *Teanga: The Irish Yearbook of Applied Linguistics*, Dublin: IRAAL, pp. 5–29.

Farr, F. and O'Keeffe, A. (2011), 'Applying corpus linguistics', *International Journal of Corpus Linguistics*, 16: 3.

Farr, F. and O'Keeffe, A. (2019), 'Using corpus approaches in English Language Teacher Education', in Walsh, S. and Mann, S. (eds), *The Routledge Handbook of English Language Teacher Education*, New York: Routledge.

Farr, F. and Riordan, E. (2012), 'Students' engagement in reflective tasks: An investigation of interactive and non-interactive discourse corpora', *Classroom Discourse*, 3: 2, 126–43.

Farr, F. and Riordan, E. (2015), 'Tracing the reflective practices of student teachers in online modes', *ReCALL*, 27: 1, 104–23.

Farr, F. and Riordan, E. (2017), 'Prospective and practising teachers look backwards at the theory-practice divide through blogs and e-portfolios', in Farrell, T. S. C. (ed.), *TESOL Voices: Insider Accounts of Classroom Life. Preservice Teacher Education*, Virginia: TESOL, 13–26.

Farrell, A. (2015), 'In the classroom', in Farr, F. (ed.), *Practice in TESOL*, Edinburgh: Edinburgh University Press, pp. 89–110.

Farrell, T. S. C. (2004), *Reflective Practice in Action. 80 Reflection Breaks for Busy Teachers*, Thousand Oaks: Corwin Press.

Farrell, T. S. C. (2009), *Novice Language Teachers. Insights and Perspectives for the First Year*, Sheffield: Equinox.

Farrell, T. S. C. (2015), *Promoting Teacher Reflection in Second Language Education: A Framework for TESOL Professionals*, New York: Routledge.

Farrell, T. S. C. (2016a), 'Anniversary article: The practices of encouraging TESOL teachers to engage in reflective practice: An appraisal of recent research contributions', *Language Teaching Research*, 20: 2, 223–47.

Farrell, T. S. C. (2016b), *From Trainee to Teacher. Reflective Practice for Novice Teachers*, Sheffield: Equinox.

Farrell, T. S. C. (2017), '"Who I am is how I teach": Reflecting on language teacher professional role identity', in Barkhuizen, G. (ed.), *Reflections in Language Teacher Identity Research*, London and New York: Routledge, pp. 183–188.

Farrell, T. S. C. (2018), 'Operationalizing reflective practice in second language teacher education', *Journal of Second Language Teacher Education*, 1: 1, 1–20.

Ferraro, J. M. (2000), 'Reflective practice and professional development. ERIC digest', *Action Research*, October, <https://eric.ed.gov/?id=ED449120> (last accessed 22 March 2019).

Firdyiwek, Y. and Scida, E. E. (2014), 'Reflective course design: An interplay between pedagogy and technology in a language teacher education course', *International Journal of EPortfolio*, 4: 2, 115–31.

Fraga-Cañadas, C. P. (2011), 'Building communities of practice for foreign language teachers', *Modern Language Journal*, 95: 2, 296–300.

Freeman, D. (1982), 'Observing teachers: Three approaches to in-service training and development', *TESOL Quarterly*, 16: 1, 21–8.

Freeman, D. (2001), 'Second language teacher education', in Carter, R. and Nunan, D. (eds), *The Cambridge Guide to Teaching English to Speakers of Other Languages*, Cambridge: Cambridge University Press, pp. 72–9.

Freeman, D. (2016), *Educating Second Language Teachers*, Oxford: Oxford University Press.

Freeman, D. and Johnson, K. E. (1998), 'Reconceptualizing the knowledge-base of language teacher education', *TESOL Quarterly*, 32: 3, 397–417.

Gardener, R. (2001), *When Listeners Talk*, Amsterdam: John Benjamins.

Garrison, R. D., Anderson, T. and Archer, W. (2000), 'Critical inquiry in a text-based environment: Computer conferencing in higher education', *The Internet and Higher Education*, 2: 2–3, 87–105.

Gatbonton, E. (1999), 'Investigating experienced ESL teachers' pedagogical knowledge', *Modern Language Journal*, 83: 1, 35–50.

Gee, J. P. (1996), *Social Linguistics and Literacies: Ideology in Discourses*, London: Taylor and Francis.

Gee, J. P. (2001), 'Identity as an analytic lens for research in education', *Review of Research in Education*, 25: 1, 99–125.

Gill, S. (1997), 'Local problems, local solutions', in McGrath, I. (ed.), *Learning to Train: Perspectives on the Development of Language Teacher Trainers*, Hemel Hampstead: Prentice Hall, pp. 215–24.

Gimenez, T. (1999), 'Reflective teaching and teacher education: Contributions from teacher training', *Linaguagem and Ensino*, 2: 2 129–43.

Golombek, P. R. (1998), 'A study of language teachers' personal practical knowledge', *TESOL Quarterly*, 32: 3, 447–64.

Gray, J. and Morton, T. (2018), *Social Interaction and English Language Teacher Identity*, Edinburgh: Edinburgh University Press.

Gumperz, J. (1982), *Language and Social Identity*, Cambridge: Cambridge University Press.

Hammadou, J. (1993), 'Inquiry in language teacher education', in Guntermann, G. (ed.), *Developing Language Teachers for a Changing World*, Lincoln Wood, IL: National Textbook Company, pp. 76–104.

Han, S. and Hill, J. R. (2006), 'Building understanding in asynchronous discussions: Examining types of online discourse', *Journal of Asynchronous Learning Networks*, 10: 4, 29–50.

Hanks, W. (1990), *Referential Practice: Language and Lived Space among the Maya*, Chicago: Chicago University Press.

Hansen, D. T. (1998), 'The moral is in the practice', *Teaching and Teacher Education*, 14: 6, 653–5.

Hawkins, M. R. (2004), 'Social apprenticeships through mediated learning in language teacher education', in Hawkins, M. R. (ed.), *Language Learning and Teacher Education. A Sociocultural Approach*, New York: Multilingual Matters, pp. 89–110.

Head, K. and Taylor, P. (1997), *Readings in Teacher Development*, Oxford: Heinemann.

Healy, M. (2012), 'A corpus-based exploration of building repertoire, linguistically shared and specific, in the hotel management training sector', at Intervarietal Applied Corpus Studies (IVACS) Leeds, 21–22 June.

Healy, M. and Onderdonk-Horan, K. (2012), 'Looking at language in hotel management education', in Farr, F. and Moriarty, M. (eds), *Learning and Teaching: Irish Research Perspectives*, Berlin: Peter Lang, pp. 141–65.

Hillier, Y. (2005), *Reflective Teaching in Further and Adult Education*, London: Continuum.

Holmes, D., Murray, S., Perron, C. and McCabe, J. (2008), 'Nursing best practice guidelines: Reflecting on the obscene use of the void', *Journal of Nursing Management*, 11: 4, 385–403.

Hubbard, P. (2009), 'A general introduction to computer assisted language learning', in Hubbard, P. (ed.), *Computer Assisted Language Learning: Critical Concepts in Linguistics. Volume I – Foundations of CALL*, New York: Routledge, pp. 1–20

Jay, J. and Johnson, K. (2002), 'Capturing complexity: A typology of reflective practice for teacher education', *Teaching and Teacher Education*, 18, 73–85.

Jenkins, J. (2007), *English as a Lingua Franca: Attitudes and Identity*, Oxford: Oxford University Press.

Johnson, C. M. (2001), 'A survey of current research on online communities of practice', *The Internet and Higher Education*, 4, 45–60.

Johnson, K. E. (1992), 'Learning to teach: Instructional actions and decisions of preservice ESL teachers', *TESOL Quarterly*, 26: 3, 507–35.

Johnson, K. E. (2006), 'The sociocultural turn and its challenges for second language teacher education', *TESOL Quarterly*, 40: 1, 235–57.

Johnson, K. E. (2009), *Second Language Teacher Education: A Sociocultural Perspective*, New York and London: Routledge.

Kagan, D. (1990), 'Ways of evaluating teacher cognition: Inferences concerning the Goldilocks Principle', *Review of Educational Research*, 60: 3, 419–69.

Kamhi-Stein, L. D. (2000), 'Looking to the future of TESOL teacher education: Web-based bulletin board discussions in a methods course', *TESOL Quarterly*, 34: 3 423–55.

Kaur, R. and Sidhu, G. (2010), 'Learner autonomy via Asynchronous Online Interactions: A Malaysian perspective', *International Journal of Education and Development using ICT*, 6: 3, 88–100.

Keenan, E. O. and Schieffelin, B. B. (1976), 'Topic as a discourse notion: A study of topic in the conversations of children and adults', in Li, C. (ed.), *Subject and Topic*, New York: Academic, pp. 333–84.

Kern, R. G. (1995), 'Restructuring classroom interaction with networked computers: Effects on quantity and characteristics of language production', *The Modern Language Journal*, 79: 4, 457–76.

Killeavy, M. and Moloney, A. (2010), 'Reflection in a social space: Can blogging support reflective practice for beginning teachers?', *Teaching and Teacher Education*, 26: 4, 1070–6.

Kinginger, C. (2002), 'Defining the zone of proximal development in US foreign language education', *Applied Linguistics*, 23: 2, 240–61.

Kiss, T. (2012), 'The complexity of teacher learning: Reflection as a complex dynamic system', *Journal of Interdisciplinary Research in Education*, 2: 1, 17–35.

Koester, A. (2006), *Investigating Workplace Discourse*, London: Routledge.

Korthagen, F. A. J. (2001), *Linking Practice and Theory: The Pedagogy of Realistic Teacher Education*, London: Earlbaum.

Korthagen, F. A. J. (2004), 'In search of the essence of a good teacher: Towards a more holistic approach in teacher education', *Teaching and Teacher Education*, 20: 1, 77–97.

Kozulin, A. (1998), *Psychological Tools. A Sociocultural Approach to Education*, Cambridge, MA: Harvard University Press.

Kramsch, C. (1998), *Language and Culture*, Oxford: Oxford University Press.

Krashen, S. (1983), *The Natural Approach: Language Acquisition in the Classroom*, Englewood Cliffs, NJ: Alemany Press Inc.

Krentler, K. A. and Willis-Flurry, L. A. (2005), 'Does technology enhance actual student learning? The case of online discussion boards', *Journal of Education for Business*, 80: 6, 316–21.

Kumaradivelu, B. (1999), 'Critical classroom discourse analysis', *TESOL Quarterly*, 33: 3, 453–84.

Kumaradivelu, B. (2001), 'Toward a post method pedagogy', *TESOL Quarterly*, 35: 4, 537–60.

Kumaradivelu, B. (2003), 'Critical language pedagogy: A post method perspective on English language teaching', *World Englishes*, 22: 4, 539–50.

Kunz, P., Dewstow, R. and Moodie, P. (2003), 'A generic tool to set up metacognitive journals and their serendipitous use', in Crisp, G., Thiele, D., Scholten, I., Barker, S. and Baron, J. (eds), *The Proceedings of the 20th Annual Conference of the Australasian Society for Computers in Learning in Tertiary Education (ASCILITE)*, Adelaide, Australia: ASCILITE, pp. 283–92.

LaBoskey, V. K. (1997), 'Teaching to teach with purpose and passion: Pedagogy for reflective practice', in Russell, T. (ed.), *Teaching about Teaching: Purpose, Passion and Pedagogy in Teacher Education*, London: Routledge Falmer, pp. 150–64.

Labov, W. (1972), *Language in the Inner City. Studies in the Black English Vernacular*, Philadelphia: University of Pennsylvania Press.

Lamy, M.-N. and Hampel, R. (2007), *Online Communication in Language Learning and Teaching*, London: Palgrave Macmillan.

Lantolf, J. P. and Appel, G. (1994), 'Theoretical framework: An introduction to Vygotskian approaches to second language research', in Lantolf, J. P. and Appel, G. (eds), *Vygotskian Approaches to Second Language Research*, Norwood, NJ: Ablex, 1–32.

Lapadat, J. C. (2002), 'Written interaction: A key component in online learning', *Journal of Computer-mediated Communication*, 7: 4, JCMC742, <https://doi.org/10.1111/j.1083-6101.2002.tb00158.x> (last accessed 22 March 2019).

Lave, J. and Wenger, E. (1991), *Situated Learning. Legitimate Peripheral Participation*, Cambridge: Cambridge University Press.

Le, P. T. A. and Vásquez, C. (2011), 'Feedback in teacher education: Mentor discourse and intern perceptions', *Teacher Development*, 15: 4, 453–70.

Lee, H. J. (2005), 'Understanding and assessing preservice teachers' reflective thinking', *Teaching and Teacher Education*, 21: 6, 699–715.

Levy, M. and Stockwell, G. (2006), *CALL Dimensions. Options and Issues in Computer-assisted Language Learning*, New York: Routledge.

Li, L. (2017), *Social Interaction and Teacher Cognition*, Edinburgh: Edinburgh University Press.

Lin, C.-W., Lin, M.-J., Wen, C.-C. and Chu, S.-Y. (2016), 'A word-count approach to analyze linguistic patterns in the reflective writings of medical students', *Medical Education On-line*, 21.

Lindquist, H. (2009), *Corpus Linguistics and the Description of English*, Edinburgh: Edinburgh University Press.

Lock, G. and Tsui, A. Y. (2000), 'Customising linguistics: Developing an electronic grammar database for teachers', *Language Awareness*, 9: 1, 17–33.

Looi, C.-K. (2005), 'Exploring the affordances of online chat for learning', *International Journal of Learning Technology*, 1: 3, 322–38.

Lortie, D. C. (1975), *School-teacher: A Sociological Study*, Chicago and London: University of Chicago Press.

Lucas, P. and Fleming, J. (2011), 'Critical reflection: journals versus blogs', in Zegwaard, K. E. (ed.), *NZACE 2011 Conference Proceedings*, Napier, New Zealand: New Zealand Association for Cooperative Education, pp. 29–33.

Lunenberg, M., Korthagen, F. and Swennen, A. (2007), 'The teacher educator as a role model', *Teaching and Teacher Education*, 23: 5, 586–601.

McCarthy, M. J. (2002), 'Good listenership made plain: British and American non-minimal response tokens in everyday conversation', in Reppen, R., Fitzmaurice, S. M. and Biber, D. (eds), *Using Corpora to Explore Linguistic Variation*, Amsterdam: John Benjamins, pp. 49–72.

McCarthy, M. J. (2003), 'Talking back: "Small" interactional response tokens in everyday conversation', *Research on Language and Social Interaction*, 36: 1, 33–63.

McCarthy, M. J. (2008), 'Accessing and interpreting corpus information in the teacher education context', *Language Teaching*, 41: 4, 563–74.

McCarthy, M. J. and Handford, M. (2004), '"Invisible to us": A preliminary corpus-based study of spoken business English', in Connor, U. and Upton, T. (eds), *Discourse in the Professions: Perspectives from Corpus Linguistics*, Amsterdam: John Benjamins, pp. 167–201.

McGarr, O. and McCormak, O. (2014), 'To conform? Exploring Irish student teachers' discourses in reflective practice', *The Journal of Educational Research*, 107: 4, 267–80.

McLoughlin, C., Brady, J., Lee, M. J. and Russell, R. (2007), 'Peer-to-peer: an e-mentoring approach to developing community, mutual engagement and professional identity for pre-service teachers'. Paper presented at the Australian Association for Research in Education Conference, Fremantle, Australia.

McLoughlin, D. and Mynard, J. (2009), 'An analysis of higher order thinking in online discussions', *Innovations in Education and Teaching International*, 46: 2, 147–60.

McPherson, M. and Nunes, M. B. (2004), 'The failure of a virtual social space (VSS) designed to create a learning community: Lessons learned', *British Journal of Educational Technology*, 35: 3, 305–21.

Malderez, A. and Bodóczky, C. (1999), *Mentor Courses. A Resource Book for Trainer-Trainers*, Cambridge: Cambridge University Press.

Mann, S. and Walsh, S. (2013), 'RP or 'RIP': A critical perspective on reflective practice', *Applied Linguistics Review*, 4: 2, 291–315.

Mann, S. and Walsh, S. (2017), *Reflective Practice in English Language Teaching. Research-based Principles and Practices*, New York and London: Routledge.

Marks-Greenfield, P. (1984), 'A theory of the teacher in the learning activities of everyday life', in Rogoff, B. and Lave, J. (eds), *Everyday Cognition: Its Development in Social Context*, Cambridge, MA: Harvard University Press, pp. 117–38.

Matsuda, A. (2012), *Principles and Practices of Teaching English as an International Language: Rethinking Goals and Approaches*, Oxford: Oxford University Press.

Medgyes, P. (1994), *The Non-Native Teacher*, Houndsmills: Macmillan.

Mercer, N. (1995), *The Guided Construction of Knowledge. Talk Amongst Teachers and Learners*, Philadelphia: Multilingual Matters.

Meskill, C. (2009), 'CMC in language teacher education: Learning with and through instructional conversations', *International Journal of Innovation in Language Learning and Teaching*, 3: 1, 51–63.

Miller, J. (2009), 'Teacher identity', in Burns, A. E. and Richards, J. C. (eds), *The Cambridge Guide to Second Language Teacher Education*, New York: Cambridge University Press, pp. 172–81.

Mishra, P. and Koehler, M. J. (2006), 'Technological pedagogical content knowledge: A framework for teacher knowledge', *Teachers College Record*, 108: 6, 1017–54.

Mitchell, A. (1997), 'Teacher identity: A key to increased collaboration', *Action in Teacher Education*, 19: 3, 1–14.

Montero, B., Watts, F. and García-Carbonell, A. (2007), 'Discussion forum interactions: Text and context', *System*, 35: 4, 566–82.

Morton, T. and Gray, J. (2010), 'Personal practical knowledge and identity in lesson planning conferences on a pre-service TESOL course', *Language Teaching Research*, 14: 3, 297–317.

Morton, T. and Llinares, A. (2017), 'Content and Language Integrated Learning (CLIL)', in Morton, T. and Llinares, A. (eds), *Applied Linguistics Perspectives on CLIL*, Amsterdam: John Benjamins, pp. 1–16.

Murphy, B. (2010), *Corpus and Sociolinguistics: Investigating Age and Gender in Female Talk*, Amsterdam and Philadelphia: John Benjamins.

Murphy, B. (2015), 'A corpus-based investigation of critical reflective practice and context in early career teacher settings', *Classroom Discourse*, 6: 2, 107–23.

Murray, J. and Male, T. (2005), 'Becoming a teacher educator: Evidence from the field', *Teaching and Teacher Education*, 21: 2, 125–42.

Murray, L. and Hourigan, T. (2006), 'Using micropublishing to facilitate writing in the foreign language', in Ducate, L. and Arnold, N. (eds), *Calling on CALL: From Theory and Research to New Directions in Foreign Language Teaching*, San Marcos: CALICO, pp. 149–79.

Murray, L. and Hourigan, T. (2008), 'Blogs for specific purposes: Expressivist or socio-cognitivist approach?', *ReCALL*, 20: 1, 82–97.

Murray-Harvey, R., Silins, H. and Saebel, J. (1999), 'A cross-cultural comparison of student concerns in the teaching practicum', *International Education Journal*, 1: 1, 32–44.

Murugaiah, P., Azman, H., Ya'acob, A. and Thang, S. (2010), 'Blogging in teacher professional development: Its role in building computer-assisted language teaching skills', *International Journal of Education and Development using ICT*, 6: 3, 73–87.

Myers, G. (1998), 'Displaying opinions: Topics and disagreement in focus groups', *Language in Society*, 27, 85–111.

Negretti, R. (1999), 'Web-based activities and SLA: A conversation analysis research approach', *Language Learning and Technology*, 3: 1, 75–87.

Numrich, C. (1996), 'On becoming a language teacher: Insights from diary studies', *TESOL Quarterly*, 30: 1, 131–53.

Nunan, D. (2017), 'Language teacher identity in teacher education', in Barkhuizen, G. (ed.), *Reflections on Language Teacher Identity Research*, London and New York: Routledge, pp. 164–9.

Nyikos, M. and Hashimoto, R. (1997), 'Constructivist theory applied to collaborative learning in teacher education: In search of ZPD', *The Modern Language Journal*, 81: 4, 506–17.

O'Keeffe, A. (2006), *Investigating Media Discourse*, London: Routledge.

O'Keeffe, A. and Farr, F. (2003), 'Using language corpora in language teacher education: Pedagogic, linguistic and cultural insights', *TESOL Quarterly*, 37: 3, 389–418.

O'Keeffe, A. and Farr, F. (2012), 'Using language corpora in initial teacher education: Pedagogic issues and practical applications', in Biber, D. and Reppen, R. (eds), *Corpus Linguistics*, London: Sage, pp. 335–67.

O'Keeffe, A., McCarthy, M. J. and Carter, R. (2007), *From Corpus to Classroom*, Cambridge: Cambridge University Press.

O'Sullivan, J. (2015) *Advanced Dublin English as Strategic Inauthentication in Radio Advertising in Ireland*, unpublished PhD thesis, University of Limerick.

Oakley, G., Pegrum, M. and Johnston, S. (2014), 'Introducing e-portfolios to pre-service teachers as tools for reflection and growth: lessons learnt', *Asia-Pacific Journal of Teacher Education*, 42: 1, 36–50.

Oxford, R. (1997a), 'Constructivism: Shape-shifting, substance, and teacher education applications', *Journal of Education*, 72: 1, 35–66.

Oxford, R. (1997b), 'Cooperative learning, collaborative learning, and interaction: Three communicative strands in the language classroom', *Modern Language Journal*, 81: 4, 443–56.

Pacheco, A. Q. (2005), 'Reflective teaching and its impact on foreign language teaching', *Revista Electrónica 'Actualidades Investigativas en Educación'*, 5, 1–19.

Parkes, K. A. and Kajder, S. (2010), 'Eliciting and assessing reflective practice: A case study in Web 2.0 technologies', *International Journal of Teaching and Learning in Higher Education*, 22: 2, 218–28.

Pennebaker, J. W., Booth, R. J., Boyd, R. L. and Francis, M. E. (2007), *Linguistic Inquiry and Wordcount (LIWC)* <http://www.liwc.net/index.php> (last accessed 22 March 2019).

Pennington, M. C. (1995), 'The teacher change cycle', *TESOL Quarterly*, 29: 4, 705–31.

Pennington, M. C. (2015), 'Teacher identity in TESOL: A frames perspective', in Cheung, Y. L., Said, S. B. and Park, K. (eds), *Teacher Identity and Development in Applied Linguistics: Current Trends and Perspectives*, London: Routledge, pp. 16–30.

Pennington, M. C. and Richards, J. C. (2016), 'Teacher identity in language teaching: Integrating personal, contextual, and professional factors', *RELC Journal*, 47: 1, 5–23.

Pennycook, A. (2000), 'English, politics, ideology: From colonial celebration to postcolonial performativity', in Ricento, T. (ed.), *Ideology, Politics and Language Policies: Focus on English*, Amsterdam: John Benjamins, pp. 107–19.

Pilkington, J. (1998), 'Don't try and make out that I'm nice!' The different strategies women and men use when gossiping', in Coates, J. (ed.), *Language and Gender: A Reader*, Oxford: Blackwell, pp. 254–69.

Porter, A., Goldstein, J. and Conrad, S. (1990), 'An ongoing dialogue: Learning logs for teacher preparation ', in Richards, J. and Nunan, D. (eds), *Second Language Teacher Education*, New York: Cambridge University Press, pp. 227–40.

Prabhu, N. S. (1990), 'There is no best method—why?', *TESOL Quarterly*, 24: 2, 161–76.

Preece, J. and Maloney-Krichmar, D. (2003), 'Online communities: Focusing on sociability and usability', in Jacko, J. A. and Sears, A. (eds), *Handbook of Human-computer Interaction*, Mahwah, NY: Lawrence Erlbaum, pp. 596–620.

Prodromou, L. (2003), 'In search of the successful user of English', *Modern English Teacher*, 12: 2, 5–14.

Pryor, C. R. and Bitter, G. G. (2008), 'Using multimedia to teach inservice teachers: Impacts on learning, application, and retention', *Computers in Human Behavior*, 24: 6, 2668–81.

Putnam, R. T. and Borko, H. (2000), 'What do new views of knowledge and thinking have to say about research on teacher learning?', *Educational Researcher*, 29: 1, 4–15.

Randall, M. and Thornton, B. (2001), *Advising and Supporting Teachers*, Cambridge: Cambridge University Press.

Ray, B. B. and Coulter, G. A. (2008), 'Reflective practices among language arts teachers: The use of weblogs', *Contemporary Issues in Technology and Teacher Education*, 8: 1, 6–26.

Richards, J. C. (1998), *Beyond Training*, Cambridge: Cambridge University Press.

Richards, J. C. (2001), *Curriculum Development in Language Teaching*, Cambridge: Cambridge University Press.

Richards, J. C. (2012), 'Competence and performance in language teaching', in Burns, A. and Richards, J. C. (eds), *The Cambridge Guide to Pedagogy and Practice in Second Language Teaching*, New York: Cambridge University Press, pp. 46–59.

Richards, J. C. (2017), 'Teacher identity in second language teacher education', in Barkhuizen, G. (ed.), *Reflections in Language Teacher Identity Research*, New York: Routledge, pp. 139–44.

Richards, J. C. and Farrell, T. S. C. (2005), *Professional Development for Language Teachers*, Cambridge: Cambridge University Press.

Richards, J. C. and Farrell, T. S. C. (2011), 'The nature of teacher learning', in Richards, J. C. and Farrell, T. S. C. (eds), *Practice Teaching: A Reflective Approach*, New York: Cambridge, pp. 15–30.

Richards, J. C. and Lockhart, C. (1996), *Reflective Teaching in Second Language Classrooms*, New York: Cambridge University Press.

Richards, K. (2006), 'Being the teacher: Identity and classroom conversation', *Applied Linguistics*, 27: 1, 51–77.

Riordan, E. (2011), 'Assessing the integration and quality of online tools in language teacher education: The case of blogs, chat and discussion forums', in Hourigan, T., Murray, L. and Riordan, E. (eds), *Quality Issues in ICT Integration: Third Level Disciplines and Learning Contexts*, Newcastle Upon Tyne: Cambridge Scholars, pp. 94–119.

Riordan, E. (2012), 'Online reflections: The implementation of blogs in language teacher education', in Farr, F. and Moriarty, M. (eds), *Learning and Teaching: Irish Research Perspectives*, Berlin: Peter Lang, pp. 195–224.

Riordan, E. (2018), *TESOL Student Teacher Discourse. A Corpus-based Analysis of Online and Face-to-face Interactions*, London: Routledge.

Riordan, E. and Farr, F. (2015), 'Facilitating identity construction through narratives: A corpus-based discourse analysis of student teacher discourse', in Cheung, Y. L., Said, S. B. and Park, K. (eds), *Advances and Current Trends in Language Teacher Identity Research*, New York and London: Routledge, pp. 161–74.

Riordan, E. and Murray, L. (2010), 'A corpus-based analysis of online synchronous and asynchronous modes of communication within language teacher education', *Classroom Discourse*, 1: 2, 181–98.

Roberts, J. (2016), *Language Teacher Education*, New York: Routledge.

Rodgers, C. R. and Raider-Roth, M. B. (2006), 'Presence in teaching', *Teachers and Teaching: Theory and Practice*, 12: 3, 265–87.

Rogers, C. R. (1969), *Freedom to Learn*, Columbus,OH: Charles Merrill.

Rogoff, B. (1990), *Apprenticeship in Thinking*, Oxford: Oxford University Press.

Romano, M. E. (2008), 'Online discussion as a potential professional development tool for first-year teachers ', *Technology, Pedagogy and Education*, 17: 1, 53–65.

Rommetveit, R. (1985), 'Language acquisition as increasing linguistic structuring of experience and symbolic behaviour control', in Wertsch, J. V. (ed.), *Culture, Communication and Cognition. Vygotskian Perspectives*, New York: Cambridge University Press, pp. 183–204.

Sachs, J. (2005), *Teacher Education and the Development of Professional Identity: Learning to be a Teacher*, London: Routledge.

Schiffrin, D. (1987), *Discourse Markers*, Cambridge: Cambridge University Press.

Schlager, M. S., Farooq, U., Fusco, J., Schank, P. and Dwyer, N. (2009), 'Analyzing online teacher networks: Cyber networks require cyber research tools', *Journal of Teacher Education*, 60: 1, 86–100.

Schocker-von-Ditfurth, M. and Legutke, M. K. (2002), 'Visions of what is possible in teacher education – or lost in complexity?', *English Language Teaching Journal*, 56: 2, 162–71.

Schön, D. (1983), *The Reflective Practitioner: How Professionals Think in Action*, New York: Basic Books.

Schön, D. (1987), *Educating the Reflective Practitioner: Toward a Design for Teaching and Learning in the Professions*, San Francisco: Jossey-Bass.

Schön, D. (1991), 'Introduction', in Schön, D. A. (ed.), *The Reflective Turn: Case Studies in and on Educational Practice*, Aldershot: Arena, pp. 1–11.

Scott, M. (2008), *Wordsmith Tools 5*, Oxford: Oxford University Press.

Sert, O. and Asik, A. (2019), 'A corpus linguistic investigation into online peer feedback practices in CALL teacher education', *Applied Linguistics Review* , <http://doi.org/10.1515/applirev-2017-0054> (last accessed 29 August 2019).

Servi, L. and Elson, S. B. (2012), *A Mathematical Approach to Identifying and Forecasting Shifts in the Mood of Social Media Users*, The MITRE Cooperation, <http://www.mitre.org/sites/default/files/pdf/12_0697.pdf> (last accessed 22 March 2019).

Shanker, A. (1990), 'The end of the traditional model of schooling. And a proposal for using incentives to restructure our public schools', *Phi Delta Kappan*, 71: 5, 344–57.

Shulman, L. S. (1986), 'Those who understand: Knowledge growth in teaching ', *Educational Researcher*, 15: 2, 4–14.

Simon, R. I. (1995), 'Face to face with alterity: Postmodern Jewish identity and the eros of pedagogy', in Gallop, J. (ed.), *Pedagogy: The Question of Impersonation*, Bloomington: Indiana University Press, pp. 90–105.

Sinclair, J. M. and Coulthard, R. M. (1975), *Towards an Analysis of Discourse. The English Used by Teachers and Pupils*, Oxford: Oxford University Press.

Skinner, B. F. (1953), *Science and Human Behavior*, New York: Simon and Schuster.

Smith, J. (2001), 'Modeling the social construction of knowledge in ELT teacher education', *English Language Teaching Journal*, 55: 3, 221–7.

Sotillo, S. M. (2000), 'Discourse functions and syntactic complexity in synchronous and asyncronous communication', *Language Learning and Technology*, 4: 1, 82–119.

Spalding, E., Wilson, A. and Mewborn, D. (2002), 'Demystifying reflection: A study of pedagogical strategies that encourage reflective journal writing', *Teachers College Record*, 104: 7, 1393–1421.

Spiro, J. (2013), *Changing Methodologies in TESOL*, Edinburgh: Edinburgh University Press.

Stacey, E. (1999), 'Collaborative learning in an online environment', *The Journal of Distance Education*, 14, 14–23.

Stanley, C. (1998), 'A framework for teacher reflectivity', *TESOL Quarterly*, 32: 3, 584–91.

Steel, D. and Alderson, J. C. (1995), 'Metalinguistic knowledge, language aptitude and language proficiency', in Graddol, D. and Thoman, S. (eds), *Language in a Changing Europe*, Clevedon: Multilingual Matters, pp. 92–103.

Stiler, G. M. and Philleo, T. (2003), 'Blogging and blogspots: An alternative format for encouraging reflective practice among preservice teachers', *Education*, 123: 4, 789–98.

Swales, J. (1987), 'Approaching the concept of discourse community', at 38th Annual Meeting of the Conference on College Composition and Communication, Atlanta, Georgia, ERIC.

Swales, J. (1990), *Genre Analysis*, Cambridge: Cambridge University Press.

Szabo, Z. and Schwartz, J. (2011), 'Learning methods for teacher education: The use of online discussions to improve critical thinking', *Technology, Pedagogy and Education*, 20: 1, 79–94.

Tajfel, H. (1978), *Differentiation between Social Groups. Studies in the Social Psychology of Intergroup Relations*, London: Academic.

Tao, H. (2003), 'Turn initiators in spoken English: A Corpus-based approach to interaction and grammar', in Leistyna, P. and Meyer, C. F. (eds), *Corpus Analysis: Language Structure and Language Use*, Amsterdam: Rodopi, pp. 187–207.

Tausczik, Y. R. and Pennebaker, J. W. (2010), 'The psychological meaning of words: LIWC and computerized text analysis methods', *Journal of Language and Social Psychology*, 29: 1, 24–54.

Thornbury, S. (2010), 'What can a corpus tell us about discourse?', in O'Keeffe, A. and McCarthy, M. (eds), *The Routledge Handbook of Corpus Linguistics*, London: Routledge, pp. 270–87.

Timmis, I. (2002), 'Native-speaker norms and International English: A classroom view', *ELT Journal*, 56: 3, 240–9.

Tsui, A. B. M. (2003), *Understanding Expertise in Teaching*, Cambridge: Cambridge University Press.

Tu, C.-H. (2002), 'The impacts of text-based CMC on online social presence', *Journal of Interactive Online Learning*, 1: 2, 1–24.

Turney, C., Cairns, L., Eltis, K., Hatton, N., Thew, D., Towler, J. and Wright, R. (1982), *Supervisor Development Programmes: Role Handbook*, Sydney: Sydney University Press.

Ullmann, T. D. (2017), 'Reflective writing analytics: empirically determined keywords of written reflection', in *Proceedings of the Seventh International Learning Analytics & Knowledge Conference*, New York: ACM, pp. 163–7.

Urzúa, A. and Vásquez, C. (2008), 'Reflection and professional identity in teachers' future-oriented discourse', *Teaching and Teacher Education*, 24: 7, 1935–46.

Vacilotto, S. and Cummings, R. (2007), 'Peer coaching in TEFL/TESL programmes', *ELT Journal*, 61: 2, 153–60.

Varghese, M., Morgan, B., Johnston, B. and Johnson, K. A. (2005), 'Theorizing language teacher identity: Three perspectives and beyond', *Journal of Language, Identity, and Education*, 4: 1, 21–44.

Vásquez, C. (2007), 'Moral stance in the workplace narratives of novices', *Discourse Studies*, 9: 5, 653–75.

Vásquez, C. (2009), 'Examining the role of face work in a workplace complaint narrative', *Narrative Inquiry*, 19: 2, 259–79.

Vásquez, C. (2011a), 'Complaints online: The case of TripAdvisor', *Journal of Pragmatics*, 43: 6, 1707–17.

Vásquez, C. (2011b), 'TESOL teacher identity and the need for "small story" research', *TESOL Quarterly*, 45: 3, 535–45.

Vásquez, C. and Reppen, R. (2007), 'Transforming practice: Changing patterns of participation in post-observation meetings', *Language Awareness*, 16: 3, 153–72.

Vásquez, C. and Urzúa, A. (2009), 'Reported speech and reported mental states in mentoring meetings: Exploring novice teacher identities', *Research on Language and Social Interaction*, 42: 1, 1–19.

Vaughan, E. (2010) *Just Say Something and We Can All Argue Then: Community and Identity in the Workplace Talk of English Language Teachers*, unpublished PhD thesis, Mary Immaculate College, Limerick.

Vaughan, E. and Clancy, B. (2013), 'Small corpora and pragmatics', in Romero-Trillo, J. (ed.), *The Yearbook of Corpus Linguistics and Pragmatics*, New York: Springer, pp. 53–73.

Vygotsky, L. S. (1983), *Sobranie Sochinenii*, Moscow, Vol. 3: Prosveschenie.

Vygotsky, L. (1981), 'The development of higher forms of attention', in Wertsch, J. (ed.), *The Concept of Activity in Soviet Psychology*, Armonk, NY: M. E. Sharpe, pp. 189–240.

Vygotsky, L. S. (1978), *Mind in Society. The Development of Higher Psychological Processes*, Cambridge, MA: Harvard University Press.

Wajnryb, R. (1992), *Classroom Observation Tasks: A Resource Book for Language Teachers and Trainers*, Cambridge: Cambridge University Press.

Wallace, M. (1991), *Training Foreign Language Teachers: A Reflective Approach*, Cambridge: Cambridge University Press.

Walsh, S. (2001) *Characterising Teacher Talk in the Second Language Classroom: A Process Model of Reflective Practice*, unpublished PhD thesis, Queen's University, Belfast.

Walsh, S. (2002), 'Construction or obstruction: Teacher talk and learner involvement in the EFL classroom', *Language Teaching Research*, 6: 1, 3–23.

Walsh, S. (2003), 'Developing interactional awareness in the second language classroom', *Language Awareness*, 12: 2, 124–42.

Walsh, S. (2006), *Investigating Classroom Discourse, Domains of Discourse*, London and New York: Routledge.

Walsh, S. (2011), *Exploring Classroom Discourse: Language in Action*, London and New York: Routledge.

Walsh, S. (2013), *Classroom Discourse and Teacher Development*, Edinburgh: Edinburgh University Press.

Walsh, S. and Mann, S. (2015), 'Doing reflective practice: A data-led way forward', *English Language Teaching Journal*, 69: 4, 351–62.

Walsh, S., Morton, T. and O'Keeffe, A. (2011), 'Analysing university spoken interaction: A CL/CA approach', *International Journal of Corpus Linguistics*, 16: 3, 325–45.

Walsh, S. and O'Keeffe, A. (2007), 'Applying CA to a modes analysis of third-level spoken academic discourse', in Bowles, H. and Seedhouse, P. (eds), *Conversation Analysis in Languages for Specific Purposes*, Berlin: Peter Lang, pp. 101–39.

Wang, Y., Chen, N.-S. and Levy, M. (2010), 'Teacher training in a synchronous cyber face-to-face classroom: Characterizing and supporting the online teachers' learning process', *Computer Assisted Language Learning*, 23: 4, 277–93.

Warford, M. K. and Reeves, J. (2003), 'Falling into it: Novice TESOL teacher thinking', *Teachers and Teaching: Theory and Practice*, 9: 1, 47–65.

Waters, A. and Vilches, M. L. C. (2005), 'Managing innovation in language education: A course for ELT change agents', *RELC Journal*, 36: 2, 117–36.

Wegerif, R. (1998), 'The social dimension of asynchronous learning networks', *Journal of Asynchronous Learning Networks*, 2: 1, 34–49.

Wenger, E. (1998), *Communities of Practice. Learning, Meaning, and Identity*, Cambridge: Cambridge University Press.

Wertsch, J. V. (1990), 'The voice of rationality in a sociocultural approach to mind', in Moll, L. C. (ed.), *Vygotsky and Education. Instructional Implications and Applications of Socio-Historical Psychology*, Cambridge: Cambridge University Press, pp. 111–26.

Wertsch, J. V. (1998), *Mind as Action*, Oxford: Oxford University Press.

Wickstrom, C. D. (2003), 'A "funny" thing happened on the way to the forum', *Journal of Adolescent and Adult Literacy*, 46: 5, 414–23.

Widdowson, H. G. (1997), 'Approaches to second language teacher education', in Hornberger, N. (ed.), *Encyclopedia of Language and Education*, New York: Springer, 121–9.

Wolff, D. and De Costa, P. I. (2017), 'Expanding the language teacher identity landscape: An investigation of the emotions and strategies of a NNEST', *The Modern Language Journal*, 101: S1, 76–90.

Wood, D., Bruner, J. and Ross, G. (1976), 'The role of tutoring in problem solving', *Journal of Child Psychology and Psychiatry*, 17, 89–100.

Woods, D. (1996), *Teacher Cognition in Language Teaching: Beliefs, Decision-Making and Classroom Practice*, Cambridge: Cambridge University Press.

Yang, S.-H. (2009), 'Using blogs to enhance critical reflection and community of practice', *Educational Technology and Society*, 12: 2, 11–21.

Zeichner, K. (1995), 'Reflections of a teacher educator working for social change', in Russell, T. and Korthagen, F. (eds), *Teachers Who Teach Teachers*, London and Washington: Falmer Press, pp. 11–24.

Zeichner, K. (2006), 'Reflections of a university-based teacher educator on the future of college-and university-based teacher education', *Journal of Teacher Education*, 57: 3, 326–40.

Zeichner, K. and Liston, D. (1996), *Reflective Teaching: An Introduction*, Mahwah, NY: Lawrence Erlbaum.

Zembylas, M. (2003), 'Emotions and teacher identity: A poststructural perspective', *Teachers and Teaching*, 9: 3, 213–38.

Zimmerman, B. J. (2002), 'Becoming a self-regulated learner: An overview', *Theory into Practice*, 41: 2, 64–72.

Zimmerman, D. H. (1998), 'Identity, context and interaction', in Antaki, C. and Widdicombe, S. (eds), *Identities in Talk*, Thousand Oaks, CA: Sage, pp. 87–106.

Zwozdiak-Myers, P. (2012), *The Teacher's Reflective Practice Handbook*, Abington and New York: Routledge.

INDEX

184